A Tactful God

This book is dedicated:

– *with love to the memory of my father, himself something of a 'gadfly' to the Church, who died while it was being written;*

– *with affection to Father Abbot and the monks of Elmore Abbey, Gregory's brothers;*

– *with gratitude to the memory of Brother Kenneth CGA, who always encouraged my writing, and at whose suggestion this biography was begun, but who sadly died in 1993.*

A Tactful God

Simon Bailey

The publishers would like to acknowledge the assistance of the Monks of Elmore Abbey in the preparation of this volume.

First published in 1995

Gracewing
Fowler Wright Books
2 Southern Ave, Leominster
Herefordshire HR6 0QF

Gracewing books are distributed

In New Zealand by
Catholic Supplies Ltd
80 Adelaide Road
Wellington
New Zealand

In Australia by
Charles Paine Pty Ltd
8 Ferris Street
North Parramatta
NSW 2151 Australia

In USA by
Morehouse Publishing
PO Box 1321
Harrisburg
PA 17105 USA

In Canada by
Meakin and Associates
Unit 17, 81 Aurega Drive
Nepean, Ontario
KZE 7Y5, Canada

Typesetting by Reesprint, Radley, Oxfordshire, OX14 3AJ
Printed by Cromwell Press, Broughton Gifford, Wiltshire, SN12 8PH

ISBN 0 85244 340 4

Contents

Foreword

by the Abbot of Elmore

It is sometimes said that Dom Gregory Dix wrote a book about the shape of the liturgy. This is partially true for that was the title of his now famous book. But what he actually wrote was a book about the meaning rather than the shape of the liturgy. Had it been the latter, the book would have been of little interest outside a circle of specialists. Not only did he write in a specialist field but he did so in a way that made the fruit of some fifteen years concentrated research and study available to a very wide public. Austin Farrer used to insist on his Oxford students reading the first one hundred pages of *The Shape* as a foundation for his theology course. He believed that it was written in such a way as to be accessible to all and that its subject was essential to a full grasp of theology. After all, what could be of greater importance than the way we worship and our reason for doing so? Dom Gregory's academic genius was combined with an unshakable faith in the importance of his subject and a deep love for the *plebs sancta Dei* — 'the holy common people of God'.[1] It was for them, no less, that he wrote.

If reading *A Tactful God* does no more than introduce you to *The Shape*, it will be immensely worthwhile. But it will do more, much more. Dom Gregory was devoted to the cause of the unity of the Church, the Body of Christ, and it was this which inspired his whole life. He never lost sight of the early vision he had of Catholic faith and order; a vision which

---

1   *The Shape of the Liturgy,* p. 744.

deepened through his priestly and monastic life, especially
in his pastoral ministry. He saw himself as a member of the
plebs sancta Dei and his gifted wit shines through a thoroughly
human being, just like you and me. He didn't hesitate to
apply it to himself. When told, 'Dix, you're as bad as ever',
by a friend, his reply is well worth remembering: 'But I've
slowed down the deterioration!' Therein probably lies the
secret of a great man who made a significant contribution to
the twentieth century.

I thoroughly recommend *A Tactful God* to you. On behalf
of the monastic community, to which Dom Gregory belonged, I wish to express gratitude to Simon Bailey for this
excellent study. He calls it, modestly, 'aspects of a life'. A
biography is long overdue and so many will welcome this
volume, including, perhaps especially, those who, though
encountering Dom Gregory Dix for the first time, will discover their indebtedness to him.

Dom Basil Matthews OSB
Abbot of Elmore
Easter 1994

Acknowledgements

I am deeply indebted in many different ways for the help and support of the Abbot and Community of Elmore Abbey, the successors of Nashdom. They not only gave me free access to all Dom Gregory Dix's papers and to other community books and records, but I also stayed with them as a guest and tasted a little of the Benedictine life. Their help and support has been more than generous—with finance, in friendship, by helpful critical response to drafts of the text, and in prayer too. I owe a special debt to Dom Augustine Morris, not only as a friend of Gregory's but also for his good memory and acute mind! Dom Godfrey Stokes too, who was Abbot when I began the research and started me off on the project, knew Gregory well and provided invaluable information, careful criticism and a fund of Dix stories! The community put me in touch with their sister house at St Gregory's Abbey, Three Rivers in the USA, which Greory helped to nurture. I am grateful the Abbot and community there for looking after me, providing fresh material and other contacts and also for photographs. Further American help and information was provided by Dr Samuel West on behalf of the Associated Parishes movement with which Gregory had contact.

A number of others generously provided valuable material especially Fr Benedict Green of the Community of the Resurrection, Mirfield, who allowed me to use his father's correspondence with Gregory. The estate of Fr Marcus Stevens with whom Gregory corresponded in the thirties provided interesting parts of that exchange, and other friends and acquaintances uncovered personal anecdotes and many other references which have been very helpful. Among them was the Revd T.F. Taylor, whom Gregory knew as 'Fish', who let me see some letters between them.

Others have been helpful in different ways. I owe a great deal to the Revd Henry Chadwick, who worked on Gregory's papers in the sixties with a view to a biography and put them in some kind of order. Further cataloguing was done more recently by Dom James Leachmann OSB of Ealing Abbey, formerly of Nashdom. I am especially indebted to a friend, Antony Pegram, who listed all the papers and so enabled me to find my way through them all.

Westminster School and Merton College, Oxford allowed me to consult documents relating to Dix and I was able to research other material among the Church of England's Records at Lambeth Palace Library, the Oxford diocesan records, the Wells Theological College records and the Bodleian Library. I was helped by the archivist of West Malling Abbey who also provided photographs of their abbey at the time when the Nashdom community moved there.

I am grateful to the late Peter Hebblethwaite for information abour Maurice Bévenot SJ and through him for contact with Fr Robert Murray SJ of Heythrop College who enabled me to see the Bévenot papers there. Fr Richard Woodward, the parish priest of St Michael's Beaconsfield, gave me access to parish records from Gregory's time there, and I also met parishioners to whom he had ministered.

Among those from Beaconsfield I am especially grateful to Joy Green, who not only remembered him but also undertook research for me into the Dix family tree. Her husband Geoffrey had been prepared for confirmation by Gregory and had many useful memories of him from then and later too. Mr and Mrs Green put me further in their debt by generously entertaining me and providing accommodation.

Nearer home, I owe more than I can say to a patient parish and a generous diocese who allowed me time to work on the book. A massive debt is owed to Jayne Cobham and especially to Jenny Bott who patiently typed all this material and made it presentable. Finally, of course, I want to acknowledge a great debt to family and close friends and many others too who patiently listened while I thought aloud about various theories concerning this or that or retailed witty stories and recondite bits of research.

Introduction

May I begin by saying that this is not a full biography. A true biography would be a comprehensive and all-embracing presentation of someone's life, rounded, detailed and whole so that the reader felt they had met the total person in their complexity, their subtlety and their variety. This book cannot hope to achieve such a complete picture for a number of reasons. The first is the inadequacy of the author to the task. A comprehensive biography of Gregory Dix would need to provide a detailed critique of the development of his liturgical scholarship and so provide a mirror to the man's mind. The present author does not have the necessary scholarship to provide such a critique. Instead, part of the book (chapter four) offers an overview of that aspect of Gregory's mind and life and attempts to see how it fits with the rest of his character.

Ultimately I have evaded the invitation to see my subject whole, and focused instead on three particular 'Aspects' of the man. Chapter two looks at Gregory as a monk and a priest; Chapter three sees him in his extensive involvement in church politics and then chapter four looks at the mind of the scholar and teacher. A fifth chapter follows Gregory on some of his travels and sees, in what must be a theme of the book, how Gregory sought to hold together the different aspects of his life.

It is not intended to suggest that these clearer facets of Gregory's life were exclusive and that there was little else to the man. On the contrary, like any human being, he contained

1

a thousand different facets, each complex, subtle, elusive and beguiling. However, any attempt at biography, even of one who died so recently (1952), must focus, concentrate, exclude, emphasise (over-emphasise) and perhaps even exaggerate. In the end the facets are not smooth, but fragments pieced together, the edges rough, and the reader must always bear this in mind, however the writing seeks to smooth over the cracks.

Biography, like any form of history, cannot help but be fairly arbitrary in its methods of selection. It depends to such an extent on the facts which survive. There are bound to be gaps, and there are particularly in this case. Readers will notice those surrounding Gregory's family and there are gaps, too, deliberate or otherwise, in the information regarding Gregory's departure from Keble College in 1926, and his long period of reflection on whether to join the Roman Catholic Church. There are, no doubt some omissions we don't even know of; 'gaps' so complete that we don't even know they are there. In consequence some of the material that does survive takes on a greater significance than perhaps it deserves; it is too easy to think that the documents we happen to have provide the total picture.

There is a question about how these 'gaps' occur. Most, of course, are accidental — the arbitrariness of history — which allows the oddest things to survive. But some must be by design, Gregory's or someone else's, as they made their attempt to influence history. Most often it is impossible to know and all we can do is work with what we have and struggle to perceive as complete a picture as possible. Every so often there is a shaft of light and it is as if the subject comes alive: the little boy with the fish slice; the laundry list; one of Gregory's delightful but barbed remarks; his daily mass.

Fascinatingly, Gregory would have known exactly what we mean. He was a historian; it was always the term he used for himself. Some lecture notes of 1930 when he was, it seems, helping with theological students at Nashdom, could have been written for this introduction. Speaking about the gospel

of St Luke but referring to history in general, and under the
general title 'Nature of historical tests of documents', his
notes say:

> Dictated by the object of History — the study of facts.
> History as a Science necessarily 'a selection of facts'. Results
> of this:
> a) Inadequacy of material without a viewpoint.
> b) Possibility of differing accounts both being 'veridical'.
> c) Possibility of reconstruction of lost facts from a repre-
>   sentative selection.
> d) Necessity of careful testing of theory by such facts as
>   we have.
> e) Necessity of accounting for all the facts we have.

Time and again in this book, as in any biography or history,
these tests have had to be applied and, when rather more of
speculation has been involved, I have tried to say so. The
result, I hope, despite the arbitrariness and selectivity, is a
portrait, not entirely personal to me, of a fascinatingly complex man.

Gregory, as a monk, as a man of the spirit, was in fact
struggling to be 'simplex' as he put it. In a book of notes on
Psalms (Ps. 105.4) he meditated on 'simplicity of heart' and
felt it must include the whole of life not just any part. In
striving for this, he added: 'My history is the history of the
deeds of God in me.'

The struggle for 'simplicity of heart' is a more complex
facet of personality for a biographer to map than any other
but in the end it was for Gregory the most significant part of
his history and, if this book can at least indicate that importance, it will not be totally inaccurate.

It is perhaps worth noting in detail the resources for this
book — they also indicate the particular emphases of the
result, and reveal some of the viewpoints for the material.

The major source of material has been Gregory's own
papers collected together into eight large boxes by his community. These include letters both personal and official,
notebooks stretching back as far as his schooldays, essays,
lectures, sermons, and many careful copies and translations

of patristic texts. Gregory had very neat handwriting and the texts are meticulously laid out in different-coloured inks, he was organised and methodical, at least at this level. There are, however, hardly any personal materials such as journals or diaries and few manuscripts for his books.

The boxes of papers also include other people's letters and papers. It is here the selection is perhaps at its most arbitrary. Why does a correspondence suddenly end and then begin again? Where is the other half of the correspondence? Where is the last sheet of a letter, or the opening note that would explain the relevance of a document? Guesses may be made but the important thing is always to be tentative. There are also the complete, revealing, comprehensive letters that say so much, like the letters to Freddy Green, and they are a great compensation.

Other secondary sources include books written by others about the same period. There are the general books of history but also the little vignettes, stumbled on accidentally, which give insight into 1930's monastic life or cast light on some aspect of Gregory's academic interests. Other records play their part here: birth, baptism and school records; college, diocesan and monastic records; church registers and visitors' books; lists which are lifeless until given a context and a setting when they shimmer into life.

Perhaps the most intriguing resources have been the memories of Gregory's contemporaries. It is over forty years since Gregory died yet some of his friends are still alive and together with two or three of his contemporaries in the community have provided invaluable insights. What is intriguing here is the way memory operates. It can be selective and arbitrary, romantic and fanciful, it can, of course, be plainly deceptive but it can also be amazingly revealing and penetrating, recalling minute detail with precision and accuracy. Sometimes, somehow, memory seems more accurate over a distance of time than with immediate experience; again at other times the 'gaps', the selectivity, are woefully obvious.

Interviewing Gregory's contemporaries provided a fund of stories and *bon mots* as well as facts and history. It was possible to feel, sometimes, how, with a character as powerful as Gregory's, stories had been honed and trimmed and refined in the telling, not least to make the most of the 'punch line'. More interestingly still, there is a kind of 'community memory', which is shared even by those who never knew Gregory. Stories are told, anecdotes recounted, and they become the property of the collective memory. This is a particular feature of monastic communities that meet for 'recreation' each day. Some of the stories recounted to me had the clear feel of much-loved and oft-repeated celebrations of Gregory's wit, refined by circulation in the monastic parlour.

These have been the main resources on which I have drawn together with other lesser materials. It is my hope, that from all these disparate elements something of the spirit and life of Gregory Dix has emerged.

The last question, especially in the light of the disclaimer made earlier, is why I should have embarked on such a complex task. Gregory Dix had died before I was born and so how do I find myself, with affection, writing this book?

When Gregory died in 1952 the Abbot together with Gregory's friends began immediately to plan a Memoir. The wave of sympathy and interest at his untimely death made this a very appropriate project. Abbot Augustine Morris approached Michael Ramsey for help with this and he initially agreed, but the scheme lost momentum and in time had been left too long to draw on the immediate interest evoked by Gregory's death.

In the sixties it was again decided that a biography should be undertaken and Professor Henry Chadwick began work on this, again supported by Abbot Augustine Morris. Sadly this too did not come to fruition. Finally Abbot Godfrey Stokes, in the mid-eighties, realised that as many of Gregory's contemporaries were by then very old and approaching death a suitable biography needed to be produced before the opportunity was lost. He mentioned this to Brother Kenneth CGA, a writer and possible biographer. He declined for himself (and sadly died in 1993) but offered to approach someone else, the present author, whom he had encouraged to write with other projects and who responded with interest.

When the project was suggested I had already heard of Gregory Dix and read his book, I had made one retreat at Nashdom and was interested in liturgy, but otherwise the connection was a remote one. Gradually and steadily I have come to feel affection and admiration for my subject and for his community. I differ from him in many of my opinions but sympathise deeply with what I have come to recognise as his great concerns and major themes. I hope, then, that I have been able to keep the distance appropriate to a biographer but at the same time to have the sympathy and sensitivity that also seem vital. The contribution of the author to the history is perhaps the last and subtlest, most elusive but pervasive, layer of the process and needs to be constantly acknowledged and borne in mind.

It may be just worth noting finally that the process has not infrequently been interesting, as it might have been to Gregory too, for distinct echoes of what must have been a parallel process in producing the gospels.... There is the timescale between the subject and the author, the fragments of history, the memories — and the nature of memory itself— the angles of the material, the arbitrary way it survives, the subtle recreative techniques of the author, the purpose of the enterprise.... In his notes about the nature of history Gregory was in fact focusing on the gospels — this attempt at biographical history is a humbler thing altogether but still the subject is elusive but attractive, a complex of nuances which every so often come startlingly alive. I hope that sometimes here, too, the subject in his liveliness and humanity with all his angles and edges can come vividly to life, as he has so often for me.

1

The Early Years

*What can be sweeter to us, beloved brethren, than
this voice of the Lord inviting us?*
From the Rule of St Benedict

The service of Benediction was over in the chapel, the French
nuns — exiled from their native country to the south of
England by the Law of Separation of 1905 — returned to
their household duties. A small boy emerged from the in-
cense-filled chapel, followed by three little girls, and headed
for the kitchen. There was no one about. The small boy took
the cook's large white apron from the back of the chair and
draped it round his shoulders. Then, on tiptoe, he reached
down the large round metal fish slice from its rack. Organising the little girls in a row behind him, the small boy set off
with cope flowing and monstrance held high above his head
as he processed around the convent, solemnly and reverently
with his little retinue.

Dix was six years old at the time that he made his visit to
the convent of Our Lady in St. Leonard's on Sea, Sussex. He
seems to have been there for some kind of nursery or kinder-
garten; by 1908 he had gone off to school.

Gregory Dix was born George Eglington Alston Dix, the
first son of George Henry and Mary Jane Dix, on October 4th
1901 in Woolwich, London. He took 'Gregory' as his name
much later, on entering Religious life. In 1905 a second son

Ronald John Eteson Dix was born and no doubt it was that
event that necessitated the older boy's care in the convent.

Despite the fact that Gregory was born this century it is
often impossible to establish details about whole areas of
his life. Of the first few years we are left completely in the
dark: no one and no documents survive to provide any
history of those earliest years. Virtually the first recorded
incident is the revealing story told above, described by a
French woman, resident at the convent, who became something of a friend to Mrs Dix.

Some of the patchiest areas of these early days are the
details about his parents, his mother in particular. The
youngest of four children, born in Preston, Lancashire, she
seems to have been involved in teaching later in her life, and
so it would appear likely that was how she met Gregory's
father. He was himself in education, first as a teacher and
then in the training of teachers. Gregory later mentions his
Lancashire Methodist lineage on his mother's side. His
grandfather and great-grandfather were both chemists. In a
letter of 1945 he says: 'My own mother was a Wesleyan and
my grandfather a most devoted local preacher in Lancashire
and I owe them both a good deal.'

A famous aside in *The Shape of the Liturgy* refers to his
Wesleyan grandmother's bizarre prejudices about the Mass.

> I remember that my own grandmother, a devout Wesleyan,
> believed to her dying day that at the Roman Catholic mass
> the priest let a crab loose upon the altar, which it was his
> mysterious duty to prevent from crawling sideways into the
> view of the congregation. (Hence the gestures of the cele-
> brant.) How she became possessed of this notion, or what
> she supposed eventually happened to the crustacean I never
> discovered. But she affirmed with the utmost sincerity that
> she had once with her own eyes actually watched this horrible
> rite in progress; and there could be no doubt of the deplorable
> effect that solitary visit to a Roman Catholic church had had
> on her estimate of Roman Catholics in general, though she
> was the soul of charity in all things else. To all suggestions
> that the mass might be intended as some sort of Holy

communion service she replied only with the wise and gentle
pity of the fully-informed for the ignorant.[1]

It is one of the only two references to grandparents among
the existing papers.

Gregory was well known for claiming Norman French
descent on his father's side but the family tree, traced back
to the beginning of the nineteenth century, only takes us to
a family of Gloucester tailors. The family name and the
family legend about their descent suggest the connection
may be further back. Gregory's father does seem to have had
links with France, not only with the nuns at St. Leonard's
but also with Bishop Amette of Bayeux and Lisieux, later to
be Cardinal Archbishop of Paris.

Gregory's father was an Anglo-Catholic. Born in 1872, he
would grow up in the heyday of that movement towards the
end of the century. He seems then to have been involved in
teacher-training at Cheltenham where perhaps he met Mary.
He may have known Father Ignatius of Llanthony; he was
certainly interested in his attempts to restore the religious
life to the Church of England. It was only later in his life,
however, that he began to feel a vocation to priesthood. After
training at Wells he was ordained in 1910 in Southwark. He
served in London churches first as curate of Wimbledon and
then as vicar of St Luke's, Kew. He remained involved in the
world of education, becoming Southwark diocesan Inspector
of Schools from 1911 to 1920. It was after this that he became
Principal, first of St John's Teacher-Training College, Bat-
tersea and then, in 1923, of the combined St. Mark and St.
John's College in Chelsea. He died in 1932 at the age of only
sixty and his sons, both by now priests, said masses for him
in St Luke's, Kew.

The *Church Times* obituary of Gregory's father stresses the
efforts he made to bring about closer co-operation between
colleges and universities to ensure better-qualified teachers.
He took his BA at the University of London (a 3rd class in
English) in 1902, the year after his first son was born. In the

1 *The Shape of the Liturgy*, A. & C. Black 1945, pp. 145–6.

year of his ordination (1910) he took an MA and in 1922
became DLitt. He not only remained involved in the University of London, sitting on its Board of Pedagogy, but also
wrote books on Religious education, the Old Testament and
Messianic prophecies. The *Church Times* calls him an 'ardent
Catholic' and a 'saintly priest, skilled confessor and director'
but Gregory himself seems rarely to have referred to his
father. One can only guess at his influence on Gregory, but
the combination of intense religion and the work of education, the effect of his father's ordination when Gregory was
nine, and his interest in religious communities must all have
been significant.

The obituary makes no mention of his wife. Gregory's
mother is somehow a much more shadowy figure. Only two
letters from Gregory to her survive but it can be inferred from
them that he wrote to her regularly. None of her side of the
correspondence survives. Gregory's letters are affectionate,
even intense, but sometimes in referring to her in other
letters he can sound slightly exasperated. She seems to have
had a drink problem. In 1935 Gregory wrote to a friend at
Wells: '... my mother has taken a change for the better... she
returns to the sacraments for Christmas.'[1]

After the death of her husband she seems to have stayed
at different times in convents, including, towards the end of
her life, at the convent in St. Leonard's, where, in 1939, she
died aged sixty-six. Gregory records this in a brief note to his
friend Ivan Young.

A photograph survives of the family at St. Mary's, Bishop-
stoke, Hampshire in 1912. Gregory's father in his still fairly
new cassock and collar and smoking a cigarette, Gregory aged
eleven in Eton collar, his hands in his pockets, Ronald smiling
shyly and their mother pretty but slightly sad and distant.

Ronald Dix was four years younger than Gregory. He also
in due course became a priest in the Church of England.
Ronnie remained in parish life but the brothers kept in close
contact. Ronnie not only visited Nashdom with his wife

1   The identity of this friend is discussed in the footnote on page 26.

Eileen but also took parties of parishioners there. It was to Ronnie's parish in Beaconsfield that Gregory went during the second world war while his brother became an Army chaplain. They continued to correspond during that period (rather confusingly addressing each other as 'Bill') and the letters provide fascinating insights into the experience of war, especially the D-Day landings, and into the religious life of soldiers. Ronnie was as catholic and as deeply sacramental as his brother; it was a vital resource to him in the pressures of war. Some of the correspondence helped to create a small booklet about Ronnie's wartime experience: *An Account of Life as a Chaplain in the Forces* (1945). He returned to parish work and was also involved in the Anglo-Catholic Congress of 1948. Ronnie at one time floated the idea of setting up a theological college, with Gregory's help, and wanted Gregory to produce a version of his *Pilot* journal (a fairly short-lived papalist publication) specially for parishes. In different ways and from different angles the brothers worked together. Unfortunately most of their correspondence no longer exists.

Gregory's parents seem rarely, if ever, to have visited him at Nashdom and how much he actually saw of them after entering the community is difficult to say. Nevertheless he acknowledged his debt to them. Slightly enigmatically he wrote to a woman friend in 1949 who had corresponded with him about her own family: 'It is only by the travail of our own mothers that any of us come into human life... some of us cost our parents much grief and suffering. I did mine.'[1]

He also, more than once, referred to 'fathers in the front rank' but, 'one's mother having to do with the roots of one's being'.

Family and ancestry are deeply influential on anyone's development. The combination of subtle influences from father and mother, mixed in with the nuances of a particular age's culture of family life, social standing, education and general nurture, these all contribute to make a person. But they contribute in such a deep way they are virtually impossible

1   21/2/49

to document and describe. The matrix has to be read back from the person that emerges.

From the little evidence that remains it is impossible to describe the personalities of George and Mary Dix and their attitudes to their children and their upbringing. Theirs was a middle-class Edwardian world in which the children went away to school, participated fully in their parents' religion and had some sense of ease about their place in society and the world at large. In many ways Gregory never lost the essence of those underlying certainties.

The letter that relates the incident with which this chapter begins describes Gregory as a quiet and pious child, even at six. He disliked the boisterous games some of the other children wanted to play and would sometimes be found in chapel: '... he would try to see if anybody was looking at him and would then pretend to be deep in prayer!'

The actor whom Gregory later recognised in himself was obviously there from very early on.... Equally the charm for which he later became renowned was also being practised then as in his befriending the sister in charge of the kitchen and inducing her to spoil him, 'for he was a bit greedy'.

'Quiet and pious' he may have been but there was clearly a spark of something else there as well. The imagination that turned apron and fish slice into cope and monstrance and caused a retinue of children to follow him was going to be increasingly significant in his life.

In 1908 Gregory went to prep school at Temple Grove in Eastbourne where he remained for seven years. The school has since moved to Uckfield but the buildings remain on the inland edge of the town but facing towards the sea with an expanse of cricket field in front. During this time his father was ordained deacon and then priest. This must have made its own impression on both boys, especially if they attended the priestly ordination. The family home moved first to Wimbledon where his father served his title and then, in 1916, to Kew. The *Church Times* obituary of George Dix describes the time at Kew as 'four intensely happy years'.

Presumably this happiness included the children too though both were by now away at school.

From Temple Grove Gregory won a King's Scholarship at Westminster School and moved there in September 1915. To begin with he was poor at Maths, better at French and better still at Classics, Divinity and English. His interest in History was by now developing steadily and was to be encouraged and deepened in the VIth by a teacher called Tanner.

Westminster School was Gregory's first real contact with a Benedictine world, albeit by now, indirectly so. The atmosphere of the school attached to the Abbey, spreading out as it does, from Dean's Yard next door to the Great Cloister, its long history and heritage began to have an effect on him. References in his school books to monasticism always accord it an important, positive role, speaking with respect of its continuous history. The same respect is already afforded to the papacy, acknowledging the popes as successors of St Peter and speaking scathingly of 'the adulteries of an apostate monk and an apostate nun' — meaning Martin Luther and his wife Catherine von Bora.

Gregory won prizes at school: the Vincent Prize in 1919 and also the Gumbleton Prize for English Verse, for which he wrote a poem about Daedalus. He indulged his gift for acting by taking part in the Latin play: the *Adelphi* of Terence in 1919. There had been no plays during the war, but Gregory took the part of Syrus in the revived performances. The part was a military one which Gregory seems to have played as a 'Tommy' and the school magazine says 'For Syrus first and unstinting praise' though it thought him to have been a 'little too drunk'.

Gregory's taste for controversy and debate led him also to active participation in the debating society where he argued against the idea that 'Might is Right'. He defended the role of conscience against the arguments of the herd and would not allow 'might' to dictate the nature of conscience. No doubt the impact of the First World War had its part to play in this argument as well as Gregory's developing religious and historical reflection. Gregory's habit of using up the blank

pages of his school books later in life means that a number
of his school books are preserved with entries ranging from
Latin translation exercises (with fairly consistently high
marks) to parody poems and jokes. He writes a poem about
'the election of juniors in 1915' — his own contemporaries.
Among them is a verse about himself:

> Myself am next upon the list
> A saintly youth, I've never been kissed.
> I've ever been kept from women free
> By ugliness, not chastity.

A more serious poem — but also a parody — reveals the
romanticism in the boy. He took the poem *Where are the snows
of winter* by Villon and created a pastiche with reference to
the Russian revolution:

> Prince, the east wind whistling fast
> through the Urals, knoweth well,
> But the east wind will not tell
> Where lies Nicholas the Last.

An essay on the subject: 'Travel as an inspiration in literature', written in the VIth, laments the dull modern world
saying: 'Travel of itself is of no avail to man without a sense
of its romance.'

Romantic ideas run through other poems and through his
writing about history: Asgard; the Holy Roman Empire; the
Blessed Virgin Mary; the *Angelus*; 'perfect knighthood and the
mystic Holy Grail'. The romantic in him no doubt matured
but it never went away.

The same process applied, however, also to the historian
in him. His capacity to enter into an age on its own terms, to
stand where they stood rather than looking from a distance,
to ask their questions rather than ours; these capabilities
were already emerging. The fascination of a period of history
in its unique many-textured wholeness had already been
caught. In one sense the important combination of the
imagination of the romantic and the diligent reasonableness
of the historian was already emerging in him.

The imagination was used in other ways too. The sense of humour and wit for which Gregory was later famous were also there in the schoolboy, if slightly less subtle. The notebooks contain a two-act '(very) Grand Opera' called *Il Profiteerio*, and 'a romance of love and intrigue' called *The Perils of Persephone*, which reads rather like Ronald Firbank. Both make allusions to current political issues such as communism and revolution and both are very flippant.

The opera contains characters such as Bisto, the Basha of Memphis and Accumalayta, his daughter, as well as Margerina and Balloonio. In very mock Italian the brief opera follows Bisto's attempt to acquire butter without queuing for it. His son Magneto, falls in love with Margerina, the butter-seller, but both eventually die for their pains. A brief quotation will give sufficient idea of the tone of the opera:

> This idea newio
> Stando in queuio
> Freezio, stewio
> It will not doio.

It seems highly unlikely that the opera was ever performed but it reveals a wilder, almost anarchic, streak in Gregory's sense of humour.

A similar zest characterises other stories of his Westminster days, undocumented but part of an oral tradition, as it were. He is said to have participated in the Shrove Tuesday 'Pancake Greaze' on behalf of his class. This was a two-minute battle over a pancake to see who could obtain the largest piece of it. Gregory is said to have been the winner on the occasion when he competed. The reward was a golden sovereign from the Dean.

An even more characteristic story concerns his determination to receive Holy Communion on Ascension Day. Apparently no provision was made for the school to attend the Eucharist on that day but Gregory wanted to fulfil his obligation so he presented himself with his request to the head master. He initially refused and threatened to discipline Gregory for his persistence but Gregory pointed out that it would look very odd in the paper next day if it said: 'Church boy expelled from church school for wanting to attend church.'

Both stories must have been told by Gregory himself later in his life and they have the air of his amused, slightly self-mocking, slightly self-aggrandising tone. The latter story, however, particularly reveals something of the continuing piety of the boy. He claimed in a later address first to have made his confession at thirteen, presumably at the time of his confirmation. He seems to have stayed doggedly with the discipline of the Anglo-Catholic tradition with which he grew up, despite the markedly different ethos there must have been at Westminster.

This was the formative world of the English public school of the early twentieth century with its combination of high academic, especially classical, expectations and near barbaric living conditions. There were no doubt additional pressures as a result of the World War being waged at the time Gregory entered the school. Boys left to become the soldiers of the trenches: this inevitably left its mark on the school and its pupils. Finding escape from the pressures of this world and the deprivation of affection and support in friendships and peer loyalties could make it all the harder to retain an independent religious devotion. Eccentricity was permitted but anything that looked like religious fanaticism would be mercilessly mocked. Then, as later, Gregory seems to have been able to combine serious religious commitment with an air of worldliness, a sense of humour and a talent for creating the atmosphere rather than, merely having to put up with living in it.

In 1920 Gregory was elected to a history exhibition, worth £80, at Merton College, Oxford and so matriculated in the university which was to remain important to him for the rest of his life. Oxford in 1920 was rather different from today. There were no suburbs, few tourists and no traffic. There was comparatively little competition for entrance. Evelyn Waugh in his autobiography *A Little Learning*, writing about exactly this period says:

At Canterbury Gate and in the Broad hansom cabs and open victorias were for hire. Bicycles and clergymen abounded, and clergymen on bicycles were, with the cattle coming to market, the only hazards of traffic. I doubt if there were thirty cars in the university owned by dons or undergraduates. Telephones were never used. It was a male community.

The community of an Oxbridge college then was in many ways small and intimate. Teaching revolved around the weekly tutorial with its essay and the occasional lecture. The college provided rooms to live in, food in hall, servants to attend and a chapel for prayer, much of which was still compulsory. Leisure time was filled with voluntary societies and clubs, rowing and other sports, friends from one's own college or beyond.

This was Oxford after the First World War and after the Russian Revolution. Communism was a topic of debate and conversation, so was the emerging science of psychology. In church terms the reform of the liturgy and of church government were developing themes; so was reunion.

Consciously or unconsciously Gregory seems to have opted for the world of religious and related issues in Oxford rather than the more directly political or secular. He joined the Church Society at Merton but never joined the Oxford Union. He does not, however, by any means, seem to have become merely pious.

A picture remains in the Merton College archives of Gregory as cox of the College boat in 1921 and again in 1922. Being small and light he had also coxed at school. In the photograph he sits on the ground in front of the rest of the crew, smartly dressed in jacket and bow tie. His thick, smooth, black hair and dark eyes suggest the French ancestry he was so proud of. The eyes twinkle. A story tells that he persuaded the crew to go to the daily mass with him before the training on the river.... Apocryphal or not, it hints at the strength, the zest, already in this little person. (The photograph tells us he weighed only 8 st. 2½ lb.)

Stories of Gregory's Oxford days seem to highlight still further an apparent contradiction. People speak of him as

quiet and even undistinguished while others recall daring
exploits and practical jokes. In many ways, perhaps, Gregory
was capable of both the quiet and the fun.

The stories of 'daring' exploits and practical jokes seem on
the whole to emanate from Gregory himself, recalled in later
years for after-dinner conversation and entertainment. He
claimed to have been a dandy. 'I wore perfectly dreadful
clothes, cloaks with coloured linings and bow ties.'

The story of the taxis comes from more than one source
and so would seem to be more than mere imagination. He is
said for a wager to have ridden down the High with two taxis,
either leaping backwards and forwards from the roof of one
to the other or, in another version, keeping one foot on each
roof and hoping the taxis kept together!

There are also two completely different versions of a story
about a gun in which Gregory either shot at a don or another
undergraduate's noisy band rehearsal. He is said to have
'hidden' the gun in the post at the porters' lodge, addressed
to himself, while the search for the culprit went on and then
had it delivered when the fuss was over. Gregory's own,
after-dinner, version of the story concluded with him talking
to the dean who claimed to have known Gregory was the
culprit but wanted to know what Gregory had done with the
gun. 'Are you asking me as a man or a dean?' said Gregory. 'He
boggled a bit, and then said "As a man". So I told him. He
took no action at all.'

The same sense of mischief emerges in a story, also recounted later by Gregory, about the visit of a psychoanalyst
from the continent. This was very topical as Freud's work was
beginning to make its impact. The psychoanalyst gave a
lecture and answered questions and provided case histories.
An Oxford professor is then said to have asked about Carl
Jung: 'Ach', said the psychoanalyst, 'Jung der appelkarten
upsetten has....' An item appeared in *Isis*, the University
paper, the next week with photographs of the continental
psychoanalyst with and without his beard....

A more serious incident is described in Dom Robert Petitpierre's book, *Exorcising Devils* (1976) in which he describes

his first experience of exorcism. This takes place in Gregory's
rooms at Merton in 1923. The College has begun to be
haunted by a man in Tudor costume, to the consternation of
many. Petitpierre and some of his friends decide that an
exorcism is required and this is to be done from Gregory's
window. Gregory finds himself holding the holy water for the
priest who reads the Roman Catholic rite of exorcism. When
the priest commands the evil spirit to depart in the name of
Christ: 'Everything on Dix's wash-stand began to shudder
and rattle in the most alarming and inexplicable way.' The
ghost, however, had departed and life returned to normal.
Knowing Gregory, it is entirely possible that it was his mischievous foot that was rocking the wash-stand

Gregory spoke of Oxford undergraduate days as 'a golden
time' but he also called them 'my most faithless period',
claiming that he barely managed to remain devout enough to
hear mass every Sunday 'usually just before midday'. There
may be some exaggeration here of his faithlessness. He was
a regular and reliable member of and contributor to the
Church Society at Merton, presided over by the chaplain F.W.
Green, who remained a lifelong friend.

The Society was linked to a University Church Society
which advertised a 'daily Communion' at St Mary the Virgin,
and the college society encouraged thought, devotion and
regular attendance at chapel. In due course Gregory joined
the Society's committee. Some of his characteristic opinions,
characteristically forcefully put, begin to emerge in the minutes of the society's discussions. Soon after joining he argued
against the Reformation as a popular movement, saying that
the suppression of the monasteries was followed by several
popular rebellions.

On another occasion, in 1922, a speaker defended capitalism and the minutes record that Gregory 'turned ridicule on
Mr Broadbent' saying capitalism was evil and the Church
must cut loose from secular power and work out a social
policy based on Christian principle.

Later in the year Gregory himself spoke on 'Disestablishment'. The minutes call it an 'harangue', 'sweeping on with

showers of ecclesiastical epigrams', 'a *tour de force* against
establishment'. Gregory seems already to be arguing that the
present time should be used to make the Church more and
more Catholic, then would be the time for disestablishment.
'To be disestablished before we were Catholic would be a
disaster, but afterwards it would be a necessity.' And already
Gregory is being accused by other members of 'mediaeval-
ism' and an 'old idea of the Papacy'. The minutes indicate
the forcefulness and charm in speaking and the clarity of
opinion which were to be so characteristic of Gregory in years
to come.

In other after-dinner reminiscences, Gregory claims to
have worked little, to have had a totally eccentric tutor at All
Souls, and to have been close to being sent down. This too
may be exaggeration. His undergraduate notes indicate methodical enough work; his tutor at Merton, Garrod, later
became a professor and, while his Upper-Second class degree
may mean that he had other interests as well, it also indicates
that history was becoming important to him, his natural field.

He clearly read other things beside history: novels and
other contemporary literature, though he never seems to
have had any particularly special place for poetry. There is
little record of his spiritual reading but his undergraduate
days saw the first contacts with Pershore, the Anglican Benedictine experiment near Worcester, later to move to Nashdom. He visited there in 1921 and again in 1923. He may
well also have visited the Cowley Fathers in Oxford along
with other undergraduates.

Among his friends were some who were to remain significant in his life. Robert Petitpierre, of the exorcism story, had
been at Westminster with him and later also became a
member of the Nashdom community. Raymond Raynes became Superior of the Community of the Resurrection at
Mirfield. Christopher Butler joined the Roman Catholic
Church and in due course became Abbot of Downside and a
Bishop. Gregory also first made contact with Tommy Strong
through the Merton Church Society.

Strong was the Dean of Christ Church but an honorary member of the Merton Society. His presence is not recorded at many meetings but he was famous for his interest in promising undergraduates with vocations. Certainly, Gregory turned to him for advice later in life when he had become Bishop of Oxford. Gregory visited Cuddesdon Palace to see him a number of times.

Somewhere in these years then, undocumented, undescribed, alongside the love of history, emerged also a sense of vocation to priesthood. So we find Gregory in January 1924 arriving at Wells Theological College for a period of ordination training. He was there for three terms and in later years could be fairly scathing about it. Lecturing to the Oxford diocesan clergy school later in his life he says:

> The first instruction on the history of Christian worship I ever received was a lecture at Wells. It left a strong and clear impression on my virgin mind — Christian worship began by being very Non-Conformist but soon got over that and became reasonably C. of E. Later on when the 'Dark Ages' were in sight it rather went to pieces and became R.C....

Gregory's notebooks contain extensive notes from this period on Old Testament history and theology and even if he found some of it superficial, it must have encouraged him to explore further both Biblical study, which he never neglected, and the ever more significant liturgical study.

The Wells College records include references to a debate in which Gregory took part arguing that socialism is a menace to civilisation: an interesting counter to his Merton attack on Capitalism and a development of his school defence of conscience. 'He dreaded the idea of the subordination of the individual to the state which he maintained led to the crushing out of initiative and the development of a mechanical type of mind.'

The same records, however, also indicate the place the religious life already had in Gregory's mind:

> G.E.A. Dix came to us almost direct from the Benedictine community at Pershore, thus bringing a new line of thought into a college which has always welcomed representatives of

all the various 'schools of thought' to be found within the
Anglican Communion. He has been able to remove many
false conceptions of the aims of the contemplative life.'

Gregory was ordained deacon on October 5th 1924, the day
after his birthday. He was not ordained to serve in a parish
but as a tutor and lecturer in modern history at Keble College
and so, after a year, he returned to Oxford. One year later, on
his birthday, he was ordained to the priesthood.

In fact, little material survives from the period at Keble:
he left after only two years to join the monastery at Pershore
in 1926, shortly before the move to Nashdom. Throughout
the time at Keble he had maintained links with the community there including a long visit in 1925. His sense of vocation
finally led to action in 1926.

There is a suggestion that he left Keble after a 'homosexual incident' and this might explain what seems to have been
a rather abrupt departure after a short tenure. There is
however no documentary evidence of any kind for this, no
record of it at Keble and no reference in any of Gregory's
papers.

It is mentioned here because it might be connected to an
intriguing poem that appears in one of Gregory's notebooks,
a poem specifically dated '15.5.1925' and entitled 'Fra Agos-
tino to Leonardo'. It is written in a re-used school book but
the dating fixes it in the Keble period. It seems to be a love
poem, mourning for lost romance but is it an exercise, a copy,
a parody? Or is it an attempt to express deep feelings? If so,
to whom? It is impossible now to say but it remains tantalising and intriguing.

The poem contrasts an 'earthly' love with a higher calling:

> Called to the heart of Infinite Loveliness
> I had complained and shrunk from His caress
> And given what was His unto my brother thief.

There is a sense of regret but determination about the
'higher calling':

Now like some Culdee of the ancient days
On the last island of dim western seas
Lord, pour the incense of my soul in praise
And tempt me to Thy cold stern ecstasies
Embittering all joy that is not Thee.

The poem reveals the still lively and romantic imagination
in Gregory, increasingly stirred by the monastic, Benedictine
ideal as well as the religious Anglo-Catholic world in general.
But the 'cold stern ecstasies' stand out with some force, a
fiercer element in his sense of vocation.

Gregory never seems to have considered marriage—perhaps
he was homosexual by nature but this poem, and the rumours
related to this period, are the only evidence linked to this
area of his life.

It may have been, then, that entering the monastery was
a final consequence of the tension faced between some kind
of relationship and his vocation. He certainly seems to have
been a frequent visitor to Bishop Strong at Cuddesdon in this
period. Strong's biographer noted this in writing to Gregory
when compiling the biography in the 1940s. Gregory's name
appeared frequently in the Cuddesdon Palace visitors' book
against the Chelsea address of his parents, suggesting that
Gregory had left Keble and returned home but was talking
with the bishop about his vocation and his future. One or two
stray notes from Bishop Strong, from later in the 1920s (after
Gregory's return from Africa) suggest that the relationship
was close and that Bishop Strong took, as he did with other
young clergy, a great deal of trouble to help Gregory.

All this is fairly speculative. The later two letters from
Bishop Strong seem to be about Gregory's desire for a licence
in the Diocese of Oxford which was eventually issued in
1935. Whether any of this was a factor in Gregory's decision
to delay his vows is impossible to say. The major factors, as
we shall see, seem to have been his illness in Africa and his
uncertainty about joining the Roman Catholic Church. He
did not take solemn vows until 1941.

In fact, if there was a crisis that precipitated Gregory's
entry into the community it was actually part of a long

process of considered vocation which reached a turning point in 1926 as he came to live with the community at Pershore.

Later in his life Gregory said that he had never, or only ever very briefly, actually doubted the existence of God. His turning at this stage of his life towards the exploration of a religious vocation was part of a deepening conviction about the nature of the world, the purpose of existence, the love and reality of God.

In an address delivered in the United States many years later Gregory reflects on the nature of God and describes an incident at this point in his life. With it we can turn from his childhood and university years to look more closely at the monk and the priest:

> Anyone who has had one little glimpse of the corner of the glory of God, or the very outskirts of His way, they will know that God is in Himself, for His own sake, lovely.
>
> It is very difficult to realise that God would have deserved all love if there had never been any creatures. I think the first time I realised that was when I was about twenty-five years of age and I walked up to a big hill in Gloucester, in England. It was a famous hill. You walk up a long dusty hill from the Gloucester side, you can't see anything except about two yards of dusty road in front of you. You come out on the top of the hill and there is perhaps the loveliest, softest landscape in the whole of England. Spread out to view is the whole valley with Gloucester Cathedral tower standing up in the middle, and this gorgeous view stretching right away to the mountains. I suddenly realised it wasn't anything in me, it was something in that view which had wrenched the admiration out of me. And that it had been just as lovely while I had been coming up the hill and couldn't see it at all.
>
> God is like that, for His own sake, in His own self, apart from what He does for me, lovely.

2

The Monk and the Priest

Therefore whoever you are who are hastening soon to reach the heavenly fatherland, first with the help of Christ carry out fully this very small rule for beginners....

Rule of St Benedict, Ch. 73

Later in his life, perhaps when he returned to Oxford to receive his Doctor's scarlet in 1948, Gregory found himself sitting on High Table in Merton next to his old tutor, now Professor, Garrod. During the meal Gregory was evidently his usual witty, caustic and amusing self. In due course the professor remarked: 'You haven't improved a bit, Dix, since you became a monk.' 'I didn't become a monk to improve', Gregory replied. 'So why did you become a monk?' asked the professor. 'I became a monk', Gregory answered, 'to slow down the deterioration.'

Gregory was not always such a realist; we have seen something of the romanticism that inspired him as a schoolboy and an undergraduate. By the time he died, however, in 1952 Gregory had spent twenty-six years living in the one religious community. He had grown and changed and deepened within it, sharing life with a group that became in effect his family. The monastic way of life, following the Rule of St Benedict, requires a seriously realistic and very basic mutual commitment of its would-be followers. Any developed attempt to live the rule would soon need practical realism and fairly

25

dogged commitment. In fact, at first, Gregory was not willing, or able, to make that full commitment but in time it became the natural development of his life, its blossoming and flourishing.

Where did his vocation come from? The papers that remain and the reminiscences of his surviving contemporaries are silent here. Perhaps this is no surprise. For most people the deepest motivations of their lives, the most strongly controlling impulses, are not to be talked about easily: they come from too far down. Gregory never describes, in any existing document, either a growing or an instant sense of calling, either to priesthood or to the monastic life. All we have is a letter to a friend[1] in 1936 when Gregory was about to enter the novitiate again. He says: 'I know now it is what I have been meant for for fifteen years past.'

The 'fifteen years' takes us back to 1921 and Gregory's first years in Oxford, as an undergraduate. We know him to have been a religious child and youth and the Benedictine heritage of Westminster may have had its part to play while he was at school there. Certainly all references in his school and college notebooks to monasticism, and the Benedictines in particular, are glowing and appreciative. An additional factor must have been his father's connections, not only with the Anglo-Catholic world in general or with the nuns at St

---

1   A number of letters exist from the middle of the 1930s from Gregory
    to a friend in Wells. There are no replies from the friend among the
    papers. The letters suggest a close friendship and reflect on common
    acquaintances but also on other interesting issues. Gregory, however,
    never addresses his friend by name; the letters are headed
    'Monsignore' (which suggests he was a canon or dignitary of some kind
    in Wells) or 'My dear friend'. It had been assumed that this must be
    a member of the cathedral chapter — the Dean, Armitage Robinson.
    Gregory perhaps does appear to have known Robinson but the letters
    seem rather familiar for a young man to write to a senior cleric,
    formerly Dean of Westminster. Most crucially the series of letters
    continues after Robinson's death in 1933. Among the remainder of the
    chapter there is no other obvious candidate. The series of letters is
    somewhat arbitrary, there may well have been further correspondence
    no longer preserved.

Leonard's, but also, although we have no direct evidence of this, with Father Ignatius of Llanthony and the attempt to revive the monastic life in the Anglican world. One might suppose that Dr Dix was also interested in Aelred Carlyle's Benedictine experiment on Caldey island but here again there is no actual evidence. However, Dr Dix does seem to have had some involvement in supporting Pershore Abbey, the Anglican successor to Caldey, and then Nashdom Abbey, the further development of Pershore. A minute in a stray notebook presents him hosting a meeting for fund-raising in aid of Nashdom in 1926 and we also find him contributing an article on the Holy Grail to *Laudate*, the community's journal, in 1928.[1]

Gregory must have grown up, then, with a much greater familiarity with the idea of 'religious life' than the average school child and, once he was at Oxford, there was nothing to prevent him travelling the forty miles or so into Worcestershire to visit the house at Pershore. His name first appears in the visitors' book, 'Alston Dix', on June 7th 1921, with three others from Oxford. He visits again in December 1923, just before going to Wells. He is remembered by a surviving contemporary as just such a visitor to Pershore, acting as subdeacon at the High Mass and memorable for the French pronunciation of his Latin.

By 1925 he is already contributing small items and reviews to *Laudate* [September 1925] and the visitors' book records that, now a priest and a tutor at Keble, he spent most of the Long Vacation of 1925 staying at Pershore. (July 11th – September 29th).

Familiarity with the world of religious communities does not necessarily lead to vocations however and we can go no further in analysing Gregory's deeper motives in those early years.

In the summer of 1926 Gregory arrived at Pershore to live. The Abbey was an ancient Benedictine foundation not far from Worcester, close to the river Avon and in sight of the

1   *Laudate*, 1928.

Malvern hills. The remains of the Abbey Church had become
an imposing parish church and within the old enclosure there
remained the Abbey house, now demolished, but from 1914
to 1926 the home of Anglican Benedictines. This community
had a fairly traumatic beginning when Aelred Carlyle's attempt at Anglican Benedictine life on Caldey Island in Wales
had foundered on the rock of Charles Gore's insistence on
some kind of conformity to Anglican ways. Carlyle had taken
most of the community with him into submission to Rome.
Three men were left, still seeking an Anglican way, only one
of whom was a professed monk. In due course the three were
offered the house at Pershore. One of those men, Father
Denys Prideaux, was an oblate of the community but around
him the new experiment began to develop. An 'oblate', in
the Benedictine way, had originally been a child dedicated
to a community by his parents (from the Latin *oblatus* — an
offering, the same root as 'oblation') In modern times the
term refers to those who, for one reason or another, wish to
be associated with the way of life without taking the full
formal vows. Father Prideaux was a priest but in many ways
a reluctant monk. It was some years before he was convinced
about the appropriateness of vows for himself and even
longer before he agreed to be Abbot. He was widely read and
spoke many foreign languages. He also had a reputation for
wandering off the subject and other eccentricities. Nevertheless the recovery of a Benedictine life in the Church of
England for men (the women were already established at
West Malling, Kent) owes its early growth to him. Perhaps it
was precisely because of his reluctance and wariness of vows
and abbacy, unlike Aelred Carlyle's exotic fervour, that the
seed was quietly sown, tended and nurtured.

It should not be inferred that there was anything easy
about this development. It was in fact extremely precarious
and in many ways haphazard. Chapter minutes from these
earliest days reveal a valiant attempt to live the life amidst
confusions over the building and its facilities, over the precise requirements of the Rule and over exactly who was
sharing in the living of the life at any given time. Discussions

in chapter ranged from the way to cense the monks during Solemn Masses to the status of jam as a 'luxury' or a 'necessary food'.

With fits and starts and some confusion the life did gradually emerge from the slightly unlikely soil and slowly a small community of committed men, under vows, was established. Stability and commitment is attractive and so the community grew until it was too big for its premises. Abbot Denys, a man of imagination, had various ideas for other houses including a London priory, but in 1926 the community purchased a large house in Burnham near Slough, West of London and moved there in September 1926.

It was just before this move that Gregory joined the community. He came from his lecturing post at Keble in Oxford, aged twenty-four, already a priest, now ready to explore a calling to live in community under vows, committed to a life of prayer. There must have been some sharp contrasts between this slightly chaotic, rather full, unevenly regulated religious house and the established comfortable, sophisticated and spacious world of an Oxford don in a High-Church college. The prospect of an imminent move can only have added to the sense of confusion and busy-ness. Yet the air of expectation, the feeling of growth and expansion must have been invigorating and inspiring too. It *was* possible to become a monk in the Church of England: to be in that Church and also fully committed to the life of corporate prayer.

Dom Gregory, of course, entered the community as 'the Reverend G.E.A. Dix', Alston Dix still, to his family and friends. As he was clothed as a novice in the traditional way he took a new name. He took the name 'Gregory'. Why Gregory? He took the name of Pope St Gregory VII, also known as Hildebrand. Gregory VII was a fierce and vigorous eleventh-century reformer of the Church, removing corrupt Church officials and staunchly, even forcefully, defending the rights of the Church against the State. There are obvious seeds here of Gregory's later work in Church affairs but the consequences too, no doubt, of his study of history, his churchmanship, his developing reverence for the papacy and a hint of his twinkling defiances.

Within a very short while Gregory had moved with the community to Nashdom. Today the community has moved on again and settled into a smaller abbey near Newbury. Nashdom has not been used since it was sold in 1987 and has developed an air of desolation and shabbiness. However, the community continues to own and tend the monks' cemetery set, as it is, away from the house among the trees. There, in addition to the abbots, are buried monks, lay brother and oblates — each under a simple cross and among them Dom Gregory Dix. The house's air of desolation is, ironically, contradicted by the perfectly still cemetery with its accumulated years of committed contemplation and living of the Rule. Overshadowed by the crucifix, the cemetery speaks of something living and still growing. The years in vows recorded on each grave speak of a vigour in prayer and a quiet, steady power in commitment that has not been abandoned.

Nashdom may no longer look like a monastery; nor did it in 1926, when the community first arrived. Although it is quite close to London and set amongst small country villages, the house felt secluded and independent. It had been built by Lutyens for a Russian, Prince Alexis Dolgoronki, hence its Russian name which means 'Our Home'. It was in a grand classical style, the walls white and the rows of shutters, green. The community adjusted its style to their own and visitors testified, as its life developed in the 30s, that it resembled nothing so much as one of the great Italian or Belgian Benedictine houses of the eighteenth century.[1] The ballroom of the prince lent itself ideally as a chapel with suitably baroque furnishings, other altars were added in various places for private masses and steadily the house was adjusted to suit the needs of a slowly growing monastic community.

1   See, for instance, Peter Anson, *The Call of the Cloister*, SPCK 1955, p. 189.

After a number of false starts by others Nashdom was the first Anglican men's religious community to order its life according, as closely as possible, to the Rule of St Benedict. A number of women's communities, such as West Malling Abbey, had been living under the rule for rather longer. As in the Roman Catholic communion, other communities have subsequently returned more and more fully to this first and clearest rule and the whole movement towards greater simplicity and clarity in the religious life which characterises recent decades has been closely linked to the rediscovery and re-examination of this 'very small Rule for beginners'.

Those who first look into Benedict's Rule are usually surprised by its sheer ordinariness, its lack of developed 'spiritual guidance', its prosaically practical and matter-of-fact tone of instruction. Its concentration on humility and obedience jar in the modern liberated ear, its quite strikingly sparse treatment of 'prayer' seems puzzling and inappropriate. Yet this little beginning, which is all that Benedict says it is, has utterly transformed the history of the Church and of Europe and indeed the world. It has done so more than once and done it in such a way that we scarcely recognise any longer its impact through the communities formed by it; and the individuals. The Holy Rule of 'Our Holy Father Benedict', as Benedictines call him, through those Benedictines, men and women, has affected scholarship and art, architecture and theology, democratic institutions and government, liturgies and spiritualities. In the Church of England alone the Benedictine spirit has infused the liturgy of the Prayer Book and its subsequent developments; has deeply coloured the lives of the cathedrals as well as their architecture and layout; has reached into church government and most recently into lay spirituality.[1] The genius of the Rule is acknowledged to be that sheer ordinariness which strikes us first: it is reasonable, not too demanding but clear in its aims, practical and not exotic. It is designed for human beings — designed to help them be, to provide one way for

1   See Esther de Waal, *Seeking God*, Collins / Faith Press 1984.

them to be, better human beings. It is not about perfection,
other ways may take you on to that, but it is about starting
out, beginning to run in the way, about discovering a realistic
way of making a start.

Of course it is ever in the nature of human beings to make
things more complicated and so the history of monasticism
is the history of exotic accretions to the rule and repeated
returns to try again for the original simplicity. This Anglican
attempt at the Benedictine way was another return to the
original; an attempt to 'establish a school of the Lord's
service'.

Abbot Denys was clearly aware of this Benedictine heritage and was widely read in Benedictine history and spirituality. He came to it, of course, with his community, through
the powerful filter of the existing Roman Benedictine world.
They did not attempt to ignore the Roman Catholic development of the Benedictine way, quite the opposite, it was
precisely that development they wanted to see implanted in
the Anglican world, as fully in bloom as possible. They
wanted there to be a sense of continuity: a continuity with
the pre-reformation English Benedictines; a continuity with
all those now living the Benedictine way and so a continuity
that could let them reach right back to the Holy Father
Benedict himself and in some way overcome and heal the
breaches and wounds of intervening centuries.

It is abundantly clear that this is very much how Gregory
saw the life. In a lecture given in the United States, probably
in 1947, he spoke on 'The religious life in the Anglican
Communion'. He argued for this sense of continuity claiming
that through Little Gidding and similar experiments, it never
actually died out. He argued that the strength or otherwise of
the life of committed contemplatives acts as a barometer in
the church, an indicator of the spiritual weather, and he went
on to claim that the religious life is there always to remind
the Church, in the face of temptation to compromises, that
no one can serve two masters. This warning function, important to Gregory's involvement in Church affairs as we shall
see later, was nevertheless ultimately secondary to the pri-

mary purpose of the life, the Prayer itself. In a sermon preached at Nashdom in 1945 he spoke on a favourite text: 'And there was silence in heaven for about half an hour' (Rev. 8.4,5). He linked the silence to the ground of contemplation and referred to the early desert monks in their: 'terrible intensity of concentration on God alone'. Thus he emphasised the absolute primacy of contemplation for monasticism and how vital this was in the economy of the whole Church.

Yet, as we have noticed, the Rule has little to say on Prayer. Towards the end of his life, though of course he did not then know that he would die soon, Gregory gave the Nashdom community a retreat on the Rule of St Benedict. Every religious community goes into retreat once or twice a year to concentrate its attention for a few days on its spiritual life; a 'holiday with God' Gregory called it. His Retreat on the Rule is a *tour de force*, a beautiful swan song. He looks carefully at different sections of the Rule in which he was clearly deeply immersed and in the eighth address comes to the subject of Prayer. He notices that there are more directions on guests than on Prayer in the Rule but shows how the idea of prayer as an 'art' is a renaissance concept and that 'psychologised' prayer in the Benedictine tradition develops after St Bernard in the twelfth century. The older idea sees prayer as a state in which the whole life 'leaps like a sparkling fountain towards God'. He quotes St Anthony of the desert (third century) from the very oldest monastic tradition: 'That monk is not yet truly praying who knows that he is praying' and he concludes: 'Prayer in its simplest elements is the going forth of your little created human spirit from itself to meet the downrush of the uncreated spirit of God.'

Gregory at other times writes in other ways about prayer and deals with some of its techniques, as we shall see, but he had learned by living the Rule that at its heart it is a state, a way of living, a deeply natural and unselfconscious 'going forth'.

This is the prayer of what in another sermon he calls: 'the little I, the individual man, so dear to God', but Gregory always stressed that prayer was an activity of the Body, a corporate thing. This is one of his most important emphases. It is there, of course, in the Rule, in Benedict's early reminder that he is writing for monks living in community under an abbot; For him the most obvious, most satisfactory, most straightforward way of running in the direction of the gospel. Consequently, therefore, prayer ceases to be a private activity but is the work of the community, its principal offering to God, the *opus Dei*. The day in the Rule is framed upon the cycle of prayer which includes scripture and psalms and the Eucharist. This daily pattern through the centuries, variously adjusted and developed, trimmed and expanded again, profoundly conditioned monasticism from its heart outwards. Whatever other good works were added on to the life at its heart this was all there was, the *opus Dei*, the offering of prayer. By the time this life reached twentieth-century Anglican England on the outskirts of London, it had been shaped and trimmed and adjusted and refashioned many times. Still its framework, its skeleton and heart, remains the work of praying together and offering worship, otherwise it is meaningless.

The Rule, as everyone notices, spends much time on the subject of the abbot, on obedience to superiors, and on humility. As we have noticed, this jars in libertarian times, but is in many ways the very natural and inevitable consequence of the emphasis on community. How do you live together in community? The life must be carefully ordered so that the gospel of love is fulfilled in the subjection of each to the other and the humble subjection of all to the rule of the abbot, who is 'believed to hold the place of Christ'. It is precisely in the last point that Benedict's idea of 'obedience' achieves maturity. As the abbot develops a fatherly relationship with his sons, working out his love for them, so in natural response the brethren live in harmony together under his benevolent rule. 'Obedience' is another word for that harmony. Such obedience belongs of course to the small, simple, balanced communities Benedict envisaged and inevitably it becomes much more difficult once that model changes, but it was never easy even there, as Benedict himself acknowledges. In many ways the history of monasticism is the constant striving to return to that model of community and that mode of obedience. Gregory learned the central place of obedience in the monastic life and having reflected on it deeply, in seeking to practise it spoke of it much in addresses and retreats and in the letters to monks and nuns which survive.

In a retreat for one of the brothers at St Gregory's, their American priory, he spoke bluntly of the monk as a slave. Once he had taken vows, his will was removed. Without using quite such strong terms, he spoke similarly of the will to the Sisters of the Church during their Christmas retreat in 1937. 'Charity makes us love as members,' he said, 'obedience makes us will as members.' Speaking on his favourite theme of membership in the Body of Christ, he reminded them that they needed each other and that their life together depended on obedience. He went on: 'Our life of obedience as religious is needed for the whole Church. In a machine the wheel that goes the most quickly needs the most perfect adjustment, so we Religious need obedience to keep us in perfect adjustment.'

His addresses to the sisters conclude, however, with an important reminder. For a Religious, obedience is a form of the incarnation. God speaks in a human voice and so he is heard in the voice of the Superiors. Like Christ there has to be a deliberate choice to be obedient to that voice.

This insight is developed further in the retreat on the Rule which he gave to his own community towards the end of his life. He points out the centrality in the Rule of humility and the summons to obey not only the abbot, but also one another. Then he emphasises that for Benedict obedience is about unity with God. For other spiritual writers obedience is simply a mortification, a discipline for the will, but for Benedict it has become something positive — a way to union with God like the union Jesus achieved with his Father by his obedience. So for Benedict, the human superior has the awesome responsibility of being identified with God and thus becomes the means by which his subjects achieve union with God. Dom Gregory, as Prior in his own community from 1948, and so a Superior, must have felt for himself that awesome responsibility in ruling the community, even as he had reflected on it in the long years of his own subjection to other superiors.

In many ways the world of the Religious life, and of all Christian living, has changed beyond recognition since Gregory gave his addresses and lived in obedience. Not only has the second Vatican Council altered the face of the Christian earth but the world has plunged further and further into secularised individualism and pluralism. Yet the question does not go away: how do you live with others in community? What do you do with the human will? How do you achieve harmony in living together? Where is Christ? What does it mean to say you 'want to obey him'?

Whatever the answers may now be, it is certainly even more true now than it was when Gregory said it in his Retreat on the Rule, that Benedict's kind of obedience and humility is a reversal of the world: 'It is the world of the Beatitudes which he has organised for us to live in.'

St Benedict's little Rule began to be lived at Nashdom according to the existing Roman Catholic pattern. Gregory, like every other monk, would have had a 'cell', a small room of his own from which throughout the day he would have made his way to join the brethren on the *Statio*, the place of assembly in the middle of the house where the Winter Garden had formerly been. From there, in procession after the Abbot, they would go together into the chapel to sing the offices. Eventually all the services were sung in Latin, taken from the Monastic breviary of the Roman Catholic Church, and were chanted according to the current plainsong of the Vatican Gradual. Gregory never claimed to have a particularly good singing voice but he took his place in this 'harmony of the community' as in its metaphorical seeking after harmony. Each day, between the (sometimes very long) services, each monk had various domestic tasks to perform around the house and grounds, as well as periods of reading and study and times of mental prayer and quiet meditation. Meals varied in time and content according to the season of the year. Pershore had a reputation for poor food (despite the jam!) and there does not seem to have been much immediate improvement at Nashdom. Meals were generally eaten in silence while one of the brethren read to the community. This was not necessarily as tedious as it may sound. Apart from the sometimes surprising contents of books piously chosen, stories abound of whole sections omitted from boring books; of monks who read every last footnote, appendix and postscript almost to the index; of one monk who corrected the punctuation; and of one monk who, in reminding the community of what had been read at the previous meal, never actually reached the starting place.

Perhaps it is important to say at this point that in general religious communities are as full of humour and the comical as anywhere else that human beings congregate. With people like Gregory Dix among them, full of wit, stories and repartee they could not help being full of life in every sense. One of the places where good humour might legitimately be enjoyed was Recreation when the community gathered each day and conversation was encouraged. Again the Benedictine common sense had no rigid 'vow of silence' but expected minimal talk in corridors, total quiet during the Greater Silence of the Night and then the encouraged conversation of Recreation. The day to which Gregory began to become accustomed would have varied seasonally and according to High Festivals or Fasts but its rough outline was something like this:

5.00 a.m.	Rising bell
5.30 a.m.	Matins and Lauds: the first prayers of the day
6.45 a.m.	Private masses: it was customary for all priests to say a mass each day at which another monk would be his server. This was Gregory's practice using the Roman Missal.
7.15 a.m.	Breakfast
8.00 a.m.	Prime
9.20 a.m.	Terce and Conventual High Mass: the eucharist for the whole community. By 1930 this was sung

every day with three ministers at the altar, communion was in one kind only but normally there would be no communions. The priest monks took it in turn to celebrate this mass.

10.20 a.m.	Work
12.05 p.m.	Sext and None
12.30 p.m.	Dinner
1.00 p.m.	Rest
2.00 p.m.	Work
3.45 p.m.	Vespers
4.15 p.m.	Tea
4.30 p.m.	Work
6.30 p.m.	Meditation
7.00 p.m.	Supper
7.30 p.m.	Recreation
8.30 p.m.	Compline, followed by the Greater Silence
10.00 p.m.	Lights out

It took some years, of course, of settling in before this fully developed pattern emerged. At first glance, with all its ingredients it might seem exotic with the Latin and the Chant and the ceremonial. For those for whom it was their life, however, it became the routine, the daily round, in which they might discover a rhythm of work, prayer and rest, together with their brethren.

At the quiet heart of it for Gregory was, of course, the Mass. Without conscious analysis the daily recitation of the accumulated prayers of the Church in the Latin Mass must have steadily worked their way deeply into him meeting with the combination of romantic and realist that was in him, feeding his imagination and his precise intellect as well as his praying spirit. In the introduction to *The Shape of the Liturgy* he argues for the importance of the praying liturgist and that was certainly where he began and ended. In the middle of his great celebration of the universal relevance of the Eucharist, towards the end of *The Shape*, he says: 'The sheer stupendous quantity of the love of God which this ever repeated action has drawn from the obscure Christian multitudes through

the centuries is in itself an overwhelming thought. (All that
going with one to the altar every morning!)'

It is clear that it was for Gregory, at least sometimes, the
place where he prayed most deeply. He was conscious through
his life of his inability to reach the place of prayer referred to
in his own retreat addresses, the place where prayer is a state,
a natural and unselfconscious offering. In letters to other
monks he admitted to being too much of an actor, too ready
to watch himself in the pose of prayer. He liked the saying of
St Antony, quoted earlier, precisely because he could see
himself there: 'That monk is not yet truly praying who knows
that he is praying.'

And yet, in writing to Dom Patrick Dalton while he was in
the United States, he could say: 'One can get out of it
(watching oneself) in prayer-time — on the lucky days —
and that's the best that can be said for me except sometimes
at the altar (and always I think at *Qui Pridie* [the beginning
of the Words of Institution] and sometimes in the confes-
sional.' At the central place in his daily mass he could feel
each day that he genuinely prayed.

Gregory was among the second or third generation of men
and women seeking to live the religious life in the Church of
England. The first horror of the establishment at this (and
indeed the first eccentricities of the earliest revivers of
English monasticism) were past. The Church of England,
and the Anglican Communion, was beginning not only to put
up with the experiment but at last to see the value and
beauty of this gift, even if, at first, the Church saw it only in
terms of its usefulness. A generation of bishops was emerging
for whom the Religious life was not frightening and foreign.
By 1930 the Bench of Bishops actually included one or two
Religious. The Lambeth Conference of 1930 warmly welcomed religious communities and, after one or two false
starts, an Advisory Council to link up the communities and
the Church at large was established. For many years it was
under the chairmanship of the very sympathetic Bishop
Kenneth Kirk of Oxford, Gregory's friend. As the Religious
life began to seem slightly less exotic and extreme it came

to be seen as a perfectly acceptable way for a man or woman to work out their Christian life.

Religious communities within the Church of England varied greatly in character from fairly loose associations of priests to communities deeply involved in active charitable and social work. Nashdom and the women's communities with which it gradually developed closer links, Edgware, West Malling, and others, were the only communities living the full Benedictine life with the Latin office and the deliberate focus on the *opus Dei*, the cycle of prayer. The Latin was important in a way that can now seem difficult to understand. When Gregory was helping to organise the Priory in the United States in 1947 he felt they needed instruction in Latin both for rubrics and the liturgy itself. He was not impressed by the existing daily office. He found that they had never sung anything and while he was there they made an attempt at Benediction. He says: 'I acted as cantor — also a very odd experience!' and he adds: 'I cheered myself up by singing the *Exsultet* without warning on Holy Saturday to the no small consternation of Brother Joseph.'

The use of Latin in the context of the full Roman usage — chant, ceremonial, constitutions — was a quite conscious and deliberate part of their religious life. Under Abbot Denys the community saw itself developing as a fully-formed Benedictine house set in the Church of England. It was not an unfortunate accident that the only model for the Benedictine life was the Roman Catholic one. It became a very deliberate offering of the fullness of that life, from the Roman world, placed in the Church of England. The 'wholeness' of the offering became crucially important as the community became more and more committed to the cause of the unity of the churches, East and West, Protestant and Catholic but especially Anglican and Roman. Within the prayer for unity Nashdom saw itself witnessing both to the catholicity of the Church of England — she could include a fully formed Benedictine way of life — and also witnessing to the Church of England that she needed to take her own catholicity seriously, take the Roman Catholic Church seriously and not least the papacy.

The community was in many ways 'Papalist' and Gregory certainly was. 'Papalism' acknowledges the place and priority of the Pope in the Church and sees the cause of unity as a return to communion with him. Mere individual submission was not appropriate, however, since that simply ignored the problem of separated churches and the reality of the continuing life of the Church in them. Papalists in the Church of England wanted to see the whole Church brought back into communion with the Roman See. The cause of unity became, then, a focus of major concern in the community, the object of its prayer. Nashdom played its part in the development of the Church Unity Octave and later, by its connections with the Abbé Paul Couturier, with the Week of Prayer for Christian Unity. The sense of the offering of the community's prayer for this object, a whole offering with no part of the life of contemplative prayer omitted, is a very deep one and affects the entire life as the first monks lived it. The Benedictine life returned to the Church of England was a contribution to the fullness of her catholicity and a call to seek the unity that alone could complete that catholicity. It was a gift, it was like a bridge, a place that made connections, it was an offering, almost a sacrificial offering.

It will be obvious that for any individual who felt like this the temptation from time to time simply to submit and to join the Roman communion must have been considerable. It is certain, as we shall see, that Gregory himself experienced this quite forcefully as did other members of the community.

Of course even in the Anglo-Catholic world of England in the twenties and thirties Nashdom's 'Romanism' was often misunderstood. By this time the children of the Oxford Movement had diversified into a range of groupings from the Liberal Catholics to the Papalists. It was, however, in many ways the heyday of the Catholic movement with the great Anglo-Catholic congresses and the massive celebrations of the Oxford Movement centenary in 1933. The Movement had made almost astonishing progress in its impact on the

Church, though it would take another generation or two for
that impact to be taken for granted. There was therefore an
air of confidence and strength, in which religious communities as well as individual monks and nuns could play their
part. The different communities: the Cowley fathers, the
Community of the Resurrection, the Society of the Sacred
Mission, the women's communities, each had their particular
contribution to make both to the wider Church but also to
each other. All this seemed to be part of the maturing of the
Religious life in the Church of England and Anglican Communion. It seemed so to Gregory who felt he had seen the
whole revived life steadily taking root. In a letter of 1950 he
describes: 'the breadth and depth and *wholeness* of response
to God' of the Benedictine way as a contribution to the
Church and, he says: 'it *is* taking root.'

Back in 1926, however, Gregory was still only a novice.
What guidance did he receive in that first novitiate? It seems
likely that the formation provided was still quite haphazard.
He would no doubt be put in touch with the standard texts
of Roman Catholic novice formation, such as Austin Baker on
Holy Wisdom, and no doubt Abbot Denys' library contained a
vast selection of Benedictine writings from which Gregory
could select. In time a more systematic method developed
and Gregory could in turn make his contribution to the
formation of others, though he was never novice master. In a
letter to Dom Hilary Powell in 1947, as he prepared for the
diaconate, Gregory emphasises the classical tradition of spirituality and says: 'Come at things in the order in which the
Church found them.' He also warns Dom Hilary not to
approach modern Biblical theology until his mind has been
formed by earlier thought especially Aquinas: 'You must have
the form given to it by passing through the Greek mind and
the discipline of metaphysical thinking before Biblical theology can be used constructively in the twentieth century.'

Gregory certainly arrived in the novitiate with an already
trained mind. He not only had the classical discipline of
school but also the training in historical method of his Oxford
days, developed as a lecturer, as well as the rather slighter

contribution of the time at Wells, to which he never gave much credit, but which may have furthered his interest in the Bible and Biblical theology.

Whatever study and discipline he may have begun as a novice, formally or informally, it was soon interrupted when Abbot Denys decided to send Gregory with Dom Bernard Clements to the Gold Coast of Africa (now Ghana).

Despite all kinds of other pressures on the infant community a connection with Ghana had begun in the early twenties when Abbot Denys had responded to the request of the bishop there for help in establishing a Benedictine house in Kumasi. It was not intended to be missionary work but clearly it could only help the Pershore community to establish its credentials at home by becoming involved in the missionary Church. Two monks went initially followed in due course by a third. By the time Gregory was due to go, the 'community' was established at St Gregory's Priory and the monks were in charge of St Augustine's Training College for African priests, as well as running the local parish of St Cyprian. The resignation of the bishop who had inspired the original idea in 1924 meant that things began to be unsettled. The new bishop began to use the monks in other places in his diocese and so the common life in the priory became disrupted, but the venture lasted until 1931 when Abbot Denys finally recalled the remaining monks.

Why was Gregory sent? No doubt because he could contribute to the teaching work in the college but also because, already a priest, he would be able to assist fully in parish work too. The Abbot must have recognised the inevitable constraints on the monastic life in the tiny priory but Gregory, by decision of the chapter, continued in the novitiate while in Africa.

There are no letters or other writings that survive from Gregory's African experience but, brief as it was — he returned home ill after about a year — it must have made its impact on him. Gregory contributed some African stories and descriptions to E.M. Almedingen's memoir of Dom Bernard Clements.This is tantalising because the focus is inevitably

on Dom Bernard, as the rector of the college and the centre
of the work, but in the background Gregory observes and
contributes and reflects.[1]

It would have been a long voyage out to the Gold Coast
and a very different world to work in once he arrived. Sandals
and a white habit were the least of the changes. Together
with sixteen African catechists they found themselves responsible for an area as large as Wales. Building was going on
at the college, out-stations needed to be visited, the students
taught, the Church organised, food grown, while at the
centre of it all the daily office said and the daily mass
celebrated. Preaching, and indeed confession, involved an
interpreter. Gregory maintained that that necessity honed
and concentrated the subsequently famous preaching of
Dom Bernard Clements — and one wonders if it also affected
his own. He describes the regular life of their house and all
its concerns, in the heat, surrounded by the vast spaces of
undeveloped Africa, with customs and culture and language
so strange and exotic. It must have seemed like another
planet to Nashdom and home:

> They all brought troubles, or requests, or just friendship and
> gossip. African students, catechists, communicants to pay
> their Church dues, husbands demanding that Dom Bernard
> deal with their erring wives or vice versa (adultery palavers
> took up endless time), Bush chiefs wanting a new school, or
> the dismissal of their schoolmaster, commissioners in Kumasi
> for a couple of days, European and Syrian traders, missionar-
> ies from the Wesleyan College, the Prefect Apostolic of the
> Northern Territories, and innumerable others, I remember
> them all coming, entirely certain that 'Father Bernard' would
> want to see them, and he did....[2]

The memoir includes a story of the blessing of a church.
About Dom Bernard, it must have been told by Gregory for
it has the ring of his voice and his ironic, understated wit.

1   1945.
2   p. 72.

The blessing was taking place in the presence of King Prempeh who as the local chief was expected to make a speech.

> He stood on the scarlet-draped platform, a small and shrivelled figure for all his important festival trappings, and looked about him, all too obviously full of Dutch courage. Then he opened his lips, began speaking haltingly enough, hiccuped once or twice, staggered and fell over. Dom Bernard got there first to pick him up. A demure Englishwoman present asked sympathetically, 'Oh dear, is it a fit?' Dom Bernard, the tiny chief held in his huge arms as though he were a baby, answered gravely, 'Yes, paralytic', and carried the old man to where his wives were waiting for him....

Whatever Gregory may have begun to gain or to contribute, his time in Africa was curtailed by illness. He found himself in hospital, at some distance from the mission, with appendicitis and other complications. How long he was in hospital before they decided to invalid him home to England is impossible to say, but he was certainly there long enough to want communion brought to him. He showed both his dogged persistence and his basic human sensitivities when at first the African priest bringing the communion was refused entry to the European hospital. It is a story remembered by his contemporaries in the community. Gregory firmly insisted to the sister that the priest must be admitted or he would see the Minister of Health. He knew the Minister to be a devout Roman Catholic fully aware of the significance of communion. His insistence gained the priest admission, but he only let the matter go when he had also acquired a letter guaranteeing the priest's future visits.

Gregory only occasionally refers to his African experience in his later letters and writings, but it did stay with him. In his 1950 lectures in Sweden, later published under the title *Jew and Greek*, writing about the difference between magic and sacraments he says:

> I remember a leading Ju-ju man of Kumawu among the beautiful Ashanti mountains in West Africa explaining to me the difference clearly and simply. He had all the aplomb and

that touch of courteous condescension which always mark
the man of science explaining to the theologian.

Earlier on in the 1930s as he pored over texts of the early
centuries of the Church he found himself making a sudden
connection. In a notebook dated 1938 as he worked through
the sermons of Caesarius (*c.* 470 – 542) he notices the early
Christian prohibitions regarding the circus and secular songs
and the like. 'The same trouble', his marginal note says,
'came up in Ashanti over the fertility dances at N'Koranga.'

On the whole, however, Africa is not referred to. Perhaps
illness and physical pain covered the rest of his experience
and contributed to rendering that slightly strange year an
episode quite separate from the rest of his life and in some
ways left unintegrated.

His return was initially a return to hospital but even when
he finally got back to Nashdom his health was not perfect.
Throughout the rest of his life his letters refer from time to
time to sickness and treatment; he rarely let it affect the life
he lived but it remained a part of him.

This may have been a factor in his decision in due course,
to become an 'intern oblate' of the community rather than
proceed to vows from his novitiate. Precisely what happened
is unclear but although the chapter minutes of October 31st
1929 record that the community unanimously elected Gregory for 'profession in the choir in temporary vows', to take
place on November 21st, this never happened and instead
Gregory changed to the status of oblate. An 'intern oblate'
shares the life of the community and makes what contribution he can and wishes to but he does not have the obligation
of the monastic vows, nor experience the full discipline of
the community's life as a community. Nor, of course, does he
experience the full impact of any dissension or difficulty in
the community and this may have been a factor in Gregory's
decision in a still struggling community. It left him on the
edge, however, and the chapter minutes include occasional
discussions of precisely where a priest oblate fitted in and
what were his obligations. On September 9th 1932 the
chapter discussed Gregory himself. The minutes record that

the Abbot raised the question of Gregory's future 'in view of the fact that his work at Bermondsey was drawing to an end [temporary parish work] and that he was seeking a curacy'. The chapter decided to ask Gregory to see the Abbot but to insist that while living at Nashdom, he should 'live the common life of an oblate'.

This reveals Gregory as unsettled and uncertain in this period about his ultimate relationship with the community. In the event he must have decided to stay there and in fact for the next seven years he chose to remain within the community but not fully of it. Some of his work at this period seems to have been paid for and Gregory appears to have readily contributed this to the community. He returned to share in the common life and the prayer and to say his daily mass but he still held back from final commitment. No doubt Abbot Denys sympathised, himself originally an oblate and, at first anyway, reluctantly an abbot. Well-read and learned, the Abbot must have encouraged Gregory to pursue the studies that now became his main concern, reading his way steadily through the writings of the early Church, extending his knowledge of appropriate languages (not only Latin and Greek but Syriac and Aramaic and some Egyptian) and moving on from the available printed texts to pore over the manuscripts of the period in the British Museum. In its manuscript room in the early 1930s he met other scholars especially Walter Frere, Bishop of Truro and a member of the Community of the Resurrection. Together they would work through, and sometimes disagree about, complexities in the manuscripts and Gregory would steadily build up the wide range of his background knowledge of the life of the early Church and its liturgy.

This was not detached and cut off from the pressures of his life or the big contemporary issues lurking in his mind, in the world, and Church around him. Gregory's instinct led him to look further and further back behind issues to their far-distant historical roots and causes. Nevertheless the silence and detachment of the manuscript room must sometimes

have felt like a cool oasis, a slightly unlikely place of self-forgetting for a would-be monk.

In amongst the complex criss-crossing web of reasons why
Gregory remained an oblate rather than continuing the pro-
gression through vows is the clear thread of his uncertainty
about joining the Roman Catholic Church. In correspondence with a Jesuit, Maurice Bévenot, in 1940, he bares his
soul and with disarming candour describes his own most
vivid, though not solitary, experience of facing this dilemma.
The pressure of Roman Catholic claims and the pressure of
Anglican inadequacies combine to lead him out of Nashdom
and to the verge of submission. The incident clearly takes
place after his return from Africa in 1928 but before 1932
since the letter implies that his father is still alive (he died
in 1932). It is difficult to date any more precisely but it does
belong to this unsettled, earlier period. In a characteristically
open, almost indiscreet, way Gregory describes it thus:

> I know perfectly well the apparent hopelessness of it, the
> perversity of it, as it must seem to you — to set out to restore
> an Anglican Church with its 'no-Popery' past, almost inextri-
> cably entangled with a mere assertion of National Sover-
> eignty, to the bosom of a Roman Church which virtually
> denies its existence as a Church. It is 'cracked' and quixotic
> and chimerical and everything else you like to call it. I faced
> all that myself one frightful afternoon for four hours in the
> Adoration Reparatrice Chapel in Beaufort Street, Chelsea. I
> had left Nashdom 'for good' a week before, to make my
> submission, spent a week fortifying myself by reading only
> R.C. books and set out from my father's house in Chelsea
> that day to find a priest to put myself under instruction, and
> went into the A.R. to say my prayers on the way. After four
> hours I went home sick at heart at the thought of not 'Poping,'
> longing to do it — as I still long very often. I saw then and
> have seen ever since what not submitting involved. It in-
> volves: (1) the duty of arresting the anthropocentric, 'Lib-
> eral' drift in Anglican theology, reversing it and replacing the
> 'classic tradition' out of which Anglicanism sprang, in the
> teeth of the whole organised machinery. (2) Disentangling
> the Anglican Church so vivified from the State. (3) Getting
> over (or round) the snag of Anglican orders (e.g. by importing

Orientals for episcopal consecrations and letting that problem solve itself, in a generation!). (4) Convincing the Roman Church that an Anglicanism thus renewed is fit for Catholic Communion and convincing the Anglican Church that it needs Catholic Communion. Furthermore the whole programme has to be faced without any assurances that it is not as mad as it looks. It involves, you will say, practically *constructing* an Anglican Church which Rome could receive into Unity.

The Adoration Reparatrice Chapel in Beaufort Street has been rebuilt and now serves as the chapel of Allen Hall, the Westminster Seminary. Then the Blessed Sacrament was permanently exposed, inviting prayerful adoration. All day a trickle of worshippers, coming and going, joined their prayers with the prayer of the Church for the salvation of the world. So Gregory faced the Blessed Sacrament, the symbol and the focus of everything that was important and meaningful and deep for him. Hour by hour his turmoil turned over and over in his mind as his eyes watched the Host as his heart went from decision to decision. The Adoration Reparatrice Chapel is by the site of the house of St Thomas More: the memory of another man's much more costly loyalty to Rome could only have added to the turmoil. It is hard to imagine all that went through his mind as he prayed: his sense of the impenetrable and immovable Anglican liberal establishment; his depression over the 1928 Prayer Book debacle when the House of Commons had overridden the Church in its desire for a new book (a book which Gregory did not think much of in any case); the dead-end of the Malines conversations between some Anglicans and some Romans which seemed to have achieved little. Through all this was infused his growing respect and reverence for the See of Rome, for its doctrinal clarity and fidelity, for its continuity; feelings fed by his patristic studies. And yet honesty would not let him deny the real nourishment the Anglican Church had given him *as* a church, the real sense that, despite everything, for so many people it *was* where, as a body, they met with God. Perhaps especially he could not bring himself to deny that the mass he said each day, and shared with his brother clergy, was

ultimately empty and had always been so. Among those
clergy was his own father and soon his brother too. Did he
discuss this with them? How would it have affected them?
And his many friends involved in different ways to different
degrees in the Church of England, not least his brethren in
the community whose very existence was owed to a decision,
in the Caldey days, *not* to submit to Rome? 'Truth' is all very
well but could he be sure enough to deny his experience?

In those few hours of wretched praying he seems to have
finally come to a hard-won and still miserable conclusion that
he must stay in the Church of England and put all his energy
and prayer into the cause of unity, hopeless though the cause
then seemed. Allowing for his own sense of the dramatic and
for the vagaries of memory after ten or more years we can
perhaps see here a reluctant and disconsolate but nevertheless dimly honest decision. His life would be in the Church
of England, his life and work and prayer would be for unity,
for greater and deeper catholicity, for ways and paths and new
routes through the mountains of Anglican indifference, igno-
rance and hostility and of Roman superiority, isolation and
lack of interest. The four objectives he elucidated in the
letter to Bévenot may not have then formed a precise set of
objectives for his life but clearly by 1940 he felt that they
characterised his work and his continuing contribution.

If the experience constituted a decision, it was not a final
decision. He faced the dilemma again and that must partly
explain why he remained an oblate in the community. Nevertheless he did return to Nashdom and may never have told
anyone there about this episode in his life.

In addition to his own reading, and the beginnings of his
writing in this period, Gregory seems to have found himself
involved in Abbot Denys' attempt at a seminary, something
he had hoped to do from as early as 1916. Almost by accident
Nashdom found itself with young men in residence, needing
somewhere to stay for their studies as they prepared for
ordination. Gregory seems to have spent some of his time
helping to develop this by providing some lectures and
tuition at Nashdom itself, no doubt with other people too.

Perhaps his experience, however brief, in Ghana helped in this. His notebooks round about 1930 include what are obviously lecture notes, including first lectures on liturgy. There is also a quite elaborate scheme for a course of study over two or three years including a good deal of Aquinas and philosophical theology. Although Gregory's own studies were taking him further and further back towards the very first years of the Church, he nevertheless seems to have found time also to read his way into the scholastic theology of the mediaeval period and to continue reading the history and theology of Europe in almost all its centuries.

The Abbey applied to formalise the seminary in 1930 but it could not fulfil many of the conditions and so the scheme passed, though there continued to be occasional ordinands until as late as 1945. Gregory's work in the early thirties comes to a climax in 1937 with the publication of his text and notes for *The Apostolic Tradition* of Hippolytus, the third-century anti-Pope. This work of scholarship was the culmination of years of hard work and research but it was also, with the scholarship behind it, the basis of so much of his future work. The title page of the book refers to Gregory thus: 'the Rev. Gregory Dix, monk of Nashdom Abbey'. By 1937 he had, in fact, become a monk again and not merely an oblate.

On May 7th 1936 Gregory writes to his friend at Wells: 'I am to enter the novitiate again. I am to be allowed to postulate as an oblate.' The latter provision would mean he could avoid the usual six months of postulancy before becoming a novice. In a letter to the same person about a week later he says: 'Now that I have fixed it I can't imagine what I hesitated about for so long', and then he remarks that he now realises it is what has been meant for him for the last fifteen years (a passage referred to earlier).

In a remark much later in his life to a woman seeking his guidance Gregory said: 'You can refuse a vocation, God's will will be done but round a corner.' Perhaps this reflection came from his own experience. He also said to her: 'When you accept a vocation you sign a blank cheque.'

Once again we have no way of knowing what led him at this point to make this decision. Perhaps at thirty-five he felt it was time to commit himself in this way. He may also have felt that there were glimmers of light on the horizon of unity in the Church and that he might actually make some progress with his four aims. Enough to justify commiting himself to this particular Anglican community in its offering for unity. The letter to Bévenot of 1940, quoted earlier, reveals that he was not entirely comfortable with life at Nashdom in the early thirties. While we know he could exaggerate when it suited him, he does say: 'Nashdom under the old Abbot's regime was disintegrating.'

At other times he acknowledged a debt of gratitude and a degree of admiration for Abbot Denys. In a letter from the United States in 1947 he notices the 'technically amateur' character of some of the communities he visits. 'What a lot we owe to Abbot Denys Prideaux,' he says, 'despite his funniosities!'

Denys Prideaux died in 1934 and Gregory found himself impressed with the new Abbot, Martin Collett. He remarked of him in a number of letters that he was: 'humble, paternal, zealous, efficient'. No doubt the new regime helped him decide to focus his own commitment and to progress with his brethren through the vows.

The novitiate, a time of supervised training and initiation, lasts a year and is followed by temporary or Simple Vows, a deeper and more demanding commitment. After three years in these vows Solemn Profession is made and life vows are taken binding the monk and his community, binding him to the Abbot and to the Rule. It is with Solemn Profession that the prefix 'Dom' (from *Dominus*, Latin for 'master') is added to the name and the monk joins the Seniors in the Choir and in the Chapter (the meeting which governs the community).

Once again Gregory's entry into the novitiate was delayed but this time only briefly and for what he called 'a rather wonderful though very frightening reason'. He wrote to his mother on September 23rd 1936 saying he was to have been clothed as a novice on September 13th but it had been delayed because the Abbot had received a number of invitations for Gregory to go and speak in France about the English Church and reunion. At the centre of these arrangements was the Abbé Paul Couturier. Gregory with his companion, Father Fynes-Clinton, found himself involved in a series of lectures and conversations in Lyons and Paris. Gregory spoke fluent French and so could make the most of the visit. Interestingly he told his mother, in a letter after the visit, that he had heard a Mass for Unity in Lyons at the Adoration Reparatrice: perhaps he remembered there his turmoil and the aims he emerged with, not so many years before in Chelsea.

This visit was something of a climax early on in Gregory's work on the question of unity. The Abbé Couturier and the Week of Prayer for Christian Unity felt like a real light in the darkness and Gregory must have felt rather more positive than ever before about what might be achieved.

He became a novice on his birthday, October 4th 1936. The ten years of his life with the community, but not fully in it, meant that he entered open-eyed and realistic. As he said to his friend at Wells: 'It won't be very easy as I know far too much about the inside of things to make a good novice.'

The Rule of St Benedict says that newcomers are not to be given an easy entry to the monastery but they are to be tested to see if they are 'really seeking God'. In one sense Gregory had made it hard for himself and done all the testing in ten years of reflection on the subject. From his letters it seems that more than once he had prepared to leave but finally he concluded that Nashdom was where he could seek God and that commitment seems only to have deepened in the years that followed.

In the next year he took his temporary vows, committing himself to three years in the common life. In these years his scholarly work began to develop further and he became more involved in Church affairs generally. From the, now more secure, base of his monastic community he could feel free to go further afield. At this time also he first made contact with Fr Maurice Bévenot SJ and between them they initiated

informal inter-Church talks. We shall look at this, and other
ecumenical contacts, more closely later. It is one part of the
slow development of Gregory's sense of vocation.

This period also saw Gregory's developing work in spiritual direction and as a confessor, not only for individuals
but also more formally on behalf of the Abbey with various
women's communities. He became Warden of the Win-
grave community and found himself for many years with
considerable responsibilities for this small women's community and the girls with learning difficulties for whom the nuns
cared.

This was a time of growing tension in Europe, as Germany
armed and appeared more and more belligerent; it is the
period of the abdication crisis and the coronation of King
George VI. Gregory's correspondence from this period barely
acknowledges these things but in a sense they are perhaps
taken for granted as the theatre in which the life is to be
lived, prayer offered and theology hammered out. A Benedictine community in England with its audible and visible
European heritage in the Italianate Latin and the baroque
setting and ceremonial can only have been fearful and prayerful about what the next years held. Although never deeply
and directly involved in the great social issues of the day, he
told Bévenot that he felt the Church in general, and the
papacy in particular, had a crucial role to play. As the full
horror of the war unfolded, and as the details of the Holocaust gradually became known, inevitably they had an impact
on Gregory's sermons and addresses and correspondence.

In the early months of the war, in 1940, Gregory's instinctive patriotism and *sang-froid* emerged in a remark he is said
to have made to a Danish count. They had been at a meeting
in London after which, to the count' s surprise, the group
fixed the date of the next meeting, Gregory told him, 'We've
faced the whole of Europe before.'

As the war was ending his tone was more restrained and
tentative. In a retreat for priests he remarked on the need
for John the Baptists to speak against the concentration

camps, on human rights and dignity, and on July 8th 1945, he preached on the Visitation at St Mary's, Slough:

> Is this a world in which it is any use — or in which we can even bear — to think of the gracious idyll of the Visitation in the springtime among the green hills of Judaea — oh so many centuries ago? When one thinks of Belsen and Dachau or of Poland — what does it mean if a young Jewish girl at the Annunciation did once take the kiss of God and quicken with the embrace of the un-created love that made the world — in Galilee 1900 years ago? Even if she did go singing over the hills to her cousin Elizabeth.... Exquisite poetry, no doubt! But even if it is true, thousands ['millions' has been crossed out...] of her race have been put to death with cyanide like rats — or suffered much worse fates — in the last five years. And that is only one little facet of a tragedy almost as wide as mankind, that has drowned the world in tears in our days, perhaps deeper than ever before. Even if stories like the Visitation are true — or were true once — what can they have of meaning for a time like ours? I think questions like this come to many of us — and they make our religion seem to us not so much 'untrue' as irrelevant and 'unreal'.

In 1940 he wrote to Freddy Green:

> I feel the war is really a liberation to faith and not a burden to it. We have, like Jeremiah, to make room in our theology for a vast evil power like Assyria triumphing temporarily over what is apparently the better cause, as an instrument of God's mercy to His own representatives.... [This was perhaps the lowest point of the war.] We may or may not be militarily victorious but Christendom will recapture its soul in what is coming, though I no longer look for any sort of external victory in my time.

Even more personally still he writes during the war on 19th October 1941, to a family of Jewish exiles he had come to know and who were grateful for his help: 'It is little enough one Christian priest can do to atone for past wickedness of Christians towards your people and the unspeakable horror of what my Christian brethren are doing today.'

The war made its contribution to Gregory's more sophisticated assessment of the human condition but it did so also

in a very practical way. He had to go to serve in the parish of
Beaconsfield as its temporary parish priest. His brother Ronald had been the priest there but he went in 1939 to be a
Forces' Chaplain and, with the Abbot's agreement, as part,
as it were, of the war effort, the monks took over. A little note
in Gregory's neat script in the church registers simply records: 'Gregory Dix temporarily serving the church.'

St Michael's Beaconsfield was in the parish of St Mary and
All Saints, Beaconsfield but it had been built in 1914–16 to
serve the new town developing around the railway. From the
very beginning it was intended to adhere to the Anglo-
Catholic tradition and, with a priest and parsonage house of
its own, it had begun to establish itself. Ronnie Dix had
arrived in 1933 and continued the tradition. The east end of
the building had not been completed then but the High Altar
and Tabernacle were nevertheless suitably appointed and
Sunday mornings involved three and sometimes four
masses: an early said mass, a children's mass, introduced
by Ronnie, at 10 a.m. and the Sung Mass at 11.00 a.m. The
English Missal[1] was used, the *Angelus* was rung, incense was in
use. Gregory had visited his brother from time to time in the
preceding years: now, on September 12th, he took over as
parish priest. Beaconsfield is not far from Nashdom and the
family connection had already led to visits to the monastery
by groups of parishioners; now the monastery came to the
parish.

Gregory was not alone in the Parsonage house, another
monk, Maurus Benson came to act as housekeeper. They
seem to have fitted quite easily into the routines of wartime
parish life. From the parsonage house the monks went next
door into the church each day to say mass. The registers
neatly record the routine, the major change being a switch
to the Roman Benedictine calendar of Saints' days in place
of the Prayer Book Calendar observed by Ronnie. The 'Benedictine martyrs' on December 1st and the 'Immaculate Con-

1   An Anglo-Catholic adjustment of the Prayer Book to the Roman
    Missal.

ception' on December 8th look slightly exotic against the
earlier plainer lists but Gregory was generally careful to
adhere to the parish's ethos — and to keep on good terms
with the Rector of St Mary's whose tradition was somewhat
different. Gregory had the advantage of his friendship with
the diocesan bishop, Kenneth Kirk, and there were clearly
times when this helped him in his work in the parish. The
registers record in Holy Week 1940:

> 'Good Friday 9.15. Mass of the Presanctified. (1 communi-
> cant) (By written permission of the Bishop of Oxford for this
> year only. He is to be written to again before next Good Friday.
> G.D.)'

The celebration of this traditional catholic liturgy of Good
Friday was very important to Gregory: he had already written
about it. The opportunity to try it in a parish setting was
obviously too good to be missed and his friendship with Kirk
made the experiment possible. By Good Friday 1941 Gregory
had left the parish and, in fact, the bishop was not written to
again nor the liturgy celebrated. The church seems to have
had fifty or sixty regular communicants, a band of trained
servers and a regular mass and instruction in a local girls'
school at Oakdene. Many baptisms, weddings and funerals
must have taken place at the parish church rather than at St
Michael's but the registers periodically record the *viaticum*
administered to the dying, a requiem and funeral, nuptial
masses and the occasional celebration of Holy Baptism. He
is remembered as a fluent, relaxed and natural celebrant, a
fluency arising from deep familiarity and comfortableness
with the movement and meaning of the rite. Gregory found
himself with a group of ten confirmation candidates whom
he set about preparing in the course of the two years he was
there.

Beaconsfield presents us with Gregory as the natural pastor. He was not shy, was at ease with children and combined
clear ideas about spiritual goals for lay people with sensitivity
to, and appreciation of, individual personality and development. Parishioners who were children at that time remember
a house full of books and papers and the smell of Gregory's

pipe tobacco. They were free to come and go and found piles of boys' comics in the house as well as Gregory's rudder, awarded for his coxing days at Merton. The monks found ways to maintain their daily recitation of the seven Hours but in most ways they gave themselves up to parish life and entered fully into all its problems and pleasures. Far from remaining in monkish enclosure, shut off from the parish apart from the services in church, Gregory seems to have enjoyed discovering the pastor in himself. He became a familiar sight around the parish in habit, cloak and wide-brimmed black hat.

He was not superficial about the work but entered seriously into the role of confessor and spiritual guide. The parish still remembers the monks with affection (a pulpit in the church commemorates their work) and numbers of individuals are grateful for careful formation in the spiritual life and for relationships that continued long after the monks' pastorate was over.

Gregory combined the range of catholic teaching and discipline with the strong attractiveness of his own personality, his wit and good humour and this made a not surprising impact especially on the young. Confirmation preparation seems to have focused on the seven sacraments, with some special emphasis on penitence and marriage, but beyond the specific teaching was the attraction of Gregory's easy gifts with people, his openness and affability. The registers note that, somehow, in the course of their time there the monks saw four women clothed as Religious but, apart from making the Religious life attractive, Gregory and the other monks helped straightforward Christian people to be just that, in ordinary, rooted-in-the-world ways. The gift of a pastor is the quite ordinary, but not so frequent, human one of paying full attention to the individuality of each person, celebrating and exploring it. Already, long ago in Africa and perhaps as a tutor in Keble, Gregory had found himself in pastoral situations. This had developed in the thirties with a growing number of penitents coming to him for confession and direction as well as the pastoral relationships that developed in connection with other, women's, religious communities. But Gregory does not seem to have needed to learn to be a pastor, it was natural in him. It is there in the letter, already quoted (p. 55) to a Jewish family and it is clear in his concerned personal attention to some of those Beaconsfield parishioners who continued to go to him for direction. He was careful not to be hasty in judging people. In dealing with the aspirants to the Priory in America he says: 'I am not a quick judge of men as a rule — at least I am very apt to be wary at the first judgement.'

His papers include a lengthy concerned correspondence with the Bishop of Lincoln, in the early forties, about a priest, a penitent of Gregory's, in trouble in his parish and there is also a touching note in 1944 from Frances Temple, William Temple's widow:

> I can't tell you how much your letter touched me — and helped me — as did our talk when you were here. I am sure you will, as far as you can feel it to be right, work as he would have hoped. I love to remember the happy side of your visits here — though I know there had to be a sad side too.

Gregory doesn't always seem to have been easy with women. In one letter he complains: 'My entire life is embittered by religious women', and elsewhere he says that he only really knows and admires five or six women. Nevertheless, at his death, many women, lay and nuns, wrote to say how they had valued his counsel and direction. He was perhaps easier with children. In 1949 he writes to 'Gregory' a boy preparing for confirmation. The letter is chatty and informative but also very personal and clear:

> Confirmation is so very important because it begins something... to help you, and because you have to be treated like a full-size Christian after you are confirmed, our Lord himself comes to you in Holy Communion at Mass. Be such a strong good Christian man that you can go often to Communion and don't just have to be at Mass without Communion like a Christian who hasn't grown up yet.

The pastoral instinct had wider implications too. From Texas in 1947 he wrote: 'Altogether I like the "deep south" immensely except for its abominable "Jim Crow" treatment of the negroes. That is very obvious and very grievous everywhere — and lynchings are still common.'

It is all in the end to do with that 'little I'. 'The little I — the individual man — so dear to God.' Interestingly those words come from the end of the sermon on the Visitation referred to earlier with its bleak view of the post-war world.

Gregory spent two years at Beaconsfield but his life was not confined to parish work. He was increasingly involved in wider church affairs, Anglican and ecumenical, and so spent time away from the parish at conferences and consultations. He was still involved in study, writing and lecturing and towards the end of this period he gave the paper to the Cowley Fathers at their General Chapter which in due course became *The Shape of the Liturgy*. In June of 1941 Maurus Benson was ordained so that he could help more fully in the running of the parish. Gregory's parish work seems to have come to an end chiefly so that he could concentrate almost entirely on turning his paper into a book and, in less than two years, producing *The Shape of the Liturgy*.

Gregory signed off from the parish with another little note in the register. After recording the service of confirmation on September 7th 1941, presided over by the Bishop of Buckingham, a bracketed note reads:

(exit Gr. D. Jesu mercy.)

He celebrated a Sung Mass of the Blessed Virgin Mary's Nativity the next morning at 6.30 a.m. and then he was gone. The register records, even at that hour, fifty-six communicants, some for the first time; a measure of affection and esteem. He was succeeded by Dom Augustine Morris but did return from time to time.

It looks as though Gregory saw a natural completeness in presenting his candidates for confirmation, six girls and four boys along with nineteen others from elsewhere, including

soldiers. He had made his pastoral contribution and then —
'Jesu mercy.'

The parish clearly made its contribution to him. The
outward evidence is in *The Shape* when, in the introduction,
he says about the present liturgical situation in England:
'Two years in a parish since the war began have left me with
an intense sympathy for the lay communicant and his parish
priest in facing those difficulties, which are ultimately not of
their making.' The inner, unspoken and more pervasive
evidence is in *The Shape's* repeated concern for the ordinary
worshipping laity.

Another event took place, however, in the course of the
two years at Beaconsfield and this must be noted now. On
October 11th 1940, together with Maurus Benson, Gregory
was Solemnly Professed at West Malling Abbey. The event
did not take place at Nashdom because of the war. While
Gregory was at Beaconsfield the monks had handed over
Nashdom to the community from Edgware, moved out of
their home with their disabled children. A few monks remained in the Guest house at Nashdom but most eventually
moved to West Malling in Kent replacing the sisters there,
for the rest of the war.

In one sense Gregory was not at home for his Solemn
Profession and he does not seem to have been much 'at home'
in any other sense either. The story is told that, the night
before, having travelled to Kent with Maurus Benson he
asked his companion for the fare back to Beaconsfield.
Maurus refused and Gregory stayed. Maurus only later reminded him that in fact he already had a return ticket!

A few years later Gregory wrote to Hilary Powell from the
U.S. at the time of his solemn profession and the letter
reflects on his own experience:

> A man only accepts his destiny once in his life, and it is always
> something that makes me want to cheer and cry at the same
> time when I see it happen. It comes to different men in
> different ways but for religious it is nearly always at final vows.
> Even priesthood, for a monk, tremendous thing that it is in
> itself, only builds upon that disturbingly decisive thing that

happens at profession. We are right to be disturbed, I think (I was terrified). It is so conclusive, so unavoidable (after a certain point of development) so alarmingly irrevocable. Henceforward one can keep one's vows or break them or mess about with them — but there they will always be — for ever and ever, to all eternity. A new relation to God — to the foundation of all existence — has been set up for me — and nothing I can do will ever alter it. As one who has kept his vows singularly badly, may I say that that alarming fact is the only comfort in the situation. I may wobble and rat — God will not. The relation binds me to Him and He remains. Don't mind being frightened. One has to make this particular leap in the dark alone. No amount of reassurance from me or anyone else can help you in it. But He does catch you when you jump alone!

So I shall pray like a steam engine for you between now and then that you may go to meet your destiny, not perhaps unafraid (that is irrelevant, anyhow) but as a man should, walking as stiffly as he may and committing himself to God humbly and creatively and filially for all that is to come of it.... I wouldn't have missed all that I have had already for anything (quite literally!) that this world has to offer.

Perhaps that was how he felt himself in 1940 as he made his own 'leap in the dark alone', struggling to 'walk stiffly', committing himself 'humbly and creatively and filially' to God.

His terror had in it the thread of questioning about submission to the Roman communion: this was the period of the Bévenot letters.

It is obvious from a letter written in June 1940 to Freddy Green, his former college chaplain and a close friend, that Gregory had once again faced a sharp attack of 'Roman fever'. It seems to be related to the events of the war and the Church's response. He had been to see the Abbot who had not wanted to hear. At a meeting with Roman Catholics about the national and international situation it had been a Roman Catholic monk, Dom Wimslow, who had persuaded Gregory to stay where he was. He had said to Gregory: 'For God's sake don't do that! It is vital at present to have some catholics who are free to speak. Your Signpost group is one of the greatest rays of light at the moment.' Well, that rather seemed to settle it.' Gregory added in brackets above 'catholics' the word '*sic!*' His letters to Freddy Green are another request for advice but, apparently without any, he settles again to the Church of England.

The chapel at West Malling is part of the old Abbey. The nuns live amongst the ruined, and partly ruined, ancient monastery and feel the sense of continuity in prayer and life. The Abbey is continuous too somehow with the beautiful, gentle Kent countryside and the pleasant and pretty English village of West Malling. Just on the edge of the village stands the great bulk of the mediaeval gatehouse to the monastery. Behind its huge bolted doors are lovely grounds, streams and flowers, and warm, solid stone buildings. Somehow the sheer bulk of the preserved gatehouse, standing in the way, across the path, echoes Gregory's terror. Monastic life has its beauty and its warmth but it is no easy, casual way: it demands a gatehouse, a threshold, a clear place of decision and commitment — Solemn Profession.

At the centre of the monastic enclosure, now surrounded by neat grass and winding paths, is a tower of the ancient church. The south transept remains, and there the nuns used to have their chapel. It is square, small, high and, in those days, quite dark. Small windows let in little light and rows of monastic stalls, a High Altar and an altar to our Lady took up the space. Moreover, a few feet from the High Altar a grille extended the whole width of the chapel — iron bars to emphasise the nun's enclosure, shutting the world out, in a startling way that has now passed from usage.

It was into this chapel, with Maurus Benson, that Gregory came to make his solemn profession, on the morning of October 11th 1940.

Around him was every reminder of the monastic world to which he was finally committing himself: the stalls and the grille and the candlelit altar; his brethren in their choir habits, his Abbot in full pontifical vestments for the High Mass. But above him, as it were, was the reminder of the world, a world he was finally leaving but a world he was also

finally committing himself to in the deepest way possible for
him. Above Kent in the autumn of 1940 raged the Battle of
Britain. The monks at West Malling often found themselves
shouting the psalms above the din of flying bombs and often
the recitation of the divine office was disrupted by monks
leaving, at the sound of the siren, to fulfil their air-raid and
fire-watching duties. In a very real sense a monk does not,
cannot, leave that world behind, outside the gate. Instead by
his vows he simply becomes committed to it, in its need and
pain and hope, in an utterly different way.

The Pontifical High Mass began in its normal way that
morning in October 1940. The full ceremonial was limited a
little by the lack of space in the chapel but nevertheless the
solemn latin and the chant would have rung familiarly in the
ears of the waiting monks. Half way through the service, at
the offertory, the moment came. The Rule requires that a
monk seeking to make his Solemn Profession writes out a
document to that effect to give to the Abbot. It must be
written in his own hand as it is his own decision, his own
responsibility, the conscious action and choice of a clear
mind. So, also, it is that 'leap in the dark alone', for life. '*Votis
solemnibus per vitam meam*' says the petition, 'in solemn vows
throughout my life'.

The petition is placed on the altar, the place of gifts, of
offering, of sacrifice and the decision is made. Then the
monk lies prostrate before the altar and, in one of those ritual
actions that are terrifyingly appropriate, is covered with a
pall. As he lies there the community chants a litany. Prostrate,
as if dying or dead, the threshold is crossed and, as the litany
ends, the new Solemnly Professed monk rises with hands
extended to intone: '*Suscipe me...*', 'Uphold me, O Lord,
according to thy word and I shall live, and let me not be
confounded in my expectation.' Three times he sings this
prayer, the note rising each time, three times the community
repeats his words. Three times for greater assurance, three
times for deeper confidence, 'Uphold me, O Lord', and three
times to hear the answering supporting reassurance of the
brethren. The 'leap in the dark alone', made prostrate under

that smothering pall, is in fact a leap into community, across the threshold to the brethren, and so to them now the monk goes, each in turn, to exchange the kiss of peace.

Then the mass continues and the newly professed monks receive communion at what was normally in those days a non-communicating service. And the host on the tongue would have brought the taste of the wider and deeper community, the Church, the Body of Christ, into which the two newly professed monks were now even more strongly bound.

The precise vows made, 'before God and his saints' are Stability, *Conversatio morum* (which might be translated 'the conversion of life') and Obedience. All these have to do with the radical and yet realistic attempt to seek God alone and to do so in community. Stability is first of all a practical commitment to remain faithfully in the one community but clearly its implications are about the fixing of the will and the desires, settling firmly even comfortably, into the routine of the committed life, the security and strength that grows from an established and clear knowledge of a sure place before God. The second vow concerns the continual, repeated and ever deeper movement towards that sure place. The rule may resist harshness and the imposing of burdens but the objective is never disguised: the seeking after perfection and the pure and true conforming of the will. There is change, conversion, repeated turning in the course of the monastic life. It is not static or idle but being always converted more and more closely to the gospel way. The third vow, obedience, as we have seen, is the inevitable outworking of the other vows in a life in community and it mirrors also the required obedience to God. Under these vows the monks together struggle, quietly, diligently, unspectacularly, to become a place where the life of the Beatitudes is lived.

The more conventional expression of the vows of poverty, chastity and obedience is not especially different from these. Poverty and chastity are also fairly inevitable and natural consequences of the desire to live the life of the gospel together in community.

'Community' is becoming something of a dead word because of its modern overuse. It was not in fact a word often
used by Gregory but it was profoundly connected with some
of the increasingly central concerns of his thinking and his
teaching, of his praying and his life. Steadily, in his scholarly
works, the idea of the Body of Christ, the organic unity of the
people of God, became more and more important. His extensive, almost exhaustive, reading in scripture and early church
literature, his study of other theologians and philosophers,
his experience of community and, in a different way, of parish
life. Perhaps above all his daily celebration of the mystery of
the Eucharist, each time reflecting more deeply upon that
mystery, combined with these other mysteries to create a
profound sensitivity to the mystical body, the people of God
in Christ. Despite the individualistic and pietistic narrowness of some of the spirituality he encountered, including
some of the literature about the Religious life itself, Gregory
began to see, from very early on, that the Christian is not
alone but exists in the Church, a member of the body. He
emphasised that life is lived in this community where prayer
is prayed, there the eucharist is offered, the offering actually
creating the community. This 'organic mutuality' he expressed as a vision for all social living, a picture of how the
world might be. In the introduction to *The Shape*, written
when the world seemed to be falling apart, he wrote:

> There is a Christian pattern of a solution which is expressed
> for us and by us at the eucharist. There the individual is
> perfectly integrated in society, for there the individual Chris-
> tian only exists as a Christian individual in as much as he is
> fully exercising his own function in the Christian society.
> There his need of and utter dependence upon material
> things even for 'the good life' in this world is not denied or
> even ascetically repressed, but emphasised and met. Yet his
> needs are met from the resources of the whole society, not
> by his own self-regarding provision. But there the resources
> of the society are nothing else but the total substance freely
> offered by each of its members for all. There too is displayed
> a true hierarchy of functions within a society organically

adapted to a single end, together with a complete equality of recompense.[1]

Here Gregory seems to be writing at once about the Church, about the eucharist itself, about his own community and about the hopes for wider society in a post-war world.

Increasingly his sermons and retreats witnessed to this emphasis on the corporate life: the church which is formed by the eucharist together offers its life to God. The concept is a very strong one. In scripture he finds the Church as the New Israel, a redeemed race, an organic whole, single and unique in its relationship to God, as the Israel of old. This was never just an academic or pious theory. When he spoke of the 'body of Christ' and of the 'redeemed race' he thought always of 'the holy common people of God', the *plebs sancta Dei*. He meant the mass of ordinary Christians whose devotion and ordinariness, their longsuffering and failures he took very seriously.

In a manuscript of an introduction to *The Apostolic Tradition*, which does not seem to have been used, Gregory writes:

> In 'the mind of the Church' the peculiar contributions of her great saints and leaders and divines are never lost, but fused and generalised and enriched, not seldom corrected and transcended, by the sure collective wisdom of the redeemed race.

This stress on the living body and trust in its development and faithfulness is crucial to Gregory's teaching and thought. It is vital to his spirituality and vocation for he saw himself as a part of that body with his own function to perform his own unique contribution to make. Always he combined the personal with the corporate. The manuscript just quoted goes on:

> Every individual in the immense dumb but praying multitudes of Christendom is a particular object of God's love and has each his or her own direct commerce with God which is

1   *Shape*, p. xviii.

no less real and true than that of the greatest saint.... Because
it is popular 'Tradition' is never reflective and intellectual.

His sense of the Church as both popular and mystical, deeply
sacramental and very personal was expressed in a favourite text
of St Augustine quoted in *The Shape* and in *The Image and
Likeness of God* (a collection of retreat addresses published
after his death).

> The Body of Christ, the Church, offers itself to become the
> Sacrificed Body of Christ, the sacrament, in order that there-
> by the Church itself may become in time what in eternal
> reality it is before God — the 'fullness' or 'fulfilment' of
> Christ; and each of the redeemed may 'become' what he has
> been made by baptism and confirmation, a living member of
> Christ's body.... As Augustine was never tired of repeating to
> his African parishioners in his sermons, 'So the Lord willed
> to impart His body, and His Blood which he shed for the
> remission of sins. If you have received well, you are that which
> you have received.' 'Your mystery is laid on the table of the
> Lord, your mystery you receive. To that which you are you
> answer "Amen", and in answering you assent. For you hear
> the words "the Body of Christ" and you answer "Amen". Be
> a member of the Body of Christ that the Amen may be true.'[1]

So there is a kind of continuity, an organic unity, between the
sacramental body of the eucharist, the body which is the
Church and Christ himself, offering himself to God. And this
unity is not static but living, growing, moving and developing. Gregory could be high-flown and almost ecstatic in his
descriptions of this but he was also practical and realistic. In
a sermon in 1945 he says: 'The first saint in heaven was not
an apostle but a penitent thief baptised not by an Apostle
but in his own blood', and more pointedly still in an earlier
sermon: 'A saint is a complete human being: not a dead
clergyman.'

The Christian life was to be worked out in the ordinary
everyday details with the help of the sacraments and the
reality of the mystery. It remains ordinary and practical and

1   *Shape*, p. 247.

mundane, vulnerable to making mistakes and falls but also open to getting up again and to correction. In the Retreat on the Rule he focuses on the importance of God's desire for our human offering:

> God does often prefer second bests in practice. It is lucky for me. He wills to be worshipped by us — and He might have created more Archangels instead — beings who never answer with the wrong side of the choir, and are never late for office or sing out of tune or time, and never start the wrong responsory, and never wander vaguely to the wrong side of the golden altar that is before the throne of God and the Lamb.

So he can be perfectly honest with the humanity of his community. In the Retreat on the Rule as he reaches the section on 'Our brethren' he says: 'we come now to speak of the thorns in our crown — our Brethren.'

They are set in this testing company precisely so that they may be for each other the instruments of God's holiness: it happens within the Body and only there. And there may truly be the possibility of holiness.

> 'Let them render one another obedience *certatim* — competitively.' What a heavenly place this would be, if we could only obey those words.... If that were the only cause of friction among us — as to who should have least of his own way! Of course, there might be a certain amount of confusion while all the people who wanted to go to the right moved rapidly to the left to please their left-wing brethren, and all the left-wings moved strenuously to the right so as not to hurt the feelings of their right-wing brethren. But at least it would be a sweet and generous confusion which superiors could sort out without any agonising displays of tact. St Benedict does exactly reverse the world's values, doesn't he? He sets before us in this chapter the *duty* of entering into a competition with one another in genuine meekness, and gentleness and kindness, considerateness and modesty and simplicity, in trying not to get my own way in *anything* in my daily dealings with others — in a spirit of deep and unaffected affection — which is to be quite unsentimental.

There is a picture of Gregory (reproduced on the cover of
this book) which was probably taken at the monastery in
America. It shows him relaxed, comfortable, filling his pipe.
His smiling mouth and eyes may be telling a story, there is
mischief, charm and wit in the face of this attractively human
figure. Sometimes the piety of the monastic tradition in the
earlier decades of this century — the end in one sense of a
long development — can seem very remote and detached.
Gregory's humanity keeps breaking through, showing him
sensitive to ordinary lives in ordinary communities with
ordinary hopes and fears and longings. His humanity kept
him in touch with the reality of human community, of human
relationships and human affection. It was a key part of his
perception of the Body of Christ.

Curiously, it is difficult to include with certainty his own
family in this. He maintained regular contact with his brother
and they corresponded, especially during the war years when
Ronnie was serving as a Forces Chaplain, but his parents
never seem to have visited the monastery despite his father's
earlier contacts. His father died in 1932 when Gregory was
still undecided about his own vows; his mother died in 1939.
The papers include no letters from his father and only two
to his mother and these are copies obtained by someone else.
Personal correspondence, if there was any, no longer exists.
In so far as he needed a family, 'that crown of thorns, the
brethren' became it and certainly stirred deep feelings in
him. Writing from the US to Nashdom he says he is homesick:
'... all the time wanting England and my Abbot and my
brethren and my friends very badly indeed.'

Gregory's sense of being 'at home' in the community was
deepened by his profession in Solemn Vows in 1940 but not
in an obvious or immediate way. He returned for the time
being to Beaconsfield and to parish work but a year later he
left the parish to live in the Guest House at Nashdom, saying
mass for the nuns from Edgware and otherwise engaged in
the study and writing that became *The Shape of the Liturgy*. He
had it finished by June 1943. Working long into the nights,
he had never slept well, sometimes becoming so absorbed

that he forgot the nuns' mass and they would have to fetch
him. While in many ways isolated, lonely work *The Shape* is
above all the combination of many influences on him and of
many of his own traits: honest scholarship, historical analysis, a sense of community in the Church, a sense of current
issues and controversies, a sense of humour, and above all else
a sense of the liturgy, and of its place in the life of the Church,
the Christian and his own life. *The Shape* is the child both of
his spirituality and of his intellect, each in the service of the
other, striving to make a contribution to the life and unity
and prayer of the Church.

It took over a year for the book finally to be published at
the beginning of 1945. Its reception changed Gregory's work
considerably. He became ever more in demand as a speaker,
preacher and retreat leader. His status in church politics rose
considerably, he found himself on committees and in pressure groups. Increasingly he was involved in publication work
for catholic causes, producing pamphlets and small books,
articles and learned papers. At the same time he maintained
his connections with Roman Catholics and others committed
to the cause of unity.

It may be that with Solemn Profession and his final commitment to the Religious life Gregory anticipated settling
into the community and so living its life more fully than ever
he had done before — working on Stability in other words.
This was not to be. In 1945 he was elected a Proctor in
Convocation by the Oxford Clergy to represent their views
in the lower House. This was a natural climax of Gregory's
growing activity and he took the position very seriously. In
fact it appealed to another side of his character. He delighted,
sometimes in a quite mischievous way, in being involved in
decisions of the Church, in the exhilaration of making
speeches and knowing that people were keen to hear him
and waiting for him to give a lead. He revelled in the
wheeling and dealing that was sometimes involved in reach-
ing decisions or in avoiding them. He enjoyed keeping the
bishops awake and alert: a 'gadfly' they called him. As a
consequence of this commitment Gregory found himself

away from the community quite frequently, coming and going to meetings and conferences.

The community returned to Nashdom from West Malling in August 1945 and slowly some semblance of their ordered life began to return. They were now twenty-strong with twelve fully professed seniors, three in temporary vows and one novice as well as three lay brothers and a novice lay brother. By 1949, as the effects of the war lifted and people settled down, there were thirty. Martin Collett was still Abbot and Augustine Morris his Prior. Other monks, like Anselm Hughes, the musician, were involved in work beyond the monastery and this was seen as part of the Abbey's contribution to the Church. It was not always easy to combine such work with stability and the contemplative life.

Things simply became busier and busier for Gregory. 1946 was the only year for which he kept and preserved a detailed diary of his activities. He clearly needed to since he became so involved in so many things. The diary is full of speaking engagements, preaching and retreats, Convocation meetings and committees, catholic pressure-group meetings, ecumenical meetings, writing and publishing and organising other publications. He travelled to Wales, backwards and forwards to Oxford, Cambridge and London, did duty in women's communities and fitted in penitents and letters and dinners. There is at least one reference to a hospital visit and one attempt to find quiet for himself. Presumably there was continued study, thought and preparation for his new publications. In the spaces of the diary no doubt he lived the rhythm of the life in the monastery but his mind must have been buzzing with so many other connections. Even so, in April 1946, he wrote to one of the monks in the US:

> I have made it a rule to be in the house more than two-thirds of my time and have succeeded in keeping it since last September when the community returned. We have made a really good start on the 'new chapter', I think. There is a zeal and a recollection in the house very different from what I remember of pre-war days — internally things are as good

and quiet and settled as one would wish. It is an intense
happiness just to be here....

From the late 1930s onwards the community had included at
least two American monks undergoing formation in the mother house ready to establish a priory or daughter house of
the community in the United States. In due course they
returned to Michigan to begin to live the life there. Things,
however, faltered and it became clear that they urgently
needed help and support. Gregory was the solution. Abbot
Martin was ill by this time and so the natural person to send,
the Prior, Dom Augustine Morris, had to stay at the Mother
house. It was decided to send Gregory to help to organise the
priory.

As soon as he arrived, he discovered extensive financial
difficulties. Soon he launched himself into another enterprise: lecturing, leading conferences, preaching and speaking
all over the US to raise money for the priory. This seems to
have been his own idea. Gregory revealed an enormous
energy for organisation and for lecturing and preaching,
combined with a considerable skill in obtaining money. He
also developed an attractive, fresh and witty style in letter-
writing which means that his American visits are well documented and fascinatingly described.

1947 saw this new and exciting field of work to which he
took with a sure instinct and some relish. It was of course,
no closer to the contemplative life than the busy-ness of 1946
had been and yet he could at least now feel that all his activity
was aimed at the establishment of the Benedictine contemplative life in the Anglican community of the United States.

The American visits will be looked at in detail later but
the letters reveal much of Gregory's continuing reflection on
monastic life and commitment. The very act of writing in the
way he did so fully to the Abbot, in letters that read as if they
were intended for all the brethren, makes a kind of extension
of the enclosure. Ruefully he complained that aeroplanes are
not really conducive to the cloistered life, but his letters
somehow manage to keep alive the connections of community. In other ways it was an episode that suited Gregory

very well giving him independence and letting him take the initiative. It included intellectually stimulating work but also new impressions and experiences and all in the course of his monastic commitment.

He was in the United States from February to September 1947, returned in July 1950 and was there until May 1951. In the years between, he remained very actively involved in the developing work. It felt like something of a child of his own especially when, after illness and incapacity, Abbot Martin eventually resigned in January 1948. Augustine Morris became Abbot and immediately appointed Gregory as his Prior. As such he became even more directly involved in and responsible for all the life of the monastery, including its American daughter.

Priordom suited Gregory's practical organising abilities but it also gave opportunity for his spiritual gifts in oversight and in the guidance of the other monks. This is particularly evident in his correspondence with Dom Patrick Dalton. Dom Patrick was sent out in 1947. It was envisaged that eventually he should replace Gregory in the American Priory and in May 1949 he was appointed Prior there. Recalled in 1950, Gregory returned again to the States. The correspondence covers all these movements and tensions in the context of their close relationship. Not only were they fellow monks but also friends and Gregory had acted for some time as Dom Patrick's confessor. In the earliest letters Gregory, after his return began tentatively to give advice to Dom Patrick to whom he was technically Superior but whom he preferred to treat as an equal. Gregory offered his own analysis of the problems of the American Priory. He identified the existing Prior's authoritarian attitude as the result of fear about his role and a general insecurity. The answer was patience ('a fine amateur recommendation of a virtue I know little about') and Gregory advised: 'Rely on grace and then try like hell.'

The correspondence resumed in 1949 when Dom Patrick had become Prior of the American house. It is advice from one Prior to another about things that might seem mutually

contradictory — self-mastery and self-forgetting. Interestingly much of the letter focused on chastity as an elementary
requirement for the practice of ruling the other brethren and
bringing about a life truly lived according to the Rule. Gregory is honest rather than merely pious about chastity: 'We
have to love chastity not just practise it (sometimes regret-
fully in my case).' This he finds the key to the necessary
'consideration' and readiness to pay attention to the other
brethren required of a Prior. Gregory recognises the power
and virtue of sexuality, emphasising that chastity is not
prudery but, 'a deliberate holocaust of a good and natural
thing'.

Later on he is more personal still: 'You and I have both of
us wanted many, many other things with our minds and
bodies, things which have loomed very large in the immediate foreground often and often...' but he stresses that in the
end what matters is the seeking after God, the honest
commitment to that: 'look for that fundamental disposition
in your subjects. If it is right they will make monks — in the
end.'

It is apparent from letters to others that Gregory did not
think Dom Patrick was an ideal Superior, so this letter, in one
sense, is part of an attempt to focus Dom Patrick's attention
on the things that will make him a better Prior. Chastity,
single-hearted concentration on genuinely living the Rule,
attention to the 'fundamental disposition' of the monks,
'seeking God'. ' "Don't fuss", "Love God", "Don't fuss", I
cling to that', says Gregory and repeats it as his summary
motto and theme.

Gregory seems to have thought Dom Patrick inclined to
be too conscious of making a success of the Priory rather than
simply concentrating on living under the Rule together as
fully as possible. The emphasis on chastity has to do with
this disciplined concentration and focused restraint.

In another letter two months later Gregory was more
flippant about being Prior: 'You just go away for weeks at a
time rooting bishops about — then when you get back
nobody can conceivably expect you to know anything about

anything or settling anything. You just say "You must ask Fr Abbot about that" and before you can be involved you go away again.'

The climax or crisis of the correspondence came when Dom Patrick was recalled to England and Gregory returned to America. Dom Patrick was clearly angry about this and must have made this clear in a letter to Gregory. Gregory's reply is exuberant, honest, almost brutal but also affectionate: 'Well thank heaven you can still spit in my eye — good rheumy, nicely bunched accurate gob too!'

Gregory claimed to have been waiting for Dom Patrick's mood to break and saw the letter as the breakthrough. Now they could face the issues: 'You talked about becoming *simplex*! You? You'll do that about half an hour before I do, I expect — in purgatory! Too bloody good an actor...' and Gregory went on to develop his idea of 'watching himself', especially in prayer, that we noticed earlier in the chapter. He stressed the central summons towards 'single-heartedness' but knew it was still far away. The acting and watching of oneself was there in Dom Patrick too. The important thing he affirmed was: 'not "building up the Priory" but the life *secundam regulam* of these men'.

On his rather humiliating return to England Dom Patrick wanted to 'vindicate his priorship'; Gregory wanted the emphasis to be on 'seeking God'. The letter ended on a gentler note, referring to the Abbot: 'So we can always rely on each other — you and I on his love and his wisdom, he on our love and trust.'

The letters, on the whole, avoided anything patronising and they contained wisdom and insights from Gregory's own experience. Fresh and honest they reveal again that ideal which Gregory pursued ('Christ the hunter' as he said in a sermon) — 'seeking God'. Single-heartedly, with the mind recollected, the spirit intently concentrated, effortlessly and unselfconsciously to go straight — simple and pure — towards God. He knew how complicated a person he was, an actor, a maverick, a still restless soul, but the goal was that simplicity and the way to it was the following of the Rule.

Between his visits to America, Gregory also lectured for two months in Sweden, and his Convocation and other work continued. He was a monk immersed in the world, holding together, often with some difficulty, all the threads of his activity and the reasons for his involvement. All the busy-ness of his activity in the States could make him feel very homesick, as could the Church affairs in England:

> This Church of England is *unbearable* and its bishops *unspeakable* (however, we beat one up in Convocation [Barnes]). They give me belly ache *at sight*. And I have given up smoking which does not improve my patience. Just one damn row after another, except when I am at home.

But 'home' was not, of course, perfect. Sometimes late for the offices, he slept badly and worked into the night as well as being so often away. This could cause resentment among the brethren who experienced stricter discipline from the superiors. Nevertheless the attachment to the monastic life, to the brethren including the American house grew. It was his home, the place where he belonged. As he left St Gregory's in the States he wrote about saying Vespers on his way and wondering whether to *add 'beato Gregorio'* to the office: 'suddenly I nearly cried, because it brought home to me practically the fact that I had ceased to belong to St Gregory's'.

All this was part of the tension in which Gregory lived. Coming and going when a monk is supposed to live in Stability, occupying himself with so many current issues and concerns when a monk is supposed to be steadily and systematically turning his life ever inwards in greater conformity to the gospel, organising his own life lectures, committees, books when a monk is supposed to live under obedience. He knew it to be a central tension and so in his Retreat on the Rule (1949) he used himself as a pointed example for self-examination. Speaking about the monk's attitude to the world he quoted the words of one of the desert fathers: 'Do I find in myself quite that estimation of the events in the world as "an empty smoke ring drifting into nothingness" or of the events of the Church, which would befit a monk?' The Religious life is not escapism. Moving to live under vows in community is, or should be, uncovering the deepest tensions of human relationships and facing the sometimes alarming reality within oneself, and then struggling together to live 'single-heartedly'.

In his address on 'The Religious life in the Anglican Communion' delivered in the United States, Gregory quotes a favourite text, used also in the Retreat on the Rule, a text that clearly moved him. It comes from the *Verba Seniorum*, what he calls the novice classes of the desert hermits: '*Mansionem praeparare in terra quietorum* — to build a lodging in the land of quiet men.' This movement out into the desert, this beginning of the monastic life, is not misanthropic but the seeking of the pearl of great price, the treasure hidden in the field. 'These were no refugees from life,' he says, 'the quiet was tense with the strength of violent men taking heaven by storm'.

The place where all this was to be worked out and lived into was the monastery: with 'the tools of the spiritual craft' chipping away to shape and fashion the life from the tensions of the world — and the tension of seeking heaven. In the words of the Rule: 'Now the workshop, where we are to work diligently at all these tasks, is the enclosure of the monastery and stability in the community.'

Gregory made a good Prior and his Abbot came to rely on him. He trusted his judgement, his efficiency and his insight. 'I am developing', he said from the US, 'the organising abilities of an archdeacon, I think.' But he enjoyed the variety of the work, with his own interests and pursuits fitted in beside it. He was in some senses a 'natural' Superior with the wisdom to give helpful advice and the self-knowledge and imagination not to be patronising or arrogant. He clearly enjoyed being in control because he knew he was capable of the work to be done and this applied in the wider Church involvement too. He knew the kind of power he could exercise, knew how to use it and did use it.

From the end of the 1940s, for all his sometimes frantic activity, Gregory seems to have become a more settled man, more sure of his place, more assured. He was still intense and passionate about the things that mattered to him but from a fixed place with a confidence in his role and ability and contribution. For all the tension he had 'built a lodging in the land of quiet men'. This is the period of his Retreat on the Rule (1949) and its sure tone, its quiet confidence and maturity was the natural result of this development in him. Sermons and other addresses of the period, including his lectures and letters in Sweden, have the same more balanced and settled tone.

This was not, sadly, to be the beginning of long years of deeper wisdom and more mature thought and insight, it was the prelude to illness and, in only a few years, death.

In New York on Good Friday 1951 Gregory, already a sick man, delivered a series of addresses for the Three Hours, meditating on the Passion of Christ. He did not think much of the tradition of long addresses and too many words on Good Friday. He preferred the silences and restraint of the ancient liturgy of the Mass of the Presanctified. However, these addresses, published after his death as *God's Way with Man* are a deep meditation on the centrality of the Passion of Christ and there is irony and sadness in knowing the state of health of the man who delivered these vivid, personal but measured and thoughtful addresses. In Michael Ramsey's foreword to the little book the point is clearly made:

> In his last preaching of the Passion we seem to find an intense concentration of heart and mind upon the ultimate verities: Calvary's judgement upon man, and Calvary's gift to him of selfless love evoking selfless love in return.

There is a poignant photograph of Gregory taken on the day of the consecration of the new chapel at St Gregory's Priory in the United States in May 1951. He was to have been Master of Ceremonies at the great service, a job he was good at and enjoyed. However, in the event, he was too ill to manage and attended the service, robed in a cope, but remaining, quiet and still, in his place. The chapel is as much his work as anyone's, indeed the reality of Benedictine life in that place is partly his too. All his intense work was coming

to fruition but in the photograph he stands in the midst a
victim too, haggard-looking, tired and ill, ill with the cancer
that would finally kill him. In a strange way there is something here of the 'violent men taking heaven by storm'. All
the activity of America, of his life, all the storms and tensions,
all the searching scholarship, the reading and the teaching,
part of this assault. The intense prayer, the daily mass, the
seeking to stand still and be quiet, the effort to live the Rule,
was part of the struggle too. Not a refugee from life but
hunting for the pearl of great price, digging in the field for
its buried treasure.

He coped with the final severe illness with his usual wit
and irony. There was still zest in his concern for other
patients in hospital, still the mind hunting for new insights,
still a monk wanting to be in his community. Surgery seemed
at first to be successful but he was tired and still uncomfort-
able. By May of 1952 he had relapsed and was dying. He was
cared for in a house near the Abbey with the Abbot in regular
attendance. He died on May 12th 1952. As he was dying
Gregory had been able to recall events and relationships for
which he was grateful. He specifically remembered a trou-
bled young man on the British Embassy staff whom he had
met on the ship returning from Sweden. Gregory had been
of help to him and had recently received a letter of gratitude
on the anniversary of the occasion. 'God is so tactful' Gregory
said. Not always so tactful himself he could perhaps feel all
the more strongly the tactfulness of God and, knowing his
own need of such tact, in dying, turn towards that divine
generosity and grace.

Gregory had a special love for the hymn *Adoro Te* — the
hymn about the Blessed Sacrament written by St Thomas
Aquinas for the feast of *Corpus Christi*. There is an echo in
Gregory of that great 'Angelic Doctor' of the Church who with
his monumental intellect yet composed this intensely devout eucharistic poem. Theirs were minds that longed to
pray as well as to think. Gregory said that the last two verses
of the hymn 'squeezed your heart out'. Here, in English, are
those verses:

Fountain of goodness, Jesu, Lord and God,
Cleanse us, unclean, with thy most cleansing blood;
Increase our faith and love, that we may know
The hope and peace which from thy presence flow.

O Christ, whom now beneath a veil we see,
May what we thirst for soon our portion be,
To gaze on thee unveiled, and see thy face,
The vision of thy glory and thy grace!

In among all the other complicated motives and issues of his
life there was a man in Gregory kneeling with 'his heart
squeezed out' before the Blessed Sacrament. What moti-
vated his prayer, what stirred his spirit, what was happening
in him when he came to pray?

It is, of course, impossible as well perhaps as ultimately
impertinent to speak of such interior things but his spirituality is central to his thought and teaching, contiguous with
the monk and the priest and so fundamental to his life, and
deserves some attention.

He sought 'simplicity of heart'. For all his acknowledged
complicatedness, 'the actor' in him, watching himself, this
goal of the contemplative life remained his goal and he
referred to it often in retreats and other addresses. 'Recol-
lection' he also calls it — that gathered concentration of the
prayerful life. In *The Image and Likeness of God*, retreat addresses published after his death, he says:

> Let us be clear that this recollection, this sort of awareness
> of God is not a matter of the imagination or of the feelings.
> Occasionally yes, they may be usefully employed or they may
> be moved by the thought of God, yet for the most part it will
> be simply a return to the *bare fact* of God. It is not so much a
> matter of thinking *about* God as of thinking *of* Him, being
> aware of Him....

This he sees as being part of the *state* of prayer rather than
the *art* of prayer on which he had focused in the Retreat
on the Rule. It concerns that natural and instinctive,
unselfconscious turning into the presence of God. In a

characteristically apposite metaphor in *The Image and Likeness of God* he puts it like this:

> The older monastic spirituality regarded prayer much more as an abiding state of the monk, which quickens into greater intensity at the fixed hours of mass and office and mental prayer. To use a metaphor, it is like the charcoal burning all through mass in the censer. When the incense is put on, it kindles a little and consumes the grains and gives off the sweet odour of the incense. But if the charcoal has gone right out, or even grown cold... you may put on as much incense as you please at the offertory, but there will be no sacrifice of a sweet-smelling savour. The spirit of prayer, a dim but unfailing awareness of the fact of God somewhere at the back of the mind, ought to be the aim of every Christian.... This dim but unfailing awareness is the fruit of recollection, the outcome of the practice of silence and self-discipline in the mind and heart.

As he put it even more simply and directly to Dom Patrick Dalton, the motto is: 'Don't fuss. Trust God. Don't fuss.'

For all his stress on the Body of Christ and corporate life in the Church, his spirituality is nevertheless intensely personal (the 'little I...' again '.... the individual man — so dear to God'). It is penitential too. *The Image and Likeness of God* begins with the realisation that the image is broken even, he says, destroyed. In general he maintains the Catholic position on an essence remaining that God can use. This means that, on the whole, his spirituality is far from gloomy and negative but capable of celebrating beauty, especially natural beauty, pleasure and happiness.

If a personally loved hymn was *Adoro Te*, a personally loved biblical text was 'And there was silence in heaven for about half an hour.'[1]

What did he love about those mysterious words? Perhaps precisely the sense of mystery, the intensity of that heavenly silence, its anticipation, its sense of fulfilment, above all the sense of a collective, deep and lasting stillness achieved and

1   Rev. 8.1.

the fathomless directness of prayer and worship, a perfected liturgy, mysterious but assured.

His spirituality, his presentation of it, can sometimes seem dated. It grew in the first half of the twentieth century before the deluge of the Second Vatican Council and all the other radical developments in religion and spirituality. These sometimes cut us off very thoroughly from even forty years ago. Yet when he found words to convey that sense of mystery in prayer and liturgy, sometimes in *The Shape*, in the Retreat on the Rule, in addresses and sermons, he speaks from his own heart within the great and timeless traditions of Christian spirituality.

The theology that works its way out from this spirituality is catholic in its emphasis on the Incarnation. Even when he is not writing specifically about that idea it colours all his thoughts. At the centre is God's revelation of himself in Christ, through the Blessed Virgin Mary, chief guardian, as it were, of the Incarnation. Christ is the sacrament of God, his reality in the world, and this continuing reality for all time is the Church, the sacrament of Christ. The 'real presence' of Christ in the Church gives her a mystical status, a dignity and a holiness not derived from her individual members. Within the Church, she maintains her own life by the sacraments. The Church is fed and fashioned by the mass, her ordinary life is sustained in all its members by Christ in his sacraments in the Church. Here is a theology which is deeply corporate, deeply Trinitarian, deeply sacramental, and its natural implications include Holy Order, the religious life, the Papacy.

For Gregory the Incarnation *includes* the atonement. The Paschal mystery is God's redemptive work achieved through his involvement and participation in creation in Christ. It is a theology which *affirms* creation and, despite the war, a goodness. We are capable, he says in the Retreat on the Rule, of making our own little movement towards God's love, it is there in us. He compares God to the Sun:

Tranquilly, unendingly from the depths of His own being His love plays upon us and He swings us unceasingly on our life's

way and holds us and draws us to Him. And we draw Him to
us. However slight by comparison with the sun's vast attraction upon the earth, the earth's little pull upon the sun is
real; it does happen.

He goes on immediately to stress that together earth and sun
influence other planets too: we are 'rooted and grounded in
love'. This corporate emphasis is specifically focused in the
Church whose life is part of Christ's offering to God, whose
life is a priesthood, a sacrificial offering for the world.

Again Gregory's background in theology is traditional,
even scholastic — certainly his philosophy is Thomist.
Clearly he read modern theology too, especially biblical
theology and criticism, and was prepared to face honestly
radical implications in his own theology.

Curiously, like others whose emphasis is on the Apostolic
and Catholic credentials of the Church, he can seem more
interested in that than in Jesus himself, the Jesus of the
gospels, a person rather than a doctrine. However in *The Image
and Likeness of God* he puts Jesus 'into' St Paul's hymn to love
and the effect is beautiful:

> 'Jesus suffereth long and is kind' — in utter self-forgetful-
> ness, though continually slandered and opposed, 'He went
> about doing good.' 'Jesus envieth not': though of royal de-
> scent, He will not supplant a Herod or a Pilate, but chooses
> the lot of a labourer.... 'Jesus vaunteth not himself', but
> proclaims as His qualification for teaching only humility:
> 'learn of me for I am meek and lowly of heart'.

The life and liveliness in all of this is Gregory's imagination.
This powerful faculty in him is crucial to his pastoral insight
and sensitivity, to his careful attentiveness as a counsellor, it
is part of his engagement with what it means to be a monk.
In all his writings, and not least *The Shape*, time and again the
language and focus of thought is fired by his imagination.
With intensity, even passion, he takes up the reader with him.
Imagination enabled him to stand where others stood, to
hear as others would have heard, to see from their viewpoint.
For the man of scholarship who was also a man of the spirit,
the gift of imagination was the means by which he could fuse

his worlds and enabled him powerfully to communicate them.

Often we decern a method in his preaching and in retreat addresses which is almost Ignatian. He created pictures, evoked and created atmospheres and settings by intense realisation of detail and feeling. We see this also in parts of *The Shape* and it is especially true of those last addresses on Good Friday 1951 in New York. He sought to lead his hearers into the experience of the Passion and thereby set them to work out its implications in their own lives. From different angles and in different ways our attention is drawn to the experience of Calvary. Ultimately that was what he was always trying to do, both for those he was teaching and for himself. The Christian life was about finding ways of 'experiencing Calvary'. So the Good Friday Meditations move from matter-of-fact description of the events of crucifixion, to a web of references to the ministry of Jesus linked into his last words, to the imaginative evocation of the effect on us now:

> There is only one way, to let go of self, to give oneself to God out of love, the love that responds to Him, manifested and demonstrated to the end on Calvary.... 'Father into thy hands I lay down from myself my spirit.' *Father* — it is the first word of the first sentence He uttered from His cross, and it is the first word of the last. All has been a giving of Himself into God's hands.

His imagination is deeply linked, also, to the Romantic in him. He saw himself as a child of the romantic, Mediterranean South of Europe. His 'French ancestry', his catholicity, his dark eyes and dark southern complexion were all part of this for him. He had little sympathy with the 'Teutonic' north with its emotionalism, which he blamed for the distortions in liturgical devotion in the middle ages and reformation.

For all his antipathy he was not, of course, himself free from strong sentiment, verging on emotionalism, even at times in *The Shape*. The Catholic, romantic, southern tradition had its own emotional, intensely personal tradition too. For Gregory these were real though at least partly unexamined divisions, part of his psychology, among his instinctive assumptions.

The positive Romantic celebration of life gave him his sense of excitement at involvement in the world and its affairs, in having and using power and influence. It gave him too the charm and courtesy with which he indulged his power over people, dazzling them and sometimes infuriating them. The Romantic informed his strong sense of continuity with that long European tradition and gave him his longing to see that tradition more fully restored in England and in her Church. Inevitably it contributed too to the dilemma of the different worlds he wanted to live in: the world of battles about current affairs in the Church, the world of thought and scholarship, the world of contemplation and monastic discipline.

Spirituality, theology, imagination: Gregory's declared focus in all of them was the eucharist. It brought everything together, both deepest mystery and practical, realistic, ordinary daily living. He was speaking of and from the best in himself, when in the Introduction to *The Shape* he spoke of Eucharistic Man:

> Over against the dissatisfied 'Acquisitive man' and his no less avid successor the dehumanised 'Mass-man' of our economically focused societies insecurely organised for time, Christianity sets the type of 'Eucharistic Man' — man giving thanks with the product of his labours upon the gifts of God, and daily rejoicing with his fellows in the worshipping society which is grounded in eternity. This is man to whom it was promised on the night before Calvary that he should henceforth eat and drink at the table of God and be a king.

In amongst all Gregory's papers, inserted as a bookmark in his hand-written Greek text of the Synaxis of the Liturgy of St Mark, is a little piece of paper. It is dated '11.4.43' and simply says: 'Dom Gregory. 1 shirt. 1 pr black stockings. 1 pants. 1 vest. 1 pr of pyjamas. 3 handkerchiefs'. The laundry list in the Greek manuscript somehow pictures his life. All that wandering, soaring careful thought and the practical, earthy, ordinariness of monastic life; all the mystery of the

Church's prayer and the inescapable necessity of being clothed, living, staying alive.

At the end of his Retreat on the Rule he considers the love of God and quotes from the final sentence of Benedict's Rule:

> *Deo protegente pervenies.* Under the protection of God you shall arrive. That is where the Rule ends, you will arrive.

'You will arrive.' He has reached a quieter confidence and trust, a deeper assurance. He can feel that the deterioration *is* slowing down — God is realistic and practical and human. God is tactful.

3

The Gadfly

'... the brethren are to proffer their several opin-
ions with all the subjection of humility, and none
should presume to maintain pertinaciously his own
opinion....'

Rule of St Benedict, Ch.3

'The house is full of Swedes', Gregory wrote from Nashdom in 1949 to Dom Patrick Dalton in Three Rivers, 'I have suggested they end their visit in the traditional manner by murdering the Archbishop of Canterbury — but some of the vigour seems to have gone out of the breed.'

It was the obituary for Gregory in *The Times* in 1952 which said that the bishops had 'lost a salutary gadfly'. By the time of his early death Gregory had earned a definite reputation for his role in Church politics and controversies. He was variously described as combative, a maverick, an *enfant terrible* — a gadfly, stinging and harrying the bishops and the whole establishment of the Church, urging it all in a more catholic, more orthodox direction. It was typical of him, characteristic of him in this role, that he claimed to have chosen 'Gregory' as his monastic name not for Pope Gregory the Great, who might have seemed the obvious choice, but for Pope Gregory VII (1021 – 1085) 'who', he said, 'deposed more bishops than any other man in history'. Why should a monk get his hands dirty, soil his prayers, with such controversy?

There was something naturally combative about Gregory.
There was an ebullience of spirit, a zest, that loved a fight
and knew that more often than not he could win, or, at least,
seem to win. His charm, wit, passion and conviction combined to make him if not a natural warrior then certainly one
seriously convinced of the need for someone to take up the
weapons; himself if necessary.

'Taking up the weapons' was also the result of his long
interior struggle and subsequent conviction about the nature
of the Church and his place in it. Consciously or not, his
involvement in Church 'politics' was partly if not chiefly the
consequence of his decision, made in about 1930, not to join
the Roman Catholic Church. As he explained to Maurice
Bévenot in the letter quoted earlier, he felt he must stay in
the Church of England working as hard as he could for her
deeper adherence to her own catholic tradition and for a
closer and stronger link to Rome. He summarised his determination in four points which lie behind his extensive involvement in Church life in the thirties and forties. 'Not
submitting to Rome', as he put it, would involve him in
working for: (1) the replacing of 'liberalism' in the Church
of England with a return to the 'classic tradition'; (2) disestablishment; (3) the regularising of Anglican orders; (4) the
Roman Church's acceptance of such a Church in her communion — and the Anglican Church's realisation that she
needs 'Catholic communion'.

In the existing documents this 'programme' (as he called
it) occurs only in the private letter to Bévenot of 1940. It
appears in no published work and is admitted in the letter
to Bévenot to seem 'hopeless', 'perverse' even 'mad'. Nevertheless, in one way or another, it lay behind his involvement
in Church life. In some ways it summarises the aims of the
whole Anglo-Catholic movement, certainly in its more papalist form.

Anglo-Catholicism developed out of the mid-nineteenth
century Oxford Movement in the Church of England. It
sought to reclaim for the Church an independence from the
State (despite Establishment), a sense of continuity with the

long centuries of the Church before the Reformation as well
as since (perhaps rather more than since) an openness to the
catholic character of the universal Church. Steadily through
the nineteenth and early twentieth centuries, sometimes
with fierce struggles but also with quiet faithful witness, the
movement brought to the Church of England a wider, deeper,
tradition, a greater emphasis on the Incarnation, a more
central place and greater reverence for sacraments, especially
the eucharist. It employed the signs and symbols of movement, architecture, clothing and music which accompany
such reverence. It stimulated a theology which took seriously
the doctrine of the Church as the body of Christ with all its
implications, and it fostered a life of prayer that grew out of
that sense of 'the body', of sacramental reverence, of a rich
tradition. One consequence of that revived life of prayer was
the re-emergence in the Church of England of forms of
monasticism. In all these ways the English Church was
rediscovering or recovering, Catholicity. Anglo-Catholicism
in the early twentieth century was the Church of England
spreading out from inside its former strictures to be a whole
Church. The movement found the vestiges of that wholeness there in the existing body and they wanted to let that
develop, grow and blossom.

Some of the detailed implications of the movement, such
as confession, frequent masses, the Reserved Sacrament,
incense, met an old English (especially an establishment)
fear of 'Popery'. The clash in turn provoked a fighting, not to
say a partisan spirit in the Anglo-Catholics. The remarkably
steady flow in due course of almost all the characteristic
features of Anglo-Catholicism into the mainstream life of the
Church of England did not diminish the sense of embattled
fervour that marked many an Anglo-Catholic protagonist.

Just such a protagonist was Gregory Dix. A child of the
movement, born into it, not a convert, he stayed with it all
his life. Its characteristics were his instincts: colourful, communal, ordered, at times flamboyant but prayerful — and
pugnacious too. Gregory had had little extended exposure to
any other tradition in the Church. Oxford and theological

college at Wells might have provided opportunities to experience other positions of conviction in the Church but Gregory seems to have opted for the active defence of his own point of view rather than the careful observation of others. Instead, in the mature development of his religion, he faced, ironically, the destabilising question posed for many an Anglo-Catholic. If it is so important to be catholic why not join the Roman Catholic Church? A steady flow of Anglo-Catholics did make its way into the Roman communion. In fact, round about 1930, when Gregory was feeling the question most acutely, a number of celebrated conversions were taking place. Even in this atmosphere, he chose to stay with the Church of England but the decision made him no less an Anglo-Catholic, rather it sharpened his sense of a purpose, almost a 'mission' in the Church he had now, in effect, 'chosen'.

It ought to be recorded that Gregory hated the term 'Anglo-Catholic', perhaps because it implied a party or sectarian group when for him the whole point was that his allegiance was to the whole Catholic Church. He was happy to be called a 'Catholic', however, and even a 'Papalist'. Mischievously, when Archbishop Geoffrey Fisher in the 1940s commissioned a group to prepare a report on 'Catholicity' and wanted to know how to refer to the group Gregory suggested 'traditional Anglican'. His suggestion was certainly tongue-in-cheek and yet in a very real sense that is precisely how he saw himself.

Gregory's skills and awareness, as well as his scholarship and reputation, developed at very much the same time as the flowering of the Anglo-Catholic movement. It reached a kind of heyday in the thirties as he too settled into his life's work.

Gregory was away in Africa and then returned ill when the 1928 prayer book crisis came to its head. Anglo-Catholicism, perhaps alone of the 'factions' in the Church, had emerged effectively unscathed, perhaps even strengthened, from this debacle. Ironically, the book had been devised in an attempt at long last to accommodate Anglo-Catholic pressures on the liturgy of the Church. It had taken two decades and more for it to emerge but it had increasingly been viewed as too

compromised, too weakened in its provision and too suspiciously clear about what Gregory called the 'police' aspects
of its implementation, for Anglo-Catholics to feel comfortable with it. When it failed to make its way through parliament in 1928 Anglo-Catholics were not disappointed but
actually pleased, not least because it provided another argument for disestablishment.

1933 saw the centenary of the Oxford Movement. It was
celebrated with a huge, confident Anglo-Catholic Congress
in London assembling 70,000 people. There was a sense of
achievement and success, if of battles still to be fought, but
the Church was rediscovering and accepting her heritage and
no one could any longer be unaffected by it. The leaders of
the Church had to take the movement seriously, some of the
bishops were actually Anglo-Catholics themselves, some of
the brightest thinkers, some of the best theology was coming
from this movement. Michael Ramsey published *The Gospel
and the Catholic Church* in 1936, Gabriel Hebert edited *The
Parish Communion* in 1937 (to which Gregory contributed) and
Gregory himself produced his seminal text of Hippolytus also
in 1936.

The Anglo-Catholic blossoming, clear, visible, tangible
religion, was of a piece with the age, shifting from scepticism
and liberal vagueness to a rediscovery of religion and faith.
In the era of the Depression, with the growing rumblings on
the European continent, positive religion was a real salvation.
As Adrian Hastings puts it in his book, *A History of English
Christianity 1920 – 1990*:

> For late 1930's man, agonised by Hitler upon the one hand
> and Stalin upon the other, increasingly frightened by what
> was just around the corner, the secular vision had indeed
> faded and he was more and more inclined to look out for God
> instead, to hope for the reassurance if not of some unforget
> table burst of light, at least of the tempered optimism of the
> crucifix.[1]

1   *A History of English Christianity 1920 – 1990*, Adrian Hastings, SCM, 3rd
     ed. 1991, p. 290.

In other ways, of course, religion like this could simply be a
means of escape, a way of hiding from the pressures of a
frightening world. In the struggles of Anglo-Catholicism in
the Church of England in the thirties and forties, to the
centre of which Gregory steadily moved, there was little
reference to the depression and the Jarrow marches, little
reference to the rise of Nazism, to the war itself and its
terrible consequences (Hiroshima, the Holocaust...) little
reference to the 'Welfare State' revolution of the forties.
Even in the context of the Church of South India, the great
bête noire of the movement in these decades, astonishingly
little reference was made to the struggle for Indian independence. Anglo-Catholicism lived with, and from time to
time reminded itself of, the famous warning of the great
Bishop Frank Weston of Zanzibar at the 1923 Anglo-Catholic
congress that it was folly to seek Christ in the Blessed
Sacrament if they did not also seek out his presence in the
poor and outcast. However in the details of Church politics,
and the preoccupations of the struggle for the Church, such
larger vision over the great issues could become forgotten
and neglected.

These 'great issues' were rarely the object of Gregory's
own passion either. Of course in sermons, and sometimes in
other writings, Gregory could make the necessary connections, as we have seen. He worked, however, in the conviction
that the apparently rarefied and narrow details he fought over
in Church politics were actually linked up with the grander
issues in the end because only a purified, genuinely truth-
filled, holy and strong Church was any use to humankind.
And such a Church was the *only* thing that *was* any use.
Nevertheless, he himself acknowledged just how frustrating
the 'details' sometimes were.

One of the things Gregory's 'programme' committed him to
(point 4) was ecumenism, a greater mutual understanding
between Churches, by which he largely meant the Church
of England and Rome (Eastern orthodoxy was an academic
rather than a political interest to him). Such ecumenism was,
of course, a natural feature both of the Anglo-Catholic move-

ment in general and of Nashdom in particular. Within the movement there was a variety of different emphases from considerable suspicion of Rome to open Papalism. Nashdom belonged solidly with the latter. Being a catholic needed to include a connection to Rome.

Gregory, newly ordained and appointed to teach at Keble in the mid 1920s must have watched, a fascinated bystander, as the Warden of Keble, B.J. Kidd, along with Armitage Robinson, Dean of Wells (a city which Gregory had just left), Walter Frere, later a friend of Gregory's, and Lord Halifax pursued the Malines conversations, discussing unity with Rome with members of the Roman hierarchy. That the conversations came to nothing was a blow to all concerned but the movement certainly learned from that experience — if only that such a method, of effectively private approaches, was far from ideal. Certainly the desire for contact was strengthened. The Church Unity Octave became a central feature, specifically focused at first on unity with Rome. In time Nashdom expanded it under the influence of the Abbé Couturier to include prayer 'for the unity of all Christian people' in its Week of Prayer.

In this atmosphere Gregory, in 1936 on the eve of his novitiate, made his visit to France in the company of Father Fynes-Clinton of St Magnus the Martyr in London. His near-ecstatic letter to his mother[1] describing his visit to lecture on 'the English Church and reunion' is mentioned in the last chapter. Again it was a strictly 'unofficial' exchange between Churches but Gregory is (almost childishly) delighted at being taken so seriously and being so welcome in French Catholic circles.

Over the years Gregory corresponded with a number of Roman Catholic scholars and established other contacts but for him the most fruitful connection was with Maurice Bévenot. This Jesuit wrote to Gregory in 1937 after reading an article by him in the Nashdom Journal *Laudate*, on Papal Jurisdiction. At first the correspondence was fairly formal,

1   p. 52.

especially from Bévenot's side, but Gregory seized his opportunity and suggested setting up a group for discussion on unity issues. Gregory strode ahead with plans for the group while Bévenot, increasingly friendly and open, reined him back. Gregory's group was to include Thornton of Mirfield, Demant, Eric Mascall and Gabriel Hebert SSM: Bévenot's side were all Jesuits from Heythrop College. The imbalance is perhaps typical. In any case the meetings of the group were less significant than the actual correspondence between the two men as the long tradition of catholic teaching, focused in Bévenot, confronted and worked with the long but differently catholic tradition in Gregory. Both had to work back through very deep-seated assumptions and both men, though Gregory probably set the pace, were sometimes surprised by each other. In the letter of January 23rd 1938 Bévenot remarked that they are not attempting a kind of Malines but simply an exercise in 'getting to know each other better' if only to agree a common vocabulary.

At first the letters were frequent but they thinned out in the subsequent years, not least as Gregory became heavily involved in other things. Nevertheless the correspondence, and friendship, continued until the end of his life and was clearly important to him.

The essay on 'Jurisdiction episcopal and papal in the early Church' in *Laudate*,[1] which began the correspondence, appeared in 1937 and in it Gregory wrote as an historian about the organic, natural authority afforded to bishops but also to the papacy in the early Church. He spoke of 'a vague general tradition (by the fourth century) that Rome set the norm of Christian belief'.

At other times he argued that the Roman primacy was a 'working fact' from very much earlier. Gregory, as an historian, felt he could not escape the sheer fact in Christian history of the Roman primacy over the Church and its jurisdiction. Soberly he argued from the documents of the primitive Church, which he knew so well, that no other conclusion was

1   Vol. IV, p. 107.

possible. A Church to be a Church had to come to terms in some way with what he saw as the solid, serious reality of Rome's pre-eminent position.

It was not, of course, a popular idea in Anglican, even in all Anglo-Catholic, circles but Gregory was the man to argue for unpopular ideas.

Amongst the documents that remain is an undated paper possibly given to the group meeting with Bévenot in the summer of 1938. In it he argues that the papacy is 'like a gland in the body — an internal influence'. 'It is greater', he says 'than any other single Christian force'. He immediately goes on to say that the early primacy was very different from the modern form. It had not been about a 'legal sovereignty' but about a 'consensual authority of leadership'. In one of the letters to Bévenot he again distinguishes the character of the early primacy: 'Like you I believe there was always a real right to jurisdiction (though I don't like to use a term of the pre-Nicene Church which the pre-Nicenes themselves did not use).'[1]

Whatever its character, he believed the papacy was vital to the Church, the whole Church, like a 'gland'. To Bévenot he wrote: 'Anglicans start by thinking of the papacy as something separable from the Church (without which the Church would still be the Church as God constituted it) what I am trying to get at is the fact that the Papacy is organic to the Church.'[2]

Gregory always remained firmly convinced that the logic of his catholic faith naturally included the papacy. He argued it just as forcefully in a paper given to the community at Mirfield in 1944, 'we are all parasitic', he said.

For Gregory it was not just an academic issue; he clearly felt the connection. In a *Laudate* article of 1936 about the Good Friday liturgy in which, as so often in *The Shape*, he remarked approvingly on the liturgical conservatism of Rome, he describes the solemn dignity of the rite and notes

1   8.7.39.
2   1.2.39.

how it must have: 'moved multitudes of common men in-
stinctively to call the Roman Church their "Mother", for all
her imperious tones and jealous ways.'[1]

His personal sense of a catholic continuity and unity that
had a focus in the papacy, his reverence for the history and
tradition of Rome, his feeling that the whole thing came
together with Rome as the last piece of the jigsaw was
mirrored in the ethos of his community at Nashdom. The
Benedictine way of life itself, measured, level, sane as it was
meant to be, belonged in one piece with the unbroken
pattern of a catholic Church with Rome at its centre. The
way of life led back in unbroken continuity, back beyond the
reformation, back to a sane, balanced and perfectly natural
connectedness with Rome. It could be taken for granted and
in the community it was perhaps sometimes possible to feel,
to want to feel, even to pretend, that the reformation had
never happened, that *Ecclesia Anglicana* was as catholic as any
other Church, that the pope for whom they prayed each day
would himself have acknowledged them as his sons. It should
perhaps be said that Roman Catholics themselves, when they
paid attention to this, could either be deeply impressed like
Couturier, or more often, rather puzzled as Bévenot surely
was initially and many of the Roman Benedictines were.
Others were covertly or openly scornful. The rest of the
world's failure to understand a point of view has never, of
course, been a valid argument against it.

Not surprisingly in Anglican circles such sentiments were
labelled Papalistic: Gregory and those who shared his views
were labelled Anglo-papalists. Jointly with Ian Young, Gregory edited a small, short lived and overtly papalist journal
called *The Pilot*. An edition for the centenary of the Oxford
Movement celebrated, in Gregory's words, 'the way in which
the Anglican revival grew to a consciousness of Rome as the
necessary goal of Catholic Unity'.

Gregory knew how unpopular his ideas were, and no doubt
that helped to make him defensive about them. He was

1   Vol. XIII.

distinctly reluctant to criticise Rome and always ready to
make concessions. In his letters to Bévenot he was ready, for
instance, to put references to his own 'mass' in inverted
commas in a way that may indicate his own personal security
about such things but which actually can sound fawning and
obsequious. (Not usual characteristics of Gregory....) So too
in his little book of 1944, *The Question of Anglican Orders*
Gregory is positively gentle in his criticism of the Bull *Apos-*
tolicae Curae (1896) in which Pope Leo XIII condemned
Anglican orders as 'absolutely null and utterly void'. (One
can imagine the savagery of his wit if it had emanated from
Canterbury....) Nevertheless the book does thoroughly criticise the Roman position and Gregory's 'papalism' is not, in
the end, an unexamined and fawning admiration.

In letters to Bévenot, Gregory was more ready to be
critical, especially of the Roman Catholic establishment in
England. He remarked on a lack of respect for Anglican
writers and the Anglican position. There had been an unhelpful lack of any attempt to take English religion seriously
(they had five hundred years to do something about it,
Gregory pointed out) and still, in the war situation, when
even the English might be ready to take a lead from the Holy
See, or so Gregory claimed optimistically, it did not happen.

It was at a meeting in 1940 with Roman Catholics that
Gregory was encouraged to *remain* an Anglican because the
Roman hierarchy was already clamping down. In England
specifically the 'Sword of the Spirit' had been a Roman
Catholic initiative in 1940 and 1941 to do some thinking and
planning about the war and the world that would follow it.
It was largely lay-led but supported and even 'headed' by
Cardinal Hinsley, the Archbishop of Westminster and head
of the Roman Catholic hierarchy in England and Wales. It
was energetic, thoughtful and also ecumenical. For the first
time cardinals were making shared statements with Anglican
archbishops and Free-Church leaders. Gregory clearly saw
signs of the Roman Catholic Church leading the way and
setting the pace. But it didn't last. The ecumenism caused
trouble among other Roman Catholics, though not, it seems,

with the Pope. Hinsley died in 1943 and the movement lost the initiative and earned Gregory's lament.

In many ways Gregory's attention to and reverence for Rome prevented him taking altogether seriously the heritage of the reformation. His abhorrence of schism and respect for the papacy prevented him facing the full reality of the need for reformation in the sixteenth century. He does not seem to have asked himself why the protestant reformers and their descendants were quite so virulently and persistently opposed to the papacy and its powers. Even in his contribution to the *Catholicity* report of 1947, in which he wrote about the 'Post-Tridentine Papal Communion', he failed, uncharacteristically, to examine this continuing antipathy. The papal reforms of Trent seem to him sufficient restoration and he could not acknowledge the seemingly permanent damage done by the earlier abuses of papal power.

Gregory was certainly 'anti-protestant' — the other face of his papalism — but he did respect convinced and thoughtful protestants. He corresponded with a number of leading figures of the day and frequently acknowledge his debt to protestant scholars such as C.H. Dodd and Newton Flew. His critique of protestantism was, however, trenchant if narrow, focusing on the centrality of the idea of 'justification by faith alone'. In *The Question of Anglican Orders* and also in *The Shape*, as elsewhere, he argued that this in the end must mean that religion was a mere matter of the personal will and associated feelings, religion becoming psychology: 'Justification happened through a man's total surrender to one particular idea and to the emotion it evoked; it happened entirely and completely inside a man's own mind.'[1]

By contrast, for a catholic, justification came through Christ in his Church and through the sacraments as something real and objective. Gregory linked this to his theories about 'Teutonic' emotionalism as opposed to the, albeit sometimes crude, objectivity of the Mediterranean south. All his own sympathies lay with the latter.

1   See *The Question of Anglican Orders*, p. 21.

In Gregory's perception, therefore, protestants had no fundamental need of a Church; it might be a helpful extra but a catholic simply did not exist without the Church. In this lies his very different attitudes to different kinds of ecumenism.

The Ecumenical Movement has been identified as the great phenomenon of the twentieth century Church. It is understood as having begun in 1910 with the Edinburgh Missionary conference where Churches committed themselves to the 'evangelisation of the world', a mission that could only be achieved if they worked together. In 1920 the Lambeth Conference issued its 'Appeal to all Christian People' stressing again the gospel principle of unity in the Church and further highlighting the painfulness and even wickedness of divisions. Steadily in the early decades of the century structures for ecumenism began to emerge both nationally and internationally.

Anglo-Catholics were involved in this to some extent but the great problem for many of them was that the Roman Catholic Church was not involved in any of it. For people like Gregory the conviction grew that this was not a move towards 'unity' in any real sense but was, and without Rome could only be, an 'alliance of denominations'. That could not be seen even as a 'step in the right direction'. Rather, the danger was that a great pan-Protestant alliance would not only divert attention and energy from the effort for unity with Rome but would also make many people feel unity with Rome was unnecessary. It would only serve to polarise the Roman and protestant positions. Gregory and other papalists and Anglo-Catholics feared, throughout this period, a 'pan-protestant' alliance. They spoke of it almost in terms of a plot or conspiracy and were alarmed by the steady, effective development of structures and institutions to service the movement. When, however, Roman Catholics showed even the slightest flicker of interest in the movement it thoroughly wrong-footed Gregory and his colleagues. Maurice Bévenot attended the ecumenical conference in Edinburgh in 1937 as a fascinated observer. Gregory's response to this seems a slightly flustered explanation that he too had been invited but too late to be able to make arrangements to go.

Gregory's fear of the Church of England's involvement in all of this became something of an important motive for all his political work in the Church. He feared it would spoil the chances of unity with Rome. The Church of England, as a still-catholic Church, could most naturally turn to Rome (unlike the more protestant denominations). If she linked herself up in alliance with these protestants she could deny her place in the 'living body' of the Catholic Church and all would be lost. In this conflict Gregory, of course, found himself up against the colossus of the age, William Temple. Temple, universally respected and revered, even in his lifetime, had been involved in the ecumenical movement from the beginning. He saw its objectives as of the greatest importance to the Church and the world. He also saw them as achievable.

Reunion with Rome, on the other hand, he always considered a very distant prospect: 'at present I regard it as almost infinitely remote', he said in 1933.[1]

Gregory's relationship with William Temple was much more complex than with any other of his 'opponents'. Like so many he could not help but admire Temple, an admiration which did not diminish the more they disagreed. To Mrs Temple, after the Archbishop's death, Gregory wrote saying that Temple's mind was 'a phenomenon of nature' and he said one had 'confidence in his wisdom even when one disagreed profoundly'.

To another correspondent Gregory wrote of Temple's successor: 'I don't feel I can trust him or love him as I loved his predecessor.'[2]

For all his admiration Gregory felt Temple was at one with an essentially liberal-protestant attitude to the Church, an attitude which lay behind the pan-protestant ecumenical movement. Unity in the Catholic Church, was an organic,

1   *William Temple*, Iremonger, p. 419.
2   To John Hay, 11.6.45.

living thing: for the protestant a loose alliance was all that
was needed.

Gregory was too good a theologian to imply that protestants were living a lie and could have no experience of the
presence of God or the life of the Spirit. Real sacraments
might only be found in the Catholic Church, but 'God is not
limited by the sacraments' he quoted, and respected the
genuine protestant experience of God. But if God is in any
case 'accessible' to protestants why all the fuss? Why so much
energy and effort expended on his 'programme' for the
Church of England?

Here we come to the vital issues. At the heart of his
political involvement, behind all his campaigning and his
harrying of bishops, was his conviction about the Church as
the living body of Christ, an organism not an organisation.
The incarnation continues in the Church. Christ lives on in
his body in the world: the catholic Church. For Gregory there
is a near-physical sense to that continuing life of Christ in
the world, a tangible incarnation.

Crucial to that body, not only living in it but also guaranteeing its life, are its sacraments, which, of course, include
its ministry. None of this is incidental to the life of the body
but it is all vital, part of its unity. And the unity of the body
is *itself* a guarantee of its life, certainly of its liveliness. Unity
in the catholic Church becomes a vital sign, and division,
separation, schism become horrible, ugly for they are real,
painful wounds in the flesh. Very naturally then it becomes
a Christian duty, and a primary, passionate one, to work for
the healing of the wounds, the restoration of unity. This must
be real unity, an organic, living connection not a mere sham
of linked, 'allied', but still separate limbs. That would be the
worst of all; a travesty, a mockery.

It is one body. This theme is stressed emphatically at the
end of *The Shape of the Liturgy*.[1] Here Gregory is not arguing
ecumenical politics but is writing theology that borders on
devotion, writing that therefore reveals more of his consid-

1   p. 750.

ered, deeper personal reflection and conviction. He quotes
from patristic sources that emphasise the 'singleness' of the
body, the unique solidarity of the redeemed race, the 'Israel
of God'. The image of God is in the unity of his human
creation. It is restored in Christ and marked by the same
unity, a singleness. He quotes Athanasius: 'Therefore the
Word of God came in His own Person, in order that, as He was
the image of the Father, He might be able to re-create *the man*
[sing.] made after the image.'[1] (The italics are Gregory's.)

His commitments and passions in Church politics focus
on the nature of that Church . In 1937, in his *Laudate* article
on papal jurisdiction, he was already declaring the importance
of this: 'For the next generation the nature of the Church rather
than Christology is certain to be the cardinal problem before
Christian thought.'[2]

Confidently he recognised a movement among protestants too in this direction. In a letter to Bévenot he notes
how protestant scholars were leading others:

> Dodd and Flew and Micklem and Whale have forced our
> people to look at the scriptures and there discover the
> Church not as a debating society or an ethical endeavour
> league but an intensely dogmatic institution which is itself
> believed in and lived in as well as believed and lived.[3]

All Gregory's concerns and efforts with regard to ministry and
sacraments grow from these basic convictions about the Body
of Christ, the Catholic Church. It leads both to *The Question
of Anglican Orders* (1944) as well as to his contribution to *The
Apostolic Ministry* (1946), edited by Kenneth Kirk, in which
he writes about the primitive episcopate. In a different way
it leads to his contribution to *The Parish Communion*, edited
by Hebert (1937), about the primitive eucharist and most
extensively of course, to *The Shape of the Liturgy*. Always over
against what he sees as the individualism of 'justification by
faith alone' he sets the organic, living body of Christ, alive in

1   Athanasius, *de Incarnatione xiii.*
2   *Ibid., p. 45.*
3   1.4.42.

its sacraments, in its ministry and, logically for him, alive in that 'gland', the papacy.

Protestantism *per se*, on the continent or in English dissent, was not, however, Gregory's real enemy. The adversary, for which he reserved his greatest energies of invective and scorn, was the woolly liberal establishment of the Church of England; not truly protestant, very far from catholic, not really anything specific at all. He referred to this as the 'National Religious Establishment' or 'NRE' and said it was epitomised in the BBC. He saw it epitomised in most of the bishops too. He said that Archbishop Fisher's creed consisted of: 'God is nice and in him is no nastiness at all.' He felt they were dealing with two religions, the Catholic Church and this National Religious Establishment. It was out of the latter and towards the former that he longed for the Church of England to move.

The 'NRE' was characterised by all its state connections, the result of the reformation and the not much modified Elizabethan settlement. Disestablishment seemed to Gregory vital if the Church was to recover a real catholicity. The state link could only sap the body's energies and result in the vague, unprincipled liberalism that seemed then to him to dominate the Church of England. The experience of Prayer Book revision in 1928, when the House of Commons had overridden the clear wishes of the Church, only served to underline the point. The Church must be free of such control.

Gregory was confident enough that catholic life could be and was being revived in the Church of England to feel that the struggle was well worth continuing. He was equally convinced that the opposition was trying to enhance its position. Reflecting on the South India controversy and the Commission established to look at it in 1946 he wrote to Dom Paul Severance[1] in Three Rivers: I don't think it will have the slightest effect, on the Archbishop and his advisers.

1   10.4.46.

They are desperate to save 'the Establishment' by bringing the non-conformists into 'the National Church'.

One of the consequences of Establishment which Gregory hated most was the Church's dependence on bureaucrats and particularly on lawyers. Knowing the history of the use of the law by the authorities against his Anglo-Catholic forebears, he had come to distrust all organisation by statute of the Church. In one of his first speeches to Convocation in 1946 he commented on: 'the unhappy operation of the theory that Christian worship was a suitable subject for organisation by the police'.[1] He added: 'I do not trust statutes. I trust the general mind of the Church.' Apart from his role in Church politics, this has interesting implications for his attitude to liturgical reform as we shall see later.

Gregory was convinced that the theological and philosophical liberalism that lay behind this other religion was well and truly on the wane. He spoke of himself, to William Temple and others, as part of a 'coming generation' of much more conservative scholars, more convinced about the Church, about authority, about dogma generally. He believed, as we have seen, this was true of protestant theologians too. He could point to continental theologians also, protestant and catholic, to Barth and Niebhur, to antimodernism at Rome, to Congar and Mersch.

Gregory seems to have made the point emphatically to William Temple himself at a small conference the bishops convened in 1940 at Breadsall Mount, the Bishop of Derby's home. It was a meeting of some bishops representing the older school with some of that 'coming generation'. The group consisted of the bishops of Derby, Coventry and York, V.A. Demant, Eric Mascall, Michael Bruce and Gregory. Gregory mentioned the conference in his letters to Maurice Bévenot telling him rather grandly: 'they have left the agenda and procedure in my hands'. Gregory wanted to talk about the Church: 'where Anglican theology breaks down every

1   15.1.46.

time' but even so he says: ' "Liberalism" as a principle is in full retreat at the moment in *Ecclesia Anglicana*.'

Temple, writing to Gregory in preparation for the conference seems to admit Gregory's point about the generations:

> I think your generation has to find its own starting point and build its own bridges. I think it is likely that one of the things most needed now, in this intensely secularised world, is a return to the standpoint of the Apostles and the Kerygma (only there we must be clear about its content) and a building of bridges more scholastic from the Revelation to the world rather than from a semi-Christian world to the Revelation.[1]

Generously, Temple even offered to withdraw: 'But (please be quite candid) am I so much a bugbear intellectually to some of the people concerned that my presence would hinder more than help the arrival at a mutual understanding?'

In his next letter[2] Temple asked Gregory to set out grounds of dissatisfaction with the bishops' theological method and outlook so that they could discuss reason and authority, nature and grace, creation and redemption.

After the conference Temple wrote to Neville Tablot: '... it was Gregory Dix who specially emphasised the greater lengths to which the still younger crowd would want to go in divergence from and denunciation of us.'[3]

Temple's generosity and openness seems here to have allowed even his profound, and deeply intelligent, philosophical and theological position to be cornered, for a moment anyway, by Gregory's exuberant brilliance and charming persuasive polemicism. The consultation was not a great turning point or watershed of any kind (though a similar group did meet again with Temple in 1944) but it symbolised, the fact of it rather than anything they discussed, a change of generation. There was a sense of a liberal era passing, at least for a while, and a more dogmatic, more emphatic era emerging. Gregory did not let this theme go.

1 14.8.39.
2 1.1.40.
3 1.2.40.

More damning still, in *The Question of Anglican Orders*, he described this liberalism as: 'trusting to a purely opportunist policy and a rather ramshackle institutionalism to guide the actual life of the Church'.[1] Most damning of all he saw the projects of this liberalism as: 'the dreams of old men'.

By this time, the early 1940s, Gregory was beginning to see himself as something of a leader of his group. In some of his statements and declarations he sounded almost like a prophet. He took the role of one who, unpopular as it may be, stands for a truth that is still to be fully understood, whose day is yet to come. He adopted a similar kind of attitude, but perhaps more vigorously still, with Geoffrey Fisher, Temple's successor at Canterbury.

Writing to him in 1945 in the light of the conflicts over the Church of South India, Gregory insisted that a change must come: '... a change as the "liberal era" recedes into the past... the change is there, it affects "Protestants" as well as "Catholics" (to use terms which are losing some of their relevance).'[2]

Gregory saw himself as part of a generation, and part of a Church, the Catholic Church, which was more international, more in tune with world-wide but especially continental trends, than the English establishment, despite its liberal claims. Writing to Fisher in 1948[3] he again referred to the 'new generation' and this time emphasised his continental contacts: Couturier, Culmann, Lutherans in Denmark and Germany, as well as the Methodist Rupp and the Congregationalist Whitehouse at home. The implication is that the catholic point of view is actually bound to be wider and more international than the liberal English establishment. In the same letter he goes on to say that people like Michael Ramsey and himself working with the Free Churches in the next generation will have to begin by undoing all the present work before proceeding with questions about unity.

1   *Ibid.*, p.90.
2   10.6.45.
3   27.7.48.

Gregory's conviction, as we shall see when we look in more detail at his involvement in the issue of the South Indian Church, was that the premises were all wrong. It had begun in the wrong place from the wrong principles. All that needed to be changed, unstitched, before progress could be made.

The focus of the 'liberal establishment' for Gregory was inevitably the bishops and for them he reserved his most scathing criticism and savage wit. More than once he said, alluding to current debate about the place of bishops, essential or simply helpful to the Church, that bishops might be of the *esse* of the Church but they were certainly not of its *bene esse*. His remark about the sign of a bishop being a crook and that of an archbishop a double cross is famous and typical. The bishop as businessman, lawyer and administrator he saw as most dangerous and unattractive. It was part of his antipathy to running the Church by statute law and state-like bureaucracy. Many times in his writings, including *The Shape*, the bishops are the victims of his wit and even invective: many quotations could be made, no wonder he earned a reputation as their 'gadfly'. There was, of course, something of the little man against the power of the mighty and secure in his attitude. This was a position Gregory actually seemed to relish though he constantly told his brethren how wearisome he found it to be.

He was, no doubt, aware of the destructive danger in over-indulging this ready source of fun. He did, after all, firmly believe in episcopacy and could see that Anglo-Catholicism had sometimes gone too far in its criticisms. In *The Question of Anglican Orders* he says: 'What we have to avoid is sinking into that sterile and embittered contempt for Anglican authority in its own legitimate field, and for "the Bishops" which did so much to frustrate the old "Anglo-Catholic" party of the 1920s.'

Gregory certainly numbered Anglican bishops amongst his friends and allies. Walter Frere, Bishop of Truro, had influenced him greatly on liturgical matters, Kenneth Kirk, Bishop of Oxford, was one of his closest friends and worked with him on many issues. Gregory could even recognise the

near-impossible situation facing many a bishop. In amongst
his papers on Church history is this comment: 'Jerome was
never a bishop — he had not the grace of suffering fools gladly
which is a necessity of the pastoral spirit.'

Nevertheless, he all too often found it impossible to resist
using his sting against 'the bishops' *en masse*. He preferred to
put his trust in the whole body, in the *plebs sancta Dei* rather
than the bishops, or even just in the English clergy. In *A
Detection of Aumbries* (1945), his little *tour de force* on the
Reserved Sacrament, he has this to say. It is classic Gregory
— clever, ironic, almost snide, but disarmingly stylish and
neat:

> It certainly would seem (and was) quite unjustifiable to
> disobey the bishops. Yet the historian grows accustomed to
> the idea that even the best and most energetic of bishops will
> one day have rest from his labours and that the lance of his
> successor often delivers the diocese from the menace of some
> different windmill. But the English clergy, with their pecu-
> liarly Northern Catholic sense of 'reverence', seem to be
> always pretty much the English clergy.[1]

Recovering catholicity in the Church of England required a
renewed episcopate: reunion schemes with various Churches
even more urgently required a clear vision of a catholic
bishop; what he could do, how he was created, why he was
so important to the Church. At least part of Gregory's antipathy to bishops was the result of his vision of what they *might*
be like. Gregory turned to scholarship to spell out how he
saw the development of episcopacy, and his essay 'The
ministry in the early Church' appeared in a book edited by
Kenneth Kirk, *The Apostolic Ministry*.[2] The book appeared in
1946, but in a letter to Bévenot in 1940 Gregory claims to be
part of its origin: 'Father Hebert and I have inveigled the
Bishop of Oxford into editing a book of Essays we are
collecting.'[3]

1   *A detection of Authorities,* Dacre Press 1945, p. 72.
2   Hodder & Stoughton, ed. Kenneth Kirk, 1946.
3   14.12.40.

Such a book at such a time was a strategically important contribution to the catholic cause: it argued that episcopacy is essential to the Church, that it comes from God. Gregory's essay sought to stress the immediacy of the episcopal vocation from God. Here, and in other places, he argued not so much for a mechanical apostolic succession, hand to head, but an apostolic 'Simultaneity' — a bishop being directly and immediately commissioned by Christ in the apostolic way. We shall turn again to his 'thesis' in another chapter, here the point is the emphasis placed on the Church as a divine institution, crucial to Christian life and witness, the living body of Christ in the world, with its ministers 'constitutive' of its life.

This was all being said in 1946 as Archbishop Fisher issued his famous invitation, in a Cambridge sermon, to the Free Churches 'to take episcopacy into their system' as the next step towards developing unity. Gregory protested to Lambeth about this. Fisher's idea of episcopacy was to do with an 'organising authority', for Gregory it was once again inviting people to begin in the wrong place. In Geoffrey Fisher, Gregory seemed to find the most frustrating and depressing example of the liberal establishment bishop. In many ways he typified everything he wanted to change.

In criticising bishops in general Gregory could turn his wit in particular on specific aspects of the issue, especially their selection. In his address to the Anglo-Catholic congress of 1948, speaking about the Church and its Ministry, he said: 'The apostolate was the only direct historical consequence in this world of Jesus of Nazareth', but he also poked fun at the English system of choosing the apostles' successors. He invited his hearers to imagine 'St Paul with letters missive and a *congé d'élire* from Pontius Pilate to the apostolate.'

However, it is also worth noting that he wrote to the Abbot from the United States: 'Some American bishops are quite intolerable.... I think perhaps we have *not* got *quite* the worst system of choosing bishops in the world.'[1]

1   29.5.47.

One more story about Gregory and bishops. He told a
friend of one occasion on which he was due to meet Headlam,
the Bishop of Gloucester, whom he particularly disliked. In
the room where he waited a little girl was in tears. She turned
out to be Headlam's granddaughter and she was in disgrace.
Gregory asked her what she had done. She told him that she
had got the bishop to go into the Wendy House and had gone
away and left him inside, unable to get out. The friend asked
Gregory what he did then: 'I gave her half a crown', he said.

Many a bishop must have asked 'Who will rid us of this
turbulent priest?' or, even more obviously why doesn't this
priest rid us of himself and join the Roman Catholic Church?
If he felt so angry about the life of the Church of England
and its bishops, if he felt the need to be so scathing, why did
he not simply leave?

Gregory loved the Church of England. He could not deny
what he felt the Church had given him, and given England,
in genuine, if not unwatered, catholic formation. The combination of Gregory the historian and the sensitive honesty
of his own imagination led him to what he called in *The
Question of Anglican Orders* a 'loving discontent' with the
Church, where the stress is on both words almost equally. In
fact, that little book about Orders, affirming as it does his
own quiet conviction about the validity of Anglican orders,
and thus of his own priestly ministry, is emphatic about the
catholicity of the Church of England. While he notes the
threats to it, he assures worriers about the authenticity of
their Church. They can only stay contentedly as Anglicans if
they can be Catholics *because* they are Anglicans.

Gregory's own struggle with all of this is extensively alluded to in the correspondence with Maurice Bévenot during
the 1940s. By this time, for a decade, Gregory had felt both
more secure of his own place in a catholic Church of England
and more secure in openly criticising the Church in its
establishment and across the whole range of issues and
events. Having examined the Roman Catholic critique of the
Church of England, including *Apostolicae Curae* and its condemnation of Anglican orders, he looked long and hard and

could not bring himself to share that condemnation. In the end, his attachment was too real and mattered too much. A touch of his feeling comes through in his summary of what is required of an assent to *Apostolicae Curae*:

> Any man might be forgiven for finding these statements difficult to believe. When he is required to make them specifically on these grounds about what has hitherto been the mainspring of the best things in his life, he may well find himself unable to do so, not through pride or perversity, but out of scruple for truth.[1]

Writing to Bévenot a few years previously and imagining a similarly bleak view of the Church of England, Gregory said: 'I cannot for the life of me, even after more than one deliberate attempt, take that nihilistic view of the Anglican Church.'[2]

Gregory was writing that letter from Beaconsfield in the middle of his, relatively brief, experience of parish ministry. There, in addition to his own inner conviction, he must have observed too what the Church of England was giving to others day by day, forming the 'mainspring of the best things in their life'.

In a sermon at St John's, Holland Road, Kensington in 1945[3] he speaks of the Church: 'this half-heretical, half-bemused, muddle-headed and wholly adorable Church of England of ours, so full of good fellowship, so full of goodwill...'

For Gregory his attachment was a hard-won and thoroughly thought-out position, both heart and head together, and so when talk of 'going over' filled the air, as it often did in catholic societies and among catholic clergy in those decades, Gregory was not among the waverers. The enervating 'teetering on the brink', over and over again, that characterised some of Gregory's correspondents did not now affect him. He was convinced about the catholic credentials of his Church.

1   *Orders*, p. 88.
2   27.1.40.
3   July 1st.

His concern was, of course, that his Church might nevertheless wilfully surrender those credentials, and so he set
himself to work as hard as he could to prevent that happening
and — more — to change the Church in an even more
catholic direction.

Gregory found allies in the catholic societies and in the
religious communities. His was not a 'one man' campaign
though he did see himself as something of a leader. All his
gifts could be brought into the service of the catholicity of
the Church: not least his scholarship. In a letter to Dom Paul
Severance in Three Rivers in 1946 we find him still working
to change the governing principles: 'Only I want to shift if I
can the whole ground of the argument so that we can get the
issues clear. It is what I tried to do in *The Shape* and have tried
again to do in my essay in Kenneth Kirk's book.'[1]

In a draft of the introduction to *The Shape* which was rewrit-
ten before publication Gregory stressed again this 'shifting of
the ground'. 'There are already advocates enough before the
Church; but it is the vocation and the justification of scholarship to illuminate the problems for the jury. More than that I
have neither the authority nor the experience to do.'

In Gregory himself this division between advocate and
scholarly provider of information is perhaps rather more
blurred then he here suggests. He was determined to use all
his gifts in the service of a catholic Church of England.

These scholarly convictions are, of course, only part of the
story and there is no doubt that he took some delight in
controversy. For all the strength of his vocation to the monastic life, his seriousness and depth in that commitment, there
was also in him a zest and spirit that was not going to be
confined to the monastery. His passion was also a mission to
the Church and his wit and imagination, his 'style' made him
a formidable controversialist. He had all the necessary gifts
of the effective polemicist: the ability to master and control
facts, to present them skilfully, to dazzle and attract by wit
and manner, to let his passion shine through convincingly but

1   10.46.

not quite overwhelmingly, and the imagination to understand his opponents.

His style amounted at times to a 'prophetic' posture and,
if in some ways he was prophetic, it was often not in the ways
he expected. He could certainly overestimate his own contribution and some of his claims to Bévenot, for instance,
sound a little overstated. Yet others, from Temple down-
wards, were ready to acknowledge his influence, infuriated
though they might be. Leslie Newbiggin the Free Church
minister, eventually to be a bishop in the Church of South
India, met Gregory and a group of other leading catholics in
Oxford at the time of the CSI crisis: 'The discussions were
dominated by Dix whom I found charming, brilliant and
totally unconvincing. We clashed vigorously at every session
and afterward he wrote me a charming letter and invited me
to arrange the second meeting at Nashdom.'[1]

Some of the influence, at least, owed its impact to the
powerful image of a somehow independent monk *contra
mundum*, his ultimate commitment was evidently outside the
political arena altogether, with an air of fearlessness, of brave
good humour, almost of exasperated but relentless vigilance.
Gregory complained especially of the tedium of Convocation
and 'the drivel showered on us from the Upper House' but
at the same time the glow of the pleasure of battle is never
far away.

This readiness 'to engage the enemy' is there from the
early thirties and his political involvement and polemicist
style, develops steadily through the decade. It has its roots
earlier and we have noted his vigorous contributions to
debate both at Oxford, at Wells, and even at school. Born
from his struggle to come to terms with his place in the C.
of E., it was rooted deep in his personality.

In reviews and early articles in *Laudate* his readiness to let
a scholarly point lead to a polemical one is increasingly
evident. He was partly, if not mainly, responsible for turning

1   *Unfinished Agenda*, Leslie Newbiggin, Wm B. Eerdmans 1985, pp.
    86–87.

Laudate from a Nashdom newsletter into a scholarly journal during the course of the thirties. He contributes in the same way to other journals; to *Theology* and the *Journal of Theological Studies*, for instance. In many ways his earlier style was less subtle, more readily savage, than it later became. One of his earliest extended disputes was with Bishop Edwin Palmer, a bishop in India, who argued in an article in the *Church Times* in 1932 for precedent in the early Church for lay presidency at the eucharist. At once, in the *Church Union Gazette* of November 1932, Gregory defended episcopacy, apostolic order, the Catholic Church, his watchwords for the next twenty years. The tone of this early controversy however is more waspish, even savage, than Gregory later became: 'In every case Dr Palmer's hypotheses signally fail to cohere with any facts but those he has selected, and consequently misunderstood.'[1]

Gregory relentlessly damned Dr Palmer, accusing him of 'investing his statements with an air of spurious scholarship'. He was similarly, snidely, damning of South India: 'These notes are not controversial but purely historical. They have nothing whatever to do with South India, an affair necessarily incomprehensible to a student of Christian antiquity.'[2]

The controversy with Dr Palmer rumbled on through a series of articles and letters, pained and gentlemanly from the bishop, waspish from Gregory, then it faded away. The controversy over South India however moved steadily into the centre of Gregory's vision as the decade went on.

On this issue, as on others, he was allied with the various catholic societies; the Church Union, the Federation of Catholic Priests, the Council for the Defence of Church Principles and others. He found himself more intimately involved with many of them as he helped Mrs Bertha Travers in the late thirties develop the Dacre Press as a publishing house for catholic material. The press published *The Pilot* which he helped to edit and all his own books, including *The*

1   *Church Union Gazette*, Nov. 1932, p. 207.
2   *Ibid.*

Shape. The sequence of the books, their dates and themes, are interesting: 1942 saw *A Detection of Aumbries*, arguing for the catholicity not only of the reserved sacrament itself but also of devotions before it; 1944 the defence of ministry in *Anglican Orders*; 1945 *The Shape* exploring the Church and her liturgy. He was instrumental too in producing a series by leading catholic writers and thinkers, called *Signposts*, which appeared in 1940. (It is interesting to note in passing what other books were being published at about this time. 1942 also saw William Temple's *Christianity and Social Order*, Dorothy L. Sayer's *The Man born to be King*, C.S. Lewis's *The Screwtape Letters*, T.S. Eliot's *Little Gidding*.)

Steadily, by involvement in this busy network of catholic publishing and by his own growing reputation, Gregory moved to central issues of Church life in the late thirties and forties, helping to create those central issues and moving to the centre stage.

The Shape of the Liturgy was, of course, the great blossoming of his reputation. With its publication and subsequent fêting he became an acknowledged force to be reckoned with, a speaker to listen to, a writer to read. The book's scholarship is profound but it is a polemic too. On the liturgical level his critique of the *Book of Common Prayer*, and of Cranmer in particular, is a *tour de force* and led to continuing controversy with G.B. Timms and others. But the book is controversial in other ways too — about the epiclesis and, of course, about the place of the eucharist in the life of the Church generally.

All this grew out of, and continued to feed, Gregory's convictions about the crucial centrality of the living Body of Christ, its continuing through history, its life expressed in the sacraments and the vital importance of defending that life now.

In the atmosphere of this deepening involvement in Church issues and his growing reputation, Gregory was elected to Convocation for Oxford late in 1945 and took his seat there in early 1946.

The Houses of Convocation, Upper and Lower, are the ancient Church equivalent of the two houses of parliament, one Convocation for each of the Provinces of York and Canterbury. Their power had been effectively emasculated by the Elizabethan settlement and the seventeenth century ecclesiastical disputes, but in recent history they had begun to recover some of their significance along with the National Church Assembly. This since 1919 had also allowed some extra-parliamentary lay involvement in Church government, if only to relieve parliament of the legislative burden. Together they have evolved since into the General Synod, the House of Clergy being the members of the Lower Houses of both Convocations. Gregory of course was all for recovering the ancient power of Convocation, not least the Lower House. It became one of his main platforms in the next decade. There he was involved in discussion on liturgical reform, on Christian initiation, on the Church of South India. In every case his concern was to ensure that the Church reached catholic conclusions — or, if she could not be helped to do that, that no decision at all was made. The decisions of the Church, as the Church, must continue to be in the flow of catholic tradition. The varying opinions of bishops and the rest of the establishment, the windmills they tilted at, were wearisome enough but they were not of ultimate concern. As private opinions they could be denounced or approved. But when the Church through Convocation came to make collective decisions that affected her very nature and definition then Gregory and his colleagues fought to ensure orthodoxy was maintained and catholicity, if possible, enhanced. There was a crucial distinction. In *The Question of Anglican Orders* he argued that Cranmer's private opinions about ministry (and the eucharist for that matter) counted for nothing, what mattered was the catholic interpretation the Church had continued to put on what was being done. The Church of England, he argued, intended to do what the Catholic Church had always intended to do: he wanted to be able always to go on saying that about the life, ministry and worship of the Church of England. Convocation was the place to defend that 'intention'.

The effect of this thinking was to make him 'vigilant'. In common with many other Anglo-Catholics, he was watching for the signs of the Church's apostasy, concerned, with every issue that came along, that orthodoxy was being threatened again, constantly wary of the 'pan-protestant' threat. It could be a tightrope existence, a destructively protective attitude towards the Church (towards God). At the same time it witnessed to a deep conviction not only about the centrality of the life of the Church's single body but also about the essential unity of all these seemingly disparate issues. They were ultimately the same question: was the Church of England intending to be the living body of Christ in the world?

It is in this same context that Gregory's work on Baptism and Confirmation emerged. He contributed to a Convocation committee on the subject, lectured on it at Oxford (1946) published his paper, wrote a memorandum with Michael Ramsey for the Convocation (1946). In all this scholarly, carefully executed work, he argued for the unity of the two events, their essentially catholic nature in the body of Christ, their necessity. He resisted what he saw as profligate concessions made by bishops for protestants. Convocation, with its committees and commissions, was a key battlefield. Tiresome and exhausting it could be but he felt its importance and believed himself to be important in defending the cause. At the same time he wanted to stand to one side of its life and influence. He did not want to feel compromised by it. He could laugh to his brethren at the slightly odd 'loyal address' from the Convocation to the King in 1947. It referred to the Princess Elizabeth: 'We have watched her growth to large-hearted and well-developed womanhood.' Gregory had objected to this as vulgar-sounding but the Upper House had left it unchanged and Gregory, present when the address was delivered, claimed to detect royal embarrassment.

As the forties developed, involvement in Church politics grew. With his fame as a writer also growing, he found himself busier and busier in Church affairs. 1946 is the only year for which a full diary exists among Gregory's papers. It is full of

speaking engagements, catholic committees, official committees, space for drafting documents and papers, letters as
well as other writing, preaching and retreats. His life became
even more complicated the following year when the Abbot
chose to send him to the United States to help with the
establishment of St Gregory's Priory, Three Rivers. His letters are full of the business of the new monastery, but also of
all that is happening at home, all the commissions and
committees he is coming back to, all the fights still to be
fought and the causes to be defended.

In one letter from the States in 1947 he lists all the
bishops, from Canterbury, to Dublin, to Barbados, who were
waiting for a reply from him on subjects as various as new
prayer books, the Lambeth Conference, retreats. He had
become a force to be reckoned with, a force no doubt inclined
to overestimate its own power and significance but still a
force, someone not to be ignored.

This force was for the catholic cause in every area of
Church life but the issue that consumed much of his attention and focused many of his analytical, emotional and polemical skills was certainly the Church of South India.

It becomes difficult, across the distance of decades, to feel
the passions and high emotions that this issue evoked. It
stirred intense intellectual debate, intense heart-searching,
intense prayer. Now it seems hard to grasp the overwhelming
significance it then seemed to have. (Perhaps in a decade or
two they will be equally puzzled about our intense concern
with the ordination of women.)

What, first of all, did it have to do with the Church of
England, this Church on the other side of the world? It was,
of course, a colonial Church. As India itself headed for
Independence and autonomy, in parallel part of the Church
too was heading towards a more independent life. Indian
Christianity had inherited European, in this case English,
denominational divisions. They did not belong to India and
it seemed time to end them. From as early as 1919, and with
support from successive Lambeth Conferences, the Churches
had been exploring ways of unity. It was the first time so large

a group had begun such an exploration. It was exciting, what ecumenism was meant to be about, and it was also dangerous. Inevitably it raised every significant issue in the Church's life from the place of baptism to the nature of ministry. The Churches involved, protestant denominations and Anglicans, steadily hammered out a process for uniting with agreed documents to cover all the issues involved. Steadily they moved towards an agreement that did include bishops and ordinations but also sought to honour the integrity of more protestant traditions.

The issue only became strictly relevant to the Church of England when the Anglican bishops of the area asked Archbishop Temple of Canterbury, in 1941, to say whether by joining the United Church they would sever communion with Canterbury. However, the issue had been alive in England for very much longer than that. It was alive as an issue in the Anglican communion, in the ecumenical movement, and in the world-wide Church.

Gregory's first recorded reactions were fairly overtly implied in his dispute with Bishop Palmer in 1932. From the beginning he was suspicious, wary, somehow threatened. His focus shifted in time but his basic suspicion never changed. He saw it as part of the pan-protestant design, the allying of all the denominations so that they would ultimately consolidate themselves together, but outside 'the Church'. Once again his concern, his increasingly passionate and intense concern was for the catholicity of the Church, for the solidarity of the Body of Christ and its living unity. That living unity is visible in the sacraments, living signs which include the sacrament of orders.

Passion and the intensity grew as the dilemma became clearer. As the scheme for the uniting Churches in South India progressed, Gregory, and catholics like him, became increasingly convinced that it did not intend to continue the 'Catholic Church' in that part of India but to make something new and different — an 'alliance'. Its documents were not clearly and unequivocally orthodox about creeds and doctrines, about sacraments and the like: its *foundations* were not catholic, so it could not be good.

And if, of course, those who had been in the Catholic Church, the Anglicans in South India, opted for this alliance they were bound to cease being 'catholics', they were bound to 'leave the body' and to separate themselves.

Further, Gregory found himself going the next fatal step in logic, any Church (or individual), which continued in communion with those who had separated themselves in this way would forfeit a place in the catholic body, cease to be a Church, sink into apostasy.

The theory is one of 'contagion': the apostasy is caught by any continued connection. However orthodox a Church may claim to be, if it fails to cut itself off from such a failure of orthodoxy, then that Church and all its members catch the same disease. We are back on the tightrope of vigilance, with this threat powerful enough to disturb the balancing act completely. No other issue in Church life led Gregory as close to leaving the Church of England as this.

He said that he 'loathed and hated' schism. In a sense, it was part of what he hated about the South India scheme: it seemed to him to amount to schism. Schism was a wound in the body, tearing off a limb, it was precisely and exactly opposite to the whole meaning and purpose of the Church's life. And yet, with deep, deep irony, if it happened as proposed, he felt his only response could be his own 'schism,' his own departure. He hated schism but he hated even more any failure to follow the truth, any failure to adhere to the catholic convictions to which he had clung so hard in the Church of England. He felt it deeply, he felt nothing quite so deeply, he might have to leave: 'though it will nearly pull my heart in twain to do it.'[1]

It brought him to tears and he describes movingly a confrontation with Temple: 'I told Archbishop Temple to his face, with tears, that I could not remain in the communion

1   Letter to M.M. Hilder, 12.2.45.

of such a Church. He wept too when we talked of it.'[1] What was so important?

Gregory became increasingly involved and concerned about the issue throughout the thirties and, with other catholics, saw the South Indian developments as a focus and concrete manifestation of their fears about pan-protestant alliances. After carefully studying the documents he acknowledged that the *desire* of the scheme was catholic union but that its working out was basically a 'protestant alliance'. In articles, books, letters and indeed at every opportunity Gregory would loudly voice his opinions against the opinions of the liberal establishment, including Temple. But it was at the point where what he considered to be mistaken opinions were likely to become officially adopted positions of the Church that he became vitally concerned. Now he was arguing for the life of the Church, fighting for its catholic faithfulness, struggling to maintain the authentic orthodoxy of the whole Church.

In one sense the issue came to its head with the publication of the Constitution and Basis of Union for the United Church. Here was the officially adopted position of the Church of South India and it seemed deeply flawed. But the issue came to a head for the Church of England when, in response to the request of the bishops in India, Convocation prepared to reply. The bishops had actually written to the Archbishops in England, not to Convocation, and Temple drafted a reply. It became an issue in Convocation whether the Upper and Lower Houses had to confirm and agree to the reply or whether they were only expected to acknowledge the reply's existence.

Temple, believing it right to leave an independent foreign Church to work out its own way ahead, had drafted a reply that simply told the bishops that a kind of 'mediate communion' would exist while the uniting Church, as planned, grew into fuller catholic order as the years went by. The Primate made no comment on the orthodoxy or otherwise of that Church's

1   *Ibid.*

Basis of Faith or its constitution as he didn't consider it his business.

Temple's draft reply was rather vague and his biographer, Iremonger, actually thinks this was because he was already ill and the loss of his usual precision and confidence presaged his imminent death. Whatever the cause, the draft reply was totally unacceptable to the Catholic groups and would lead the Church of England, officially and formally, into apostasy, to a declaration that, after all, she was not concerned to maintain catholic teaching, faithfulness and unity.

In this crisis crystallised two quite different approaches. The catholics accused the Archbishop of 'a charity that has escaped from the discipline of truth'.[1]

In reply William Temple made exactly the opposite point. He called it: 'an instance of allowing concern for purity of faith to defeat charity.'[2] Behind this lay worlds of quite different attitude to dogma and the pursuit and possession of Truth.

The Superiors of Religious Communities (men's it seems) worked together to issue a warning to the Archbishop. Gregory, not a Superior, seems to have been instrumental in bringing this about: he certainly seems to have drafted the letter which the Superiors sent to the archbishop. (Temple is reported to have said to Gregory that: 'The hand was the hand of certain Religious Superiors but I thought I detected a different voice.' 'Jacob speaking, your Grace', was Gregory's reply.) He was certainly instrumental in ensuring its publication by the Dacre Press in 1943. Here, no doubt, he felt the Religious communities had a special role to play — a warning role. As he told a women's community in retreat, Religious communities could remind the Church that it could not serve two masters. The Religious communities, working together, could be a prophetic voice, a voice of truth and catholic faithfulness. They were not dependent on the

1 *Open Letter of Superiors of Religious Communities to the Archbishop of Canterbury*, Dacre Press 1943.
2 29.3.44.

establishment, were not beholden to anyone, but could speak boldly and openly. It is a kind of extension of Gregory's own personal vocation: here the communities together could make the voice louder and the stance bolder.

Of course by the very nature of their freedom to do this the communities were not homogenous and so not all equally sympathetic with this approach to the Archbishop.

A draft copy of the letter went to the Archbishop with the suggestion that his reply might be published together with the original letter (by the Dacre Press). However the letter from the Superiors contained a strong reference to the Religious communities' readiness to leave the Church if necessary if nothing was changed.

Temple was horrified by the threat because he also hated schism but also because it could seem like blackmail: he asked for the removal of the reference. The Superiors refused this and so their open letter was published separately — talk of schism included.

To what did they so strongly object? The letter expresses more or less exactly Gregory's personal views — not surprisingly if he was the drafter. They felt the Constitution and Basis of Faith gave no clear place to Tradition in the life of the Church; they were concerned that creeds need have no place in public worship; the necessity of baptism for regeneration was not mentioned: there was no definition of episcopacy even though the united Church was to have bishops. The letter argued, as Gregory argued, that appearing to accept such consecrations would cast doubt on the Church of England's own intentions in consecrating bishops. Throughout it all Gregory felt there was a clear shift towards a liberal attitude to doctrine which left the Church's teachings as a series of opinions from which to make a selection — not a faith, not the Truth.

Earlier issues of lay presidency of the eucharist, and so the question of orders generally, still came into this, but for Gregory the ultimate issue was much greater. 'What is contemplated is a wholesale transformation of faith into opinion by all those Anglicans who enter the united Church', he said.

Temple was confident the united Church would grow into orthodoxy and full 'catholic faith and order'. He was prepared to wait and let it emerge rather than prescribe it and insist that it was perfectly tidily orthodox from the very beginning. In writing about the whole business Temple maintained that the Church of South India would have the full apostolic ministry imparted to *it by* the Scheme: 'The fact that they do not receive it as such does not greatly trouble me. I have bestowed it on many young men who did not accept it as such, most of them knew later what they had received and valued it.'

Such liberal generosity and open-mindedness seemed to Gregory not merely complacent and superficial but utterly misconceived, a betrayal of the Church and the indication that the Church of England was ready, after all, to cease to be a true Church. The balancing act he had struggled to maintain with such vigilance was about to end as the Church tumbled from its tightrope.

The different conclusions of the two men, representing, as they do, the views of many other people similarly divided, stand for two basically different attitudes of mind and thought. Temple admired Gregory's mind but was ultimately puzzled by it: 'It is perfectly true that in terms of syllogistic logic your case is immensely strong, but I have the feeling all the time that it is cogent argument from premises narrower than the facts.'[1] This is part of a general feeling on the part of Temple that Gregory's opposition here is altogether too narrow.

Others shared the Archbishop's view that Gregory's attitude was persuasive, even dazzling, but somehow did not feel quite right. 'What a curious mind he has!' remarked Rawlinson, the Bishop of Derby to Bishop George Bell of Chichester.[2] For Gregory this was the liberal establishment at its polite and imprecise worst. He could not accuse Temple of stupidity but he did feel he started from utterly different

1   4.4.44.
2   Letter, 27.6.50.

foundations. He said of him in a letter to a friend[1] written after his death, that he had been 'constitutionally unable to see what was involved in the South India Scheme'. He felt that his own catholic foundations were actually the ones being rediscovered for the future (all over the Church).

Temple had died in November 1944. With the rest of the Church Gregory was devastated. For all their quite fundamental disagreements Gregory had felt a deep affection for this archbishop. He did not feel the same about his successor, Geoffrey Fisher. He continued to have regular and close contact with Lambeth and Fisher seemed to feel he needed always to take account of Gregory.

As Fisher moved to Lambeth in 1945 Gregory was becoming increasingly prominent as a spokesman for the Catholic party. His writings, especially *The Shape*, only enhanced his reputation and it was later the same year that he was elected to Convocation. Fisher seemed to see in Gregory a force to be reckoned with, but there was little affection in the relationship.

In November 1946 Gregory could write to Dom Paul Severance in the USA saying how much easier it was to say 'no' to Fisher than to Temple, but he did also add:

It's all the difference between resisting a prophet, who was also lovable as very few men I have met were, and being firm with a very likeable ecclesiastical diplomat. But he is courageous and determined and he sees no way but his — and he is astute and able...

Even that measure of respect was not always apparent in their relationship and Gregory could make Fisher the butt of some of his most acerbic scorn. In 1949 they became embroiled in an icily polite but unpleasant correspondence about an indiscreet remark Fisher had made about Gregory being 'devilish'. Fisher wrote to Gregory to tell him before anyone else did. The remark arose from a comment of Gregory's about the Upper House of Convocation's cavalier

1   17.12.44.

attitude to the Lower House. Gregory's remark was reported in confidential minutes which the Archbishop had been sent anonymously, should not have seen and should not have commented on. Gregory took the opportunity in replying to be as politely withering and devastatingly self-righteous as he had every justification to be in the situation. The correspondence can only have made their relationship colder, more formal and more distant. Even so, Fisher could not ignore Gregory's place among the leaders of the Catholic party and so, on more than one issue, he continued to deal with him directly.

The Archbishop took the opportunity of his succession to Canterbury in 1945 to have a fresh look at the South India situation. He wrote to Gregory in May 1945 proposing a 'change of atmosphere'. This would involve both a fresh scrutiny of the CSI Scheme itself and some more careful examination of the presuppositions being made by different groups. Here may be the first germ of the subsequent *Catholicity* report (1948) and the reports that emerged outlining the presuppositions of other groups in the churches.

Gregory replied, grateful for the breathing space, but unable to resist a somewhat ungenerous suspicion of the primate's motives. Was the delay to gain time to find a solution or was it because a solution simply did not exist? Gregory seemed to think the latter, indeed he almost seemed to *want* it to be the latter.

One of the reasons Fisher chose to write to Gregory at this moment may have been because the *Church Times* had published Dix's article on the Church of South India Scheme. Entitled 'Is the English Church uncommitted?'[1] it was critical of the minimal discussion and legislation there had been in England about the situation even though fullest acceptance by the Church of England of the Scheme seemed to be on offer to the South Indians.

Fisher proposed a commission of Convocation to look into the issue, and Gregory was appointed to it. At the same time

1   *Church Times*, 13.4.45.

he had published his book on *Anglican Orders*[1] made up of reworked letters from his own correspondence on the subject but not indirectly aimed at the South India Scheme. No wonder Fisher felt the need somehow to keep this man, his mind and his loyalties, directly involved in the continuing deliberations.

In fact, Gregory had now taken the huge psychological step of talking seriously about breaking away from the 'National Religious Establishment' — separation. There had been vague 'threats' before from Catholic societies and the like (also from Gregory himself) now it seemed a real possibility. As it became a concrete idea Gregory's enthusiasm became curiously engaged.

Such a separation had been mentioned, to Temple's dismay, by the Superiors in the letter which Gregory had drafted for them in 1943. In 1945[2] he spelt it out in more detail to the federal council of the Fellowship of Catholic Priests meeting at Oxford. He outlined to them his feelings about the two religions in England, the National Religious Establishment and 'the ancient English Church', and he said that he felt the time had come because of South India for the two to part. Choosing a fairly dramatic, semi-military metaphor he told them they might need 'to remain at your post and leave the communion of Canterbury'.

He said they would become 'Continuing Anglicans' (was this the first use of the phrase?) because they could no longer be in communion either with the Church of South India itself or with anyone else who was in communion with the Church of South India.

This may have been one of Gregory's first public declarations of the idea of separation and it seems to be made without a great sense of inner turmoil or crisis. This is probably for two reasons. First because it was not new to him and secondly because the inner logic of the declaration had come to feel inexorable. The speech to the Federation of

1   1944.
2   3rd July.

Catholic Priests in 1945 may have been the first public
declaration of the idea by Gregory but in it he said that he
had been thinking about it seriously for 'some fifteen
months'. In fact he had also outlined a plan for a 'non-juring'
Church to Kenneth Kirk as long ago as 1942, so the idea had
been in his mind for some years.[1]

It was, after all, a result of the logic of his whole purpose
in remaining an Anglican. When a point was reached at which
the Church of England compromised itself so much that it
could no longer be called 'catholic', what else could he do
but leave? This possibility, was inevitably, for better or worse,
always hovering in the background. It could be inferred in
much of what he wrote and said and sometimes he was more
explicit. Speaking to the Society of Saint Edward in 1944 he
reflected on the temptations of priesthood and added: 'It
may be that to our Church as a Church in the years not far
hence there will be made the ancient offer — All these
things...'[2]

At another level, as that quotation hints, the drama, even
the melodrama, of separation appealed to the romantic in
Gregory. His imagination was stirred in a complex mixture of
ways by the sense of crisis, by the possibility of his leading
role in it, by the sense of history and destiny and a rediscovered vocation for the Church. He did not want to hurt the
Church but part of him, at least, enjoyed the excitement, felt
a thrill at being part of it, and knew how to play his part as
the cool, clear, decisive but thoughtful leader to the full.

He was clear and consistent that the answer was not to
become a Roman Catholic; he had fought that struggle long
ago. To the FCP he said: 'It does not seem to me that any of
these present difficulties affect by one iota any of the reasons
which have prevented my becoming an R.C. long ago.'

Writing to Kenneth Kirk after the Draft reply of the
Archbishops to the South Indians had been published Gregory said:

1   *Kenneth Kirk*, Eric Kemp, Hodder and Stoughton 1959.
2   4.12.44.

I am fairly sure that I shall never settle down with a good conscience in mediate communion with South India — though I think I should have an equally uneasy conscience signing up for *Apostolicae Curae*. So far as I can see I am not going to be very happy whichever I do. If it were not for my vows I might join the Barrage as a Roman Catholic Private (with my insides so defective no other service would take me), but that is equally against my conscience as things are. So the only thing is to await helplessly death by drowning in the last ditch.'[1]

Dix also indicated to Kirk that some other priests were already 'deciding for Rome' but it seemed to him too much like making a convenience of the Roman Catholic Church.

The 'crisis' stirred him to a vision of a renewed Church. Far from depressing him it seemed to be a fresh opportunity, even perhaps the opportunity for which he had been waiting. To Dom Paul Severance in the United States he wrote in 1946:

I have come to believe with a quite new intensity in the Anglican vocation and the Anglican heritage. But to save them we may have to go outside the communion of Canterbury. I have foreseen this possibility for some years now....

A 'free Church of England' could — and I believe would — after a period of great difficulty — re-evangelise the country. The tragedy is that the Protestants over here are moving quite fast and would be ready before long for a union on the lines of a purified and scriptural Catholicism if this wretched Scheme, which is really the dregs of an outworn liberalism, had not come in to wreck the prospect for the future.[2]

It was often in these letters to America that Gregory spoke most openly, even indiscreetly, of his thoughts and ideas. He could sometimes seem sensationalist and melodramatic and rather to exaggerate his own role but at others his deeper hopes and visions surfaced too. A 'continuing Church', a 'free Church of England' seemed to him a real possibility, a valuable one, a God-given catholic way forward.

1   *Kirk*, p. 154.
2   10.4.46.

Gregory's does not seem to have been a widely shared vision. He worked with the catholic religious societies in this crisis and found himself a leader among those catholic Proctors in Convocation elected in 1946, specifically on the South India issue. For many others the situation was more a disturbing crisis than the opportunity for vision that it was for Gregory. One major difference, as he readily acknowledged, was that it was easier for the Religious Communities, having fairly independent life and resources, to talk of separation than it was for 'secular' clergy and laity, more dependent on the Church. Gregory expected the secession to be led by the Religious Communities with a few bishops. The secular clergy could not be expected, as he put it in his dramatic way, 'to make children starve'. It was not that it was merely easier for the Religious Communities to lead such a separation it was also part of their very purpose. They were there in the Church to keep the vision clear, to lead the way, not to let the rest of the Body compromise. He saw them as the tiny spinning wheel, perfectly adjusted at the heart of the machine, moving the most quickly, almost setting the pace.

Even that spear-head did not really come together as Gregory visualised. Opinions were more varied, attitudes more diverse and plans more mundane and immediately realistic; even among the Religious let alone the bishops.

One of Gregory's great allies in all this was Kenneth Kirk, the Bishop of Oxford. Kirk fought hard in the Upper House of Convocation for the Catholic point of view though he did not perceive it in quite the same terms as Dix. The Bishop found himself forced on the one hand to be a moderating influence on Gregory but also found himself treated by Gregory as a kind of fellow-conspirator. Some of Dix's letters to Kirk had an almost boyish enjoyment of plotting and conspiring. Kirk's response was always more serious and solemn and somehow more realistic. Where Gregory saw plots and conspiratorial policies among the bishops Kirk placated and reassured him. Gregory was not always convinced and in another of his very frank letters to America revealed some frustration with Kirk:

KO (Kenneth Oxford) behaved very tiresomely, threatened
to resign his see, proposed two totally impossible schemes,
again threatened to resign and was repudiated by the whole
catholic minority except myself... he was quite irresponsible
and I had to save his face.'[1]

Nevertheless the two men were great friends and worked
well together; so much so that their reputation produced a
famous rhyme:

> How happy are the Oxford flocks!
>   How free from heretics!
> Their priests securely orthodox,
>   Their bishop ortho Dix.

When Gregory was dying Kirk wrote of him as 'my closest and
oldest friend[2] and the most brilliant man in the Church of
England'.[3] This was quite an accolade from a man who would
himself be a rival for that title.

What happened to the Church of South India? The union
came about in 1947 and gradually, in accordance with the
Scheme, the ministry of the united Church became more and
more acceptably episcopal and 'catholic'. In the Church of
England a compromise was reached involving a moratorium
on official decisions and declarations about the Church but
effectively leaving the Church in 'impaired communion'
for the meantime. The catholic party in England saw this
as enough of a victory to save their faces. Gregory was not
entirely happy but saw that talk of separation was no longer
sensible and so he made the best of the compromise.

In a letter of 1950 to Dom Patrick Dalton in the USA he
appeared to claim for himself the credit for the compromise
moratorium: 'I have proposed a rather desperate solution
which might save us from a schism in early June and George
Bell has agreed to draft it.'[4]

---

1   22.1.50.
2   They had probably met at Oxford, where Kirk was a tutor from 1919
    and later professor of Moral and Pastoral Theology.
3   *Kirk*, p. 204.
4   22.1.50.

In writing to Kirk Gregory suggested that this could be
seen as preserving the interim policy established by William
Temple and so be presented as a tribute to him. He said that
the compromise had: 'the two advantages we sought, I think.
No mixed bathing (i.e. celebrating bishops etc. in C. of E.
and dissenting places) and no decision between "maj." and
"min." '

The moratorium was to be for five years.

As for the Continuing Church, when the moratorium
ended in 1955, the Church of England agreed a relationship
of 'growing intercommunion' though still those not ordained
by a bishop were unable to celebrate in England. A number
of Anglican priests submitted to Rome but there was no
'continuing Church'. By then of course Gregory was dead.

In 1950 Gregory clearly felt the moratorium rescued the
Church from the brink but it put him back on another brink
or rather on the tightrope of former years. He was back with
the muddling and compromising and the constant checking
to see if the Church was still catholic. By this time, heavily
involved in other more 'domestic' matters, he toured the
States raising money for the new monastery there. His intense focus on the ecclesiastical politics of England blurred
slightly and the emphasis shifted.

Was the threat of separation ever a real one? For all his
sense of drama he was theologically convinced about his
proposal. Unlike submitting to Rome, however, it required a
group, a movement, to make it at all meaningful. There never
seems to have been quite such a definite group ready to
separate. There was no body with a clear theology and sense
of identity to provide the strength and motivation for the
separation. Perhaps if there had been, they would have done
so, anyway, despite the eventual compromises. Of course
Gregory had many allies and many close friends in the catholic movement. In addition to working with other Religious
Communities and the catholic societies he worked with
Father Ian Young particularly on *The Pilot* journal. He was
close to Father Gabriel Hebert of the Society of the Sacred
Mission. The two men had different minds. In many ways

Hebert was more Anglican than Gregory and more ready to be positive about the Reformation and protestantism. Nevertheless they both sought to widen influence of the catholic movement in the Church. They shared intellectual ability and academic interests and a deep desire to apply those interests practically in the Church, especially in the area of liturgy. There were other friends too but there was in no sense an organised group, thinking like Gregory and preparing with him to leave if necessary.

Although probably not inclined to leave entirely on his own his theology remained clear and maintained the tension of his situation. Too much of what he saw in the decisions of the Church was mere expediency rather than principle. As William Temple pointed out, however, Gregory's principles were distinctive:

> [Gregory's main ground for secession] was lack of assurance concerning the faith of the united Church arising from the failure to include Creeds in its public worship. This seems to me inevitably to pre-suppose the major premiss that we should not be in communion with persons or bodies unless we have a guarantee that they hold the full Christian faith, whereas to me it is axiomatic that we should seek to be in communion with all persons or bodies claiming that they hold the full Christian faith unless we have grounds for assurance that they do not....
>
> Many of our troubles seemed to me to be the drawing of negative conclusions from positive premisses.... Thus it seemed to be assumed that everyone would say the Creed if he could; if he does not it must be because he does not believe what it contains.[1]

Temple's analysis highlights the key differences in approach of the two men, and the two 'schools' they represented. Temple's was a kind of maximalist, open and liberal attitude which his critics called 'woolly'. Gregory's attitude tended towards the limiting and purist, it required constant vigilance,

1   Letter, 28.2.44

even suspiciousness and could be criticised for narrowness and pedantry.

From early on Gregory had tended to imply that belief was always a thing to be stated and declared before it could be recognised. He asserted this unambiguously in 1933 in his controversy with Bishop Palmer, using the example of the Primitive Church and its requirement that converts should explicitly declare their new faith and equally explicitly deny their former errors.[1]

In subsequent years his attitude mellowed but he never fully shifted from his clear conviction that to be a catholic an explicit declaration and conscious, stated belief was involved. He was convinced that the woolliness, vagueness and imprecision of so much of the Church lay behind many of its problems and crises.

Some awareness of this difference of approach must have contributed to Geoffrey Fisher's desire to examine the presuppositions of catholics in the Church of England to see 'whether any reunion with Protestants is possible'. He wrote about this in a letter to Gregory in 1945 when seeking 'a change of atmosphere' on South India.

Gregory's response, although in some ways suspicious, was to suggest an *ad hoc* rather than an official committee. Here no doubt were the seeds of the *Catholicity* report. Soon Gregory was writing to the Archbishop suggesting the involvement of leading protestants and in November of 1945 Fisher invited him to set up a Catholicity group proposing that other groups should meet in the same way to state the principles of their outlook in preparation for the Lambeth Conference of 1948. Fisher insisted on providing the terms of reference for the report so that they would be comparable, and after some to-ing and fro-ing with the Archbishop on this, a committee met and began work. Michael Ramsey, then a professor in Durham, took the chair, Gabriel Hebert SSM was the minute secretary and Gregory became the formal secretary. They assembled a group of fourteen leading catholics

1   *The Church Union Gazette*, Feb. 1933, vol. LXIII, no. 748, p. 49.

from different branches of learning, shared out themes for each to concentrate on and met a number of times in 1946 and 1947.[1]

The report came out in 1947. Gregory contributed the chapter on 'the Post-Tridentine Papal Communion', and his influence is apparent in other places too. Throughout the catholic theme of the Body of Christ was emphasised declaring the Church as the place of salvation. All was in the context of God's work in creation, affirming the goodness of what he has made and with a sense of strong continuity between creation and redemption, Israel and Church, scripture and tradition.

The report acknowledged the distortions of the mediaeval Church and viewed the Reformation as, ironically, further distortions in the attempt to reform. The chapter on the Protestant Reformation, by Gabriel Hebert, was indeed generous to the reformers but finally criticised the failure to hold on to the idea of 'the image of God' and so to something truly positive about creation and all that that implies.

Similarly the report acknowledged the positive principles of liberalism but highlighted its dangerous 'belief in Man' with all its consequences.

Gregory's chapter on 'the Post-Tridentine Papal Communion' was very positive about the papacy and its post-Reformation self-cleansing. He claimed that Rome absorbed 'much that was vital in the Protestant reaction from humanism'. The essay argued for the necessity of a central institution such as the papacy.

Why, asked Gregory, had the papacy not yet re-absorbed Protestantism? He found political, theological and practical reasons not the least of which were to do with the *curia*, as opposed to the papacy, revealing once again something of his own antipathy to lawyers and bureaucrats running the

---

1 The members were: Michael Ramsey, Eric Abbott, Harry Carpenter, V.A. Demant, Gregory Dix, T.S. Eliot, Austin Farrer, Freddie Green, Gabriel Hebert SSM, Robert Mortimer, Reeves, Charles Smyth, the Bishop of Southampton, Lionel Thornton CR.

Church. Even here, in a chapter contributed to a committee's report, Gregory allowed himself a lyrical commendation of the papacy:

> The Papacy can still command the attention and to a large extent secure the following of all Christians, and it is the only Christian institution which can do so. It is at the head of a full half of Christendom, and that one, moreover, which shows no sign of diminished vitality and coherence. It is at once the strongest single bulwark of the historic tradition of Christian civilization in Europe and pioneer of the modern Christian social teaching by which it is sought to remedy the desperate sickness from which that tradition now universally suffers. It is also the largest single missionary force in the world mission-field of today. Above all, it has never wavered in its adherence to the central Christian truths of the Trinity and the Incarnation and Redemption, for its mighty witness to these all orthodox Christians of the 19th and 20th centuries have had cause to be deeply grateful.

The final parts of the report were positive and hopeful in their vision of a developing sense of spiritual unity from which organic unity might begin to grow. It would be a clear and positive unity set over against 'vague and undogmatic faith'. The report seemed to present a catholicity as sure of its teaching and faith as Gregory would require, positive about creation and the Church, but also as open as Temple would want it to be. No doubt the chairmanship of Michael Ramsey had something to do with this.

The Evangelical group produced a report for the Archbishop entitled *The Fulness of Christ: the Churches' Growth into Catholicity* and in due course (1950) the Free Churches also produced a reply entitled: *The Catholicity of Protestantism*.

In some ways the Catholicity report, produced not much more than a hundred years after the rediscoveries of the catholic character to the Church of England was a milestone. Measured, positive, hopeful, it was not the battling report of a strident minority but the quietly magisterial and intelligent reflection of a group of very distinguished men. With it Gregory could perhaps feel that he had once again genuinely contributed to the catholic character of the Church of England.

In July 1948, alongside the Lambeth Conference, another Anglo-Catholic Congress was held and here too Gregory made his contribution. His brother Ronnie was one of the organisers and many of the contributors to *Catholicity* were involved, including Michael Ramsey. Gregory spoke on the Church and Ministry , emphasising again the 'singleness' of the Church and its divine character. More significantly perhaps he also presented his demonstration of the Primitive Liturgy which he had been using during his lecture tour of the States. The report of the congress describes this as both informative and spiritually moving and we shall return to look at this device in the next chapter.

Gregory died in 1952 and was seriously ill for some time before his death: he was never again as intensely involved in Church politics as he had been in the late 1940s. No doubt, if he had lived, and been in good health, the situation would have been very different.

How very tempting it is to indulge a flight of fancy and speculate on what he might have done had he lived. One way or another he would no doubt have remained involved in the South India issue until its further resolution in 1955. It is difficult to believe he would not have been drawn into the liturgical developments of the sixties. In 1982 Colin Buchanan contributed an essay to the book *Liturgy Reshaped* edited by Kenneth Stevenson. He listed this as the third of his nightmares: 'Just suppose that Gregory Dix had lived. Suppose his mischievous, maverick, learned perversity had been charming, beguiling and bewitching the liturgical commission and all its works. How then would the course of revision have gone?'

No doubt the liturgical work would have gone on but there would have been other books too and other issues of Church politics? What about women's ordination?

During Gregory's lifetime the ordination of women had not come to the fore as a major issue. It was occasionally mentioned however and Gregory's immediate reactions were typically Anglo-Catholic, referring scathingly to 'priestesses'. Curiously, at another level, he did perhaps sense this was a coming issue. In amongst all his notebooks, translating and annotating the texts and documents of the primitive Church, there are collections of references to the ministry of women as widows and virgins and also as 'deaconesses' and 'presbyterresses'. There is also a tantalisingly incomplete paper on 'Female ministry'. Undated, it is the beginning of an essay planned as the development of that wide research. He says of the essay in the incomplete introduction: 'I have reason to fear that neither the advocates nor the opponents of a female clergy will be wholly pleased with its contents.'

He acknowledges the shock, even the repulsiveness, at first of the idea of female ministry but goes on to say how difficult it is to find a good argument against it. He says the exclusion of women is only one of discipline and the Church's discipline can and does change. He finds difficult the idea of a woman being 'incapable' of the sacrament of Holy Order since she is capable of all the other six sacraments. How could theology justify her exclusion from this one only? There the introduction abruptly ends.

Two drafts of five pages remain of a section on 'The Ministry of Women in the Old Testament' (headed 'III'). Here Gregory deftly outlines the importance and power of women in 'prophetic' Ministry (Miriam, Deborah) and also as 'singing women' in the Temple. But he notes the rigid and continuous exclusion of women from the Hebrew priesthood, despite the prevailing Mediterranean pattern. He links this to the equally rigid and ancient exclusion of any idea of a goddess from Hebrew religion. He argues that goddesses invariably require priestesses:

> Where the original non-sexual theological tradition of Yahweh's nature held firm as at Jerusalem, the priestess was not found. It is a curious parallelism of doctrine and practice we shall find exemplified over and over again in later Christian history.

But he goes on also to admit: 'Of course, from certain points of view, it was unfortunate that either sex exclusively should be chosen to represent a God of whose nature sex was no attribute.'

Unfortunately, this is the last page of the fragment and, apart from making it clear that the exclusion was not related to an 'undue depreciation of womanhood' in ancient Israel, the argument is undeveloped.

These fragments do not take us very far except to see that Gregory was thinking for himself, using his scholarship and presenting the issue in the light of scripture and tradition. He probably also enjoyed upsetting both his usual enemies and his customary friends.

Speculating about Gregory's contribution to the Church had he lived may be tempting but what of his actual contribution before his early death?

His 'gadfly', *enfant terrible*, image says something both of the accuracy of his attacks, his keen observation and perceptive insight, and also speaks of his zest and energy. He clearly enjoyed the battle, loved the chance to indulge his wit and 'dexterous unkindness' and used the powerful combination of his charm, intelligence and tactical skill to maximum effect. In some ways he saw all that he did as serving the purpose of making the Church more catholic. As early as 1933 he spoke of preparing an edition of the *Didache*, 'in view of the inevitable row about primitive church order in a year or two...' The scholarship would serve the argument about a catholic ministry.

Is this how he saw his Religious vows too? As the best means of furthering the catholic cause? There is a tension here. He certainly did see the Religious Communities as having a vocation to hold the Church to its principles, to show what the Church was supposed to be like, and so his own work in Church politics was a continuation of that. However he felt too the pull of the contemplative life. He recognised the tension between his vow of stability and his constant travels away from the monastery with the inevitable interruptions to his life of prayer. The Benedictine spirit is not about total exclusion from the world, it is much more about leavening the lump, being the salt, reminding the world of other possibilities. Gregory lived with and recognised the tensions. The remark from his *Retreat on the Rule*, quoted at

the end of the last chapter is worth quoting again here: 'Do
I find in myself quite that estimation of the events in the
world as "an empty smoke ring drifting into nothingness" or
of the events of the Church, which would befit a monk?'[1]

It was 'the events of the Church' that were, of course, a
more real temptation to Gregory than anything else — the
temptation to let them become more important than they
deserved. He struggled with this, and from the evidence it
would seem the monk did not always prevail even though in
some ways it was precisely his religious character that gave
him a status and weight greater than even he deserved.
Ironically, just at the point where he was most at risk from
'the events of the Church' it was his monastic status that
gave weight to his point of view and the vigour and force of
his argument.

Was it worth it? Was the weight given sufficient to warrant
the risk? To put it another way, did he succeed to any extent
in his 'four-point plan' outlined to Maurice Bévenot?

We have noticed Gregory's inclination to overstate his
contribution and exaggerate his influence. This was most
marked in letters to other monks but it affected also his
correspondence with Bévenot himself. He wanted to persuade himself that it was worth the effort, worth the risks to
vocation, worth the temptations. On the other hand, many
people have been ready to acknowledge his influence and
importance. His relationships with William Temple and later
with Geoffrey Fisher indicate something of the role he had
played. Michael Ramsey and Kenneth Kirk readily acknowledged Gregory's importance for the catholic cause. So how
much nearer was the Church of England to Gregory's 'four-
point plan' than when he formulated it in the early 1930s?

The first hope was to arrest the liberal drift of the Church
and see the 'classic tradition' restored. Here Gregory's own
scholarship joined to that of like-minded Anglicans was in
fact part of a general shift in the Church towards a more
conservative theology, a more 'classic' teaching. He rode an

1   p. 85.

incoming wave and felt that he had been able to make a contribution to this shift. He was probably too optimistic in his hope that this would soon bring about a wide consensus among all Christians, protestants and catholics alike. In fact, the new conservatism had effects he did not predict, not least in the growth of fundamentalism and the conservative evangelical revival-type rallies of the fifties and sixties.

Similarly his hope for disestablishment within a generation was not fulfilled although the Church steadily continued to reclaim its own character and dignity. Few formal legal moves were made to end Church-state links but many, smaller shifts of atmosphere contributed to a sense of ever greater separation. Gregory's passionate concern for the dignity of the Church, its independence and integrity made its contribution to this evolving rather than revolutionary separate-ness.

His specific third hope of 'getting round the snag of Anglican orders' remained unaddressed. Indeed, the crisis came from the other side with the whole South India issue threatening the integrity of Anglican orders quite apart from Roman recognition. He felt, though, he had helped to preserve catholic order over that issue and the question of Roman recognition had to be left for another day, another generation.

His final hope was of Rome recognising a catholic Church of England and Anglicans wanting that recognition. Again, if the Church of England seemed to begin to move in that direction it was not quite in the way Gregory had hoped and expected. His work with Couturier and his community's efforts for unity helped the many others who were beginning to long for unity. Certainly after the war a very slow thaw began, becoming a deluge later with the Second Vatican Council.

It was none of it quite what Gregory had meant but it was a more Anglican development. There were genuine changes but they were more haphazard, more compromised, less dogmatic, less principled than Gregory would have chosen. He had, of course, acknowledged from the beginning that his programme was 'mad', 'perverse', 'hopeless'. Nevertheless he made his contribution and the Church had slowly moved as he pushed.

His major contribution to a changing Church was, in one sense, not in that 'four point plan' (not specifically at least); it was in liturgy. As he would have been the first to acknowledge, subtly, deeply, pervasively, liturgy affected the Church from the bottom upwards and from its heart outwards. Here above all he contributed to this profoundly catholic influence not only in his lifetime but in the decades that follow. His sense of a praying Church, a whole body before God, offering its prayer in Christ through the eucharist was his special contribution above all else to the Church of England's continuing struggle to rediscover itself as a Church. We shall explore this further in the next chapter.

To Brother Leo, one of the monks of St Gregory's Priory, Three Rivers in the United States, Dix once said: 'Every two-to-four-hundred years something happens to cleanse the Church — this Church needs cleansing.' It is a very typical Gregory remark: dramatic, pithy and full of insight. He saw himself as a contributor to that cleansing process but typically too it did not happen in his dramatic way. Instead the Church took his contribution, recognised its value, and used it — is still using it — in its own way.

4

The Scholar and Teacher

Idleness is the enemy of the soul. Therefore, the breth-
ren should be occupied at certain times in manual
labour, and at other fixed hours in holy reading.
Rule of St Benedict, Ch. 48

A friend in Scotland wrote to Gregory having read *The Shape of the Liturgy*, shortly after it was published: 'You are clever to have made it so exciting for an ignorant layman.' These sentiments mirrored those of many others writing to Gregory and reviewing the book at about the same time.

Dix was a gifted scholar with the dedication, intellect and skill to contemplate an ancient text and begin to penetrate the layers of its meaning in its context. He was, at the same time, a teacher eager and able to communicate information, fill background, present nuances of context and go on to apply the information thus presented to life. Gregory acknowledged and appreciated the place of the detached, objective scholar poring over the minutiae, he claimed it for himself, but there was always in him the urge to apply, the desire to pass the information on, to share the enthusiasm. His was the desire to 'use' scholarship for the sake of the Church and in that word 'use' lie some of the tensions of Gregory's scholarly career.

There are few developed studies of Dix's contribution to liturgical or ecclesiological scholarship although it is always referred to in surveys of the development of liturgical study

in English-speaking countries. Kenneth Stevenson wrote a
short study in 1977[1] Gregory is the subject of a doctoral thesis
by a Roman Catholic monk and Paul Bradshaw looks extensively at Gregory's work in his recent book *The Search for the
Origins of Christian Worship*,[2] but there is no major, single
considered assessment. Nor is this book intended to be a
study of Gregory's scholarly contribution but in this chapter
aims to see where that learning and teaching fitted into the
rest of his life.

It may very well be (others must use their greater skill to
judge) that a definitive assessment will conclude that Gregory's great contribution to the study of liturgy in the twentieth century was not so much in original ideas or
revolutionary new insights or newly-discovered documents
but rather in the skill with which he made the material
accessible to a very wide audience. He made it 'exciting for
an ignorant layman'. *The Shape of the Liturgy* remains a major
landmark in liturgical study in the twentieth century because
— unlike so many other books on liturgy — it is readable,
often witty and rarely dry. It is infused with the author's
convictions about the Church and the place of the liturgy in
that community compelling him to share what he had learnt
with as many people as possible. Gregory the published
scholar was very much Gregory the 'teacher' although he
hardly did any formal teaching throughout his life. His two
years at Keble as a lecturer in modern history may have
developed his skill as also his brief period teaching in Ghana.
The rather shadowy theological teaching project at Nashdom
in the early 1930s may well have had Gregory's help, to judge
from some of his notebooks. In general however, his teaching
skill, his love of communicating, seems to have been a deeper
instinct; his ability and desire to make theological things
accessible for a wider audience a natural propensity.

It is this 'accessibility' and this readiness to 'apply' his
scholarship which I wish to highlight in this present chapter.

1   Grove Booklets, 1977.
2   see Bibliography.

I am not a liturgical scholar and so I find myself closer to the 'ignorant layman' excited by Gregory's presentation of the subject than to the precise scholars who notice Gregory's mistakes and false conclusions and overstatements. Those need to be noted — Gregory would have wanted them to be — but this chapter will try to look at his scholarly work in the light of its general impact on the Church, in the setting of his other activities and within the shape of his complex personality.

The scholarship and writings were not conducted in some ivory-towered, isolated seclusion from the rest of his life nor were they confined to some specific period before he became involved in other things. Instead the scholar, the monk and the politician are all mixed in with each other, sometimes happily, sometimes not. This chapter seeks to isolate, in so far as it is possible, the scholar while acknowledging the ultimate impossibility of the task. He is a complex whole.

How did Gregory see himself? His most frequent self-designation is as an 'historian', a role which fitted easily with his vocation as a monk. Conscious that he stood in a long tradition of scholarly contributions to the Church from the monastic communities he happily described himself on the title pages of books as 'Gregory Dix, monk of Nashdom Abbey'. This designation was also a device, however, and a wilful simplification of the much more complex role he was actually playing.

Throughout *The Shape* Gregory insists that he is operating as an historian recording and examining what history reveals. However, in the introduction to *The Shape* he clearly distinguishes between the role of the 'pure historian' and the actual role he is exercising — that of 'the liturgist'. He goes on to define the liturgist as: 'a student of Comparative Religion, who is himself a believing Christian, exercising his science especially on the practice of worship in his own religion', and in a footnote he insists on both the scientific element and the believing element otherwise 'much insight is lost'.

In many ways this is consistently Gregory's position even when he is being most scientific and objective. It acknowledges what all fields of study have come to admit, that you cannot study or write without a point of view. This is not for him a problem but part of his purpose.

He writes as a 'believing Christian' in his concern for other 'believing Christians' and not just the scholarly community but: 'the innumerable millions of plain nameless sinful Christian folk for whom in different ways the eucharist has always been the universal road to God'.

He sets himself against what he deems liturgy-as-archaeology for: 'The plain man rightly refuses to pray on strictly archaeological principles.' Gregory's interest is in the way that plain man worships.

There are pitfalls in this approach which, if he did not always avoid, he was aware of. In writing to Bévenot in 1939 Gregory, taken up with parish work at Beaconsfield and involved in scholarly and ecclesiastical projects, wrote: 'I am not a philosopher or theologian and with a parish on my hands I am ceasing even to have pretensions to being an historian and becoming simply a hack.'

He always found the tension between the extremes of historian and hack very real: polemic might take over and passion for the cause smother the precise love of truth. Nevertheless, Gregory's training as an historian was deeply grounded and shaped his whole mental approach. In every situation his profound intellect brought to bear his extensive knowledge of and sensitivity to the variety and complexity of human history.

What did Gregory mean by the term 'historian'? In a sermon preached in Uppsala in 1950 he reflected on this role. The historian must have something of the angels' view of Church history. He did not mean simply detached and 'objective', he knew that to be elusive, but a view that had 'the perspective of the moment', coloured by everything occurring at that point, a sensitivity to every context and contingent factor.

Much earlier, in 1932, in his controversy with Bishop Palmer[1] he had written:

> ....history is not composed of isolated facts and statements in documents. It is a stream of life, a continuous process, and a whole. Every single fact is unintelligible or misleading without its reference to its setting. This involves for the historian the accumulation of a great mass of detail on his period, in order that institutions may be recognised in their workings and indirect effects, and that the presuppositions and unquestioned assumptions which form the mental background of an age may be made plain to us as they were not plain even to those who held them....

Gregory acknowledged the subtlety of the historian's task. Even so, perhaps he was too confident that the historian really can recreate and enter into another time and place, though he did acknowledge throughout his life the difficulty of the task. We quoted at length in the Introduction from his early (1930) reflections on the science of history where he acknowledged that 'history' was necessarily 'a selection of facts'. As an historian Gregory generally admitted the possibility of constructing an overall picture from that selection. It was not the historian's role merely to stay with the 'selection of facts.' Perhaps, again, it was something of the romantic and imaginative spirit in him that gave him confidence to construct and not merely to record.

Gregory's formation as an historian began at Westminster School and continued as an undergraduate at Merton. By the time he went to Wells Theological College for two terms in 1924 to prepare for ordination he was combining history with an interest in theology. We know that he did not think much of his time spent at Wells. Already, presumably, he was reading extensively and forming his own mind while discovering his own particular interests and concerns.

Unlike some writers and thinkers Gregory was not the product of a particular school of thought nor the pupil of a particular teacher. He rarely referred directly to influences

1   p. 116.

on his work though he clearly fits into the complex of schools
of thought developing and changing in the first part of the
twentieth century. He was a child of Anglo-Catholicism,
reading its scholars, eventually working with them, becoming
one of them. He read the Oxford fathers of the movement
as well as the Caroline divines of the seventeenth century
but quickly diversified also into the much wider world of
international catholic scholarship. Theologically he was at
home in the scholastic catholic tradition. His approach to
theology was that of a Thomist but he clearly read modern,
even modernist, catholic writers and kept carefully abreast
of theological development. He admitted difficulty with
theological German, but was fluent enough in other languages to keep abreast of continental theology. All his instincts were with the Catholic authors and their Latin
orientation rather than the Protestant Germans.

He became steeped in monastic writings as well as other
branches of ecclesiastical study but gradually found himself
focusing on the earliest years of the Church's life. The
existing texts of the pre-Nicene Churches, in their original
languages, were studied in particular depth.

In time this involved working with the actual ancient
manuscripts and Gregory became a regular visitor to the
British Museum. In the early thirties this brought him into
contact with other liturgical scholars, British and continental, and avoided the isolation of solitary study. He noted that
this was how he got to know Walter Frere, the great English
liturgist of the previous generation. Acknowledging his debt
in a Memoir of Frere Gregory wrote: 'I owe him more than I
can say, not only for teaching, of which I am proud to speak,
but also for affection of which one does not speak.'[1]

Frere linked Gregory with the generation of Armitage
Robinson, Burkitt, Figgis, Abbot Butler, A.J. Mason, Swete
and Dom R.H. Connolly. Dix saw them as successors of
Westcott, Lightfoot and Hort in the nineteenth century; in

1   *Walter H. Frere*, ed. Philips, 1947 Faber.

turn, Gregory and his contemporaries were the next succeed-
ing generation.

In the Memoir Dix continued:

> There are those to whom their successors turn naturally for
> texts and 'information' — Bona, Eusebe Renandot, Materie,
> the Blessed Tommasi, le Sieur de Moleon, le Brun, Forbes,
> Wilson, Brightman.... There is another group — Mabillon,
> Claude de Vert, Probst, Ceriani, Edmund Bishop, Wilmart are
> representative — no less equipped with facts, but to whom
> one turns rather for their aperçus, their general judgements.

Gregory included Frere in the first group, his own place must
surely be in the second.

If Frere and his contemporaries were an influence, Gabriel
Hebert SSM became very much a companion. They seem to
have met in the mid-thirties and to have worked together on
a number of projects from then on. Hebert was more obviously 'Anglican' than Dix and more generally open to the
influence and contribution of the Protestant reformation.
But both were Religious, both were deeply concerned for
unity (Hebert was part of the discussions with Bévenot) and
they shared a deep commitment to applying scholarship to
the everyday life of the Church and its people.

By the time he came to write *The Shape*, Gregory could
claim: 'With the exception of three series of Origen's *Homilies*
I have read every sentence of every Christian author extant
from the period before Nicaea, most of it probably eight or a
dozen times or oftener.'

He could write of the period with confidence and a sure
touch as a result of years of study and reflection. It was in the
second half of the thirties that Gregory began to contribute
more publicly to the world of scholarship. It is also then that
he began to enter the world of ecclesiastical politics. This
coincides with his re-entry into the novitiate (1936) and the
granting, by the Bishop of Oxford, of a licence to preach and
minister outside the Abbey (1935). In the late twenties and
early thirties, while wrestling with other and personal issues,
such as the appeal of Rome, he was steadily working at an
ever deeper absorption in the texts, issues and atmosphere

of that earliest Christian period. Those ten years or so of
relative quiet (with the exception perhaps of the time in
Ghana) were crucial to the work that was to follow. His study
was not confined to Patristics and the Pre-Nicene Church.
He absorbed a great deal of Biblical and specifically New
Testament study. Although he was not as assured as in his
preferred field his books nonetheless reveal a familiarity and
confidence in Biblical criticism, a breadth of reading and a
deft originality with New Testament material. He rightly
recognised no real division between the texts with which he
was so familiar and the New Testament. They came from the
same period, from the same part of the world, from the same
group of people: they all belonged together.

A conservative in his scholarly attitudes he did not however share with some Anglo-Catholics a fear and rejection of
Biblical criticism. For all his scathing attacks on 'liberalism'
Gregory acknowledged scholarly developments and was not
afraid to use the resulting conclusions. He acknowledged his
debt to Biblical scholars like C.H. Dodd remaining free to
criticise their methods.

There was, in fact, an element of ambiguity in Gregory's
developed attitude to liberalism in scholarship. In his letters
to Freddy Green, for instance, he was blunt and emphatic
about his campaign, for example in *The Shape*, against the
liberal approach but he acknowledges too the danger on the
other side from some of his own contemporaries and the
'younger men':

> If you knew the amount of my time which has had to be
> wasted in commenting on defences of the Pauline authorship
> of Hebrews and/or real lions for Daniel, and similar stuff,
> during the last four years.... If I thought any way of salvation
> for theology was to be found along that line, I should have
> turned Papist ten years ago.... I think that there was a truth
> which liberalism was fumbling after which it is necessary to
> rescue from the liberal fiasco, and that the time is coming
> soon to begin to make spoil of the Egyptians.[1]

1   Letter 1943.

Significantly, he goes on to add: 'It is partly — probably mostly — because I think Rome would hardly be able to allow us — anyhow at present — to work at this, that I am so anxious to see the C. of E. remain tolerably habitable for historical Christianity.'

So, ironically, Gregory's scholarship was offered in the service of a Church that could not, at that time, accept it and this partly because Gregory's armoury against the 'Liberal heresy' included weapons taken from the liberals.

The earliest fruits of Gregory's scholarship appear in the early thirties in *Laudate*, the Nashdom journal, and in due course in other learned journals such as *Theology*. His very first review in *Laudate* appeared in 1925 over the initials 'G.E.A.D.' The book was *An Anthology of Mediaeval Latin* and the short review already has the sharp, distinctive Dix tone. Gradually he contributed more and longer reviews of books and also learned articles. His first contribution to *Theology* came in 1932[1] with an article called: 'The use and abuse of Papias on the Fourth Gospel'. The article, an attack on Canon B.H. Streeter, already had the characteristic anti-liberal stance, but from a thoroughly scholarly base.

Articles and reviews all in varying degrees combine his confident scholarship, skilful use of the material in making points and sometimes his flights of romantic advocacy of his themes. From this period we have already noticed the controversial articles against Bishop Palmer in the *Church Union Gazette*. Other articles and reviews reveal Gregory's distinctive 'Mediterranean' and Latin bias, and articles from 1937 and 1938 in *Laudate* on 'Jurisdiction, episcopal and papal, in the early Church' caught the eye of Bévenot and others. They were re-published in 1975 by the Church Literature Association as *Jurisdiction in the Early Church*.

Already the later tone and style of the writer is well-developed, making the writing attractive to read, sometimes amusing, occasionally unpleasantly scathing. As he wrote more he seems to have concluded that gentler and more

1   *Theology*, Vol. 24.

ironic techniques actually made greater impact and more
readily achieved his objectives.

Behind this and all the later work lie the notebooks of this
period. In neat, careful handwriting, with different coloured
inks for each language and textual cross-reference, Gregory
worked his way through early document after early document. Sometimes the notebooks contain minor commentary
but mostly they are meticulously textual and constitute the
precise and thorough workmanship on which he based his
developing work.

This first period of scholarship came to its climax in 1937
with the publication of his text and translation of *The Treatise
on the Apostolic Tradition of St Hippolytus of Rome*.[1] Usually
referred to as the *Apostolic Tradition*, this document of the
early Church dates from the early third century. It was
already widely seen as one of the most important of early
texts, describing as it does the practices of the Christian
community in, Gregory maintained, a very conservative way,
making it a good evidence of practices from long before its
actual date. Gregory sought to provide a critical text that
would make the document widely available. This required
weaving his way through the variety of early translations and
versions of the original from all over the primitive Church,
attempting to discern the original and also acknowledging
the work of his own contemporaries on the text. In his
preface Gregory acknowledged that scholarship has not yet
developed far enough to produce a definitive text but he
hoped his contribution would bring that nearer.

This is Gregory's most straightforwardly scholarly work: a
scholarly text, the result of four years' careful work and
years of contributory study. He planned a second volume to
include a much lengthier consideration of the text's contents
and their implications. This volume never appeared though
much of the material informed *The Shape*. However the 1937
volume included a General Introduction which was historical
as well as textual.

1   SPCK.

The work was well-received and has continued to be used by students of the period even though other editions of the original have since been produced involving further extensive scholarly work. Henry Chadwick produced a second edition of Gregory's text in 1968, reissued in 1992 by an American publisher.

In the *Apostolic Tradition* the seeds of much of his later work can be seen. Particular themes, ideas and emphases begin to emerge. In the Notes on the text and its translation he defends his use of the Greek word *anamnesis*, untranslated, maintaining that there is no suitable English translation for this word which indicates the 're-presentation' in the eucharist before God of the entire sacrificial activity of Christ. He emphasises that this includes the whole Paschal Mystery, crucifixion and resurrection, the eucharist making the coming alive in the Church of its root-cause and life-origin. This is very much a theme returned to in detail in *The Shape* and one fundamental to his ideas of eucharistic sacrifice. The Introduction also gives notice of another major concern — the Jewish influence still apparent in the Church's liturgy:

> Hippolytus reveals clearly for the first time how firmly the Jewish liturgical basis persisted in the catholic cultus after a century-and-a-half of Gentile Christianity. That is a fact — not yet adequately appreciated — which must have great weight in such questions as the alleged influence of Hellenistic Mysteries on primitive Christianity.[1]

On the other hand, the *Apostolic Tradition* also gives an early indication of Gregory's antipathy to the *Epiklesis* — the phrase in the Great Thanksgiving Prayer which asks the Holy Spirit to make the bread and wine the Body and Blood of Christ. In the Orthodox East this prayer has become vital but it has a much more chequered history in the West. It was much in dispute in the drafting of the 1928 Prayer Book. Gregory vigorously maintained that an *Epiklesis* was a later addition to Hippolytus and that such prayers did not belong, in a consecratory way, to the most primitive traditions. Dix

1   p. xliii.

was criticised for his treatment of the epiklesis in his *Hippolytus* text and it remained, a matter of controversy in his writings and was to be dealt with again at length in *The Shape*.

Overall, Gregory's work on this text was a foundation of subsequent work. This was true for other liturgical scholars as well and for the developing liturgical movement. Gregory seems to have intended it to be part of a much wider textual base. Apart from his proposed second volume of Hippolytus, there is evidence that he hoped to publish texts of other early documents, some of them equally complex. His notebook version of *The Didache* seems to have been aimed at publication, for instance. These never appeared but perhaps he had a vision of a whole collection of available and usable texts on which his reflections on the primitive Church could be securely based.

The temptation was, of course, always to press on with wider reflection rather than staying with the technicalities. Even in the *Apostolic Tradition*, his most technical work, the Introduction declines to stay with critical niceties and happily explores the wider context of its origins and the Church that produced it.

Gregory's view of himself as an historian enabled him to do this. In a letter to Freddy Green[1] he even attributed to this to what he thought of as his 'Mediterranean' temperament:

> I think I realise that a certain 'Frenchiness' of mind seeks for *les idées claires*' and dislikes the Germanic fog in all its consequences.... I think what worries people in my writings is the piling up of little bits of evidence. But I don't see how else one can study ancient history as history. It is the only way the secular classical historian works — from little bits of evidence built together to form a complete picture. That is as a matter of fact the only scientific way to work on ancient history, because of the nature of the evidence. It is the lack of this patient and docile study of the Christian evidence which has been so disastrous in the study of ancient Christian history....
>
> Old Stubbs taught me in my youth that 'history presents a chain of recognisable causes and consequences', (if it is

1   23.12.43.

studied patiently enough and above all from all round and
from within and from the contemporary background) and
that it is the duty of the historian to lay them bare.

There is a confidence in Gregory's reconstruction of the past
which is not shared by every historian. He worked from the
conviction that it is possible to enter into the mind and life
of another era, even with quite sparse material: the strength
of his imagination had its role to play in this as did the
strength of his convictions.

In many ways liturgists have moved in the other direction
since Gregory's day. They have become more tentative and
more circumspect. Paul Bradshaw, for instance, in his recent
The Search for the Origins of Christian Worship[1] argues that new
evidence and further research mean that we can only be more
insecure in our conclusions about the earliest documents.
Specifically he argues that Gregory's confident dating of
documents, assigning of authorship, linking of influences are
all more definite than the evidence warrants. Dix's general
conclusions can actually only be one possibility among many
alternatives. For all his knowledge of the texts, there is
simply not enough clear evidence to construct an accurate
picture of that primitive situation.

Gregory knew this, as we have seen in his letter to Freddy
Green, but he was simply not content to remain an observer,
a technical scholar concerned with refining particulars. He
acknowledged the primary importance of the accurate and
precise exploration of the texts but wanted to make judgements, to take a step further, sometimes quite a large step.
It was as a matter of judgement, based on what he understood
to be the facts but with a step beyond them too, that he chose
to omit the *epiklesis* from his text of Hippolytus despite its
appearance in more than one of the versions he was working
with. Judgements inevitably involved working on the basis
that a 'point of view' is inevitable. There can be no interpre-
tative vacuum, no ultimate objectivity. For Gregory the only

1   SPCK 1992.

consistent point of view, the only justifiable one, was that of
the Catholic Church (or what Gregory meant by that).

Liberal detachment and objectivity was not for Gregory;
he deemed it was spurious in any case. All his writing came
within the sphere of the Church and was, in a sense, under
its authority. That had always been the case throughout
history. In an early article in *Laudate* he wrote about the
magisterium of the Church:[1]

> In the gospels, long before they have been presented to us,
> the facts have been interpreted from a particular standpoint
> dictated by a definite theological conception. It is what we
> might expect: from 'J' to Karl Marx that is the only way the
> Jew has written history.

He went on to argue that a *magisterium* (but which?) has
already provided the teaching behind the gospels: 'The New
Testament itself is only the first and supreme product of the
teaching *magisterium* of the Church which it presupposes and
echoes, not initiates.'[2]

Gregory's kind of scholarship ultimately involved advocacy
too and he had just the gifts of imagination and skill in writing
to move from dry facts to absorption in a particular period of
history and on to convey that in a living, attractive way in his
writings.

Even so, the tension of scholarship and advocacy was never
allowed to distort or misuse the facts, but there is no doubt that
at times he allowed what he wanted to advocate to justify going
a step further than perhaps the facts strictly allowed.

One consequence of this scholarly advocacy was Gregory's
involvement in publishing. Through the Dacre Press, referred to in Chapter 3 (p. 116), he hoped to combine scholarship and catholic teaching, bringing together leading
thinkers, who could write attractively for the ordinary reader.
The 'Signpost' group of the early 1940s was just such. Writing
to Freddy Green, Gregory says:[3]

1   Vol. xl, Dec. 1933, p. 208, 'Northern Catholicism'.
2   p. 227.
3   16.7.40.

'The Signpost men' are a small group of my friends[1] — who (except for Demant who is older and stands a little apart) are all a year or two (some more) younger than I. We believe in the Catholic Religion, that is, that Catholic Theology (resting on Scripture and Tradition), is the right because revealed answer to the whole of the riddle of human life, intellectual, moral, political and practical... and are trying to say why we believe it. We do include the encyclicals of the Pope from Leo XIII to Pius XII in the Catholic *magisterium*, but only as part of it.... We are publishing a series of 12 one-shilling books, once a month, this year, at the Dacre Press (which is us under another name) to explain just why 'Liberalism' is from the abyss.... They are selling in thousands.

In an earlier letter[2] Gregory had put the same group at the centre of his reasons for staying in the Church of England. His opportunity for, and skill at, 'scholarly advocacy' was thus vital to his vocation. The letter describes to Freddy Green the London meeting of the 'Signpost men' with a group of Roman Catholic clergy. One of those clergy. Dom Winslow, argued with Gregory about his joining the Roman Church:

... he clutched my arm saying 'For God's sake don't do that! It is vital at present to have some Catholics (*sic*!) who are free to speak. Your Signpost group is one of the greatest rays of light at the moment . Don't do anything that might wreck it. You are still free to write and think and guide.

'Writing' and 'thinking' and 'guiding' were very much what Gregory wanted to do. His involvement in publishing ventures of different kinds was only one expression of this desire. His lecturing, preaching and writing and, in a different way, his involvement in Church politics, were part of this 'scholarly advocacy', through writing, thinking and guiding. It was all in the service of catholic Christianity and against the monster of liberalism. It was for the living Church.

1 J.V.L. Casserley; D.M. Mackinnon; E.L. Mascall; G.B. Bentley; T.M. Parker; P. McLaughlin; V. Demant; D.G. Peck; A.H. Rees. Casserley and Mascall were in fact the General editors.
2 26.6.40.

In a lecture of 1943 to an Oxford diocesan clergy school Gregory stressed the living Church.

> Neither the second century nor the sixteenth century can be a very sure guide for us, who have to be Christians in the twentieth century. We can learn from all in our condition.... That we don't try to set up an unreal golden age. That we don't try to read back any one period into another, but suffer each one to tell us for itself how it loved the one Christ and believed the one faith.

The 'one faith', the living Church, is an all-controlling idea — more than an idea — in Gregory's work. Perhaps no other concept is more fundamental and crucial to his thought and life. He felt strongly that it should be the dominant issue of everyone's reflection. In his articles in *Laudate* in 1937[1] he said: 'For the next generation the nature of the Church rather than Christology is certain to be the cardinal problem before Christian thought.'

It is worth examining in more detail what he himself meant by the 'nature of the Church'.

As we have noticed already, he did not see the Church first of all as an institution or organisation, still less a convenient meeting of Christian individuals. It was a living organism, a divine creation, the Body of Christ.

Gregory always expressed this in the strongest possible terms. In a lecture on *The Apostolic Ministry*, undated but probably delivered in the United States he said: 'The Incarnation did not "found" the Church — Christ redeemed it.'

He went on to argue that the Church, the community of the faithful, is as old as, and vital to creation. By the Incarnation God renewed and restored that community and fashioned it to be the continuation of his presence in creation. So the Church is now the continuity of Israel, God's chosen race, it is Israel's renewal and enlargement, and it is a single entity, a unity before God, one Body.

In notes from the early thirties, perhaps made for lectures to ordinands, he was already stressing the corporate nature

1   Vol. xv, p. 45 ff.

of the Church and her liturgy. Individuals are 'incorporated into a regenerate race' and he added: 'By baptism we are taken into the perfect worship of Christ our High Priest.'

The Israel of God is not one race or nation but a stronger, deeper universal unity and is designed for worship. This 'organism' organises itself locally in particular churches but it is first of all the 'Israel of God', the divine creation, the catholic Church.

A powerful sense of the Body of Christ led him to emphasise the place of the ordinary worshipper, the *plebs sancta Dei*. In his introduction to his text of *Hippolytus*[1] he spoke of: 'the immense dumb but praying multitudes which form the strength of Christendom'.

Those 'praying multitudes' continued to be a major concern and became a focus of his attention, as in *The Shape of the Liturgy*.

The theology of this emphasis on the Body of Christ has many consequences and implications for all Gregory's work, some of which we shall look at in more detail. One slightly more curious connection deserves noticing first.

Gregory felt very strongly that his argument in all this grew from the heart of catholic tradition. When he spoke of the 'catholic tradition' he not unnaturally looked to Rome — but he also seems to have looked to the Roman setting, to the Mediterranean 'milieu' and the whole Latin world, what he called 'the basis of our civilisation'. This is surely linked to his feelings about his own French descent and his clear preference at almost every point for Latin, 'catholic' culture. Over against the Latin he sets the Northern or sometimes 'Nordic' or 'Teutonic' or even 'Germanic' culture. Among other factors, distance from Rome allowed for growing variation and the differences of temperament could account not only for varieties of devotion but also for the Reformation itself and for the characteristics of continuing Protestantism. His implication was that England lies somewhere in between

1 1937.

these two 'cultures', closer to the North but affected by the South.

The 1930s were in many ways the heyday of racial theories, not least in Germany. Gregory does not overuse these ideas, but they occur with some prominence in *A Detection of Aumbries*[1] and in a rather different way in *Jew and Greek*[2] where his contrast is between Greek and Syriac cultures. From time to time they occur in or behind other writings including some early articles in *Laudate*.

In *A Detection of Aumbries* for instance he wrote:

> Whereas the Latin or Southern mind in general finds it natural to regard a man or an institution or a thing chiefly in the light of its prescribed purpose or end, the Northern mind is apt to concentrate upon the thing in itself without looking further.... The temper of the Latin mind is thus what its admirers call 'logical' and those who dislike it will doubtless continue to call 'legalist' or 'formalist' in religion. The Northern mind is by contrast more 'affective' and 'out-flowing' in the things of the soul and often seems to itself more reverent and devotional than that of the South.[3]

Generally speaking, of course, Gregory's bias was always towards the South, even when trying to be fair. Sometimes the ideas were simply used for sarcastic fun. In a letter in 1935 to Marcus Stephens, a friend and SSM novice who was perhaps beginning to be taken by the idea of a distinctive 'Northern Catholicism', Gregory wrote:

> ... the grand old Book of 1548, that was used by Bede and Aldhelm and good King Alfred, when Englishmen were really English and Nordic and whiskered and sank their horns of mead in a he-manly way. You see what I mean — real 'Northern Catholicism' — further North and more Catholic and none of your minging Continental stuff, brought in — like Cranmer's Dutch 'wife' — surreptitiously from overseas in a herring barrel.

1   1942.
2   1953.
3   p. 51.

Behind all this presumably lay an instinctive defence of a single catholicity which Gregory did not want to see divided into distinctive 'cultures'. It seems generally to mean that the Southern and Latin is normally to be taken as the truly catholic.

Out of the fundamental theme of the all-pervading importance of the idea of the Church, the Body of Christ, emerged a series of closely-related secondary themes. Some were more controversial than others. We shall look particularly at the Ministry in the Church and the related issues of Authority and the Papacy; at Initiation in the Church; and at liturgy in particular that of the Eucharist.

Gregory's convictions about the Ministry of the Church are the natural consequences of his thinking about the sacramental nature of the Body of Christ. The continuing life of Christ in the world is lived through a sacramental structure given to the world at Christ's command. This is no arbitrary command but a provision deliberately and graciously adjusted to the needs of humankind providing the best way in which to enter fully the richest communion with God through Christ. This sacramental structure extends from the beginning of the process in Initiation through all its landmarks and finds its most regular expression in eucharistic worship. It includes those who are the ministers of this structure. The Ministry does not merely administer the system but is itself a visible and organic part of it all, itself a witness to the reality of Christ's life in the Church. Here is the reason why ideas about the Ministry and the defence of catholic teaching in this area were so important to Gregory. A sacramental ministry (ministering sacraments and itself a sacrament) was a vital part of the Catholicity he was defending. It was a guarantee of genuine catholicity as well as useful and creative and attractive in itself.

Gregory saw this threatened by the 'pan-protestantism' of his day and by many of the moves towards unity emerging in the thirties. It was just too easy to avoid offence and achieve a superficial unity by ignoring or glossing over real historical differences in ministerial doctrine. All Gregory's defensive

instincts rose up here producing some of the more controversial writings of his career.

He was not merely being defensive but arguing for what
he clearly felt to be a precious gift of God to the Church in
the form of the apostolic, catholic ministry. Here was a gift
to be cherished, shared and restored where it was lost, not
to be discarded or ignored.

'A precious gift of God to the Church' was actually not
quite how Gregory saw it. His argument about the ministry
was more startling and surprising. In more than one place he
maintained that Jesus founded a *ministry* rather than a
Church and that ministry is creative of the renewed Church
and not vice versa. So Apostolic Ministry in the Church
ceases to be merely a helpful extra but becomes crucial,
fundamental and indispensable. Whether there is, in fact,
quite so clear a distinction between the first apostles and the
Church is a debatable point, but Gregory felt that his emphasis emerged from his characteristic exploration of Jewish
ideas behind the Greek words that had become so central
here: *ecclesia, episcope, apostolos.*

In his paper *The Apostolic Ministry* delivered in the USA he
set this in the context of the Church as the redeemed
community, the Christian community continuing and fulfilling the old Israel. What is new in the community is the
Ministry, created by Christ. Gregory says that the Twelve
were: 'the only direct historical consequence of Jesus of
Nazareth. They were endowed with his own Messianic Spirit
to act for him.' They were his plenipotentiaries.

Gregory made an important distinction which he emphasised, perhaps over-emphasised, in other places too: the
apostles were to carry on fulfilling the earthly role of Christ.
In doing so they were appointed within the Church but were
also 'sent' (the root meaning of *apostolos*) to it. Their commission was not so much from the Church but from Christ
— in the Church.

Ideas in this area were developed most substantially in the
long essay 'The Ministry in the Early Church (c. AD 90–410)'
published in Kenneth Kirk's book of 1946, *The Apostolic*

Ministry. This was the book that Dix claimed (to Bévenot) that he and Hebert had persuaded Kirk to edit. They envisaged it as a catholic contribution to the growing debate about ministry especially in the national and international ecumenical scene (not least in the context of South India). Gregory's essay is far and away the longest in what is a small book in its own right. Among the least influential of his writings, it gained less general acceptance than, say, his ideas in *The Shape.* Interestingly enough the two were being written fairly simultaneously and both under wartime conditions. *The Apostolic Ministry* had been on the go since 1940 and was published in 1946. Gregory, we know, was out working on *The Shape* throughout the same period. Michael Ramsey found himself unconvinced by Gregory's arguments about 'the Shaliach' and Gabriel Hebert, commenting in 1962, felt Gregory had overstepped the mark.[1] Even so, letters survive about a possible French translation of Gregory's essay (not the whole book...) with developments to take into account the continental situation. This was at the time of Gregory's death and nothing, in fact, ultimately came of it.

The essay has as its starting point the *Apostolic Tradition* of Hippolytus and argues from there that the liturgical provisions it contains show us a great deal about the place of the Apostolic ministry both in the third-century Church and the preceding century and even back to sub-apostolic times. It locates two distinct places of origin for the Church's ministry, both profoundly influenced by a conviction of the strong continuity between Jewish and early Christian institutions. The Christian presbytery or council of elders is seen as a direct descendant of the *zeqenim* or council of the synagogue and as such as a body for government, discipline and ordering of the community life. The episcopate, on the other hand, even with the Sanhedrin of presbyters around it, descends from the *shaliach* — the Hebrew concept perceived behind the New Testament 'apostle'. This is the 'plenipotentiary', the one endowed with all the power of his master, fully and

---

1 *Apostle and Bishop*, Faber, 1962.

directly, sent, like the apostles by Jesus, sent, like Jesus by
God. Thus the origins of the episcopate are dynamic and
charismatic. It is a function derived directly from God and
expressed in the leadership of worship, the grace and power
to teach, the charism to lead a local Church, to connect it
with the Church through history and with the Church in
other places. The unique gift of the Holy Spirit in the
consecrating of the bishop is emphasised, the apostolic succession being an addition to the number of the apostles
rather than a succession to them. This is called 'apostolic
simultaneity'. It is less as a kind of mechanical 'contagion'
derived from the other consecrating bishops than as a direct
charismatic gift from God with which the bishop succeeds to
the inheritance of his predecessors in the see. In this essay
Dix says:[1]

> 'Do Thou now pour forth' (in the prayer of Hippolytus)
> indicates that what is here expected is a fresh creative act of
> divine power making the elect a bishop, exactly analogous to
> but not simply dependent upon the imparting of the Spirit
> to the original band of apostles.

Gregory notes how, steadily in the fourth century, and from
then on, the characteristics of episcopate and presbyterate
begin to be transferred to each other. The presbyterate
shares the liturgical function and at 'parish' level takes it over,
the episcopate takes on an increasingly ordered and eventually administrative role in jurisdiction and government. Even
so, the episcopate never loses hold of its special function in
ordination and consecration and here in the bestowing of the
Spirit the bishop continues to come into his own.

The argument was criticised for paucity evidence, Jewish
or otherwise, on the idea of the *shaliach* and for reading too
much into, or out of, very little. Gregory's theory of an
intermediate 'apostolic man' who bridges the gap between
the twelve and later bishops was shown to have very little

1   p. 200.

evidence. The essay does serve to show very many of his characteristic concerns in this area and in general.

He wanted to demonstrate that the Church emerged as a dynamic living organism with an integral leadership and that legalistic and jurisdictional concepts and concerns only came later. This organic character did not make the ministry a less vital part of the Church but actually more crucial and important as the ministry becomes a fountain of the Church's life, directly created by God. Its life flows then into the Body and it becomes guarantor as well as representative.

In *The Apostolic Ministry*, Gregory paints a picture of this Church and its leader:[1]

> The pre-Nicene bishop is, indeed, in a singular sense 'the man' of his own Church — its priest, offering its corporate sacrifice by which 'it becomes what it is', the Body of Christ, which is at once the climax and source of its being as a Church; and the minister, in person or by delegation, of all sacraments to all its members. He is also, by his liturgical sermon, the guardian and spokesman to itself and to the world without of his own Church's doctrinal tradition, by which the apostolic function of 'witness to revelation' is discharged. He is the creator of its lesser ministries; its representative to other Churches: the administrator of its charity; the officer of its discipline; the centre of its unity; the hub of its whole many-sided life, spiritual and temporal, inward and outward.

But Gregory never wants to lose sight either of the implications for the corporateness of the Church and the effect that has on the ministry. In an undated paper entitled *The Petrine Primacy and Special Function of the Roman Church in Christendom*, he paints a picture of this early Church and its ministry which tries to keep the balance between these different elements. He argues that only a possessor of the Apostolic Spirit, directly bestowed in consecration by God, could occupy the bishop's throne. He only acquired his authority as a bishop, however, by the election of the community and his

1   p. 198.

enthronement by the local Church. Here Gregory distinguishes between a consensual authority of 'leadership' and a
juridical authority of 'jurisdiction'. In this early period the
bishop is always surrounded by the presbyterate. Gregory
argued that while he had no formal power over them they,
nevertheless, had a duty to follow him. The bishop was not
merely 'chairman' of this council but more like 'High Priest'.
He stood before God for the Church and before the Church
for God — and he stood before other Christians for his own
Church. All this was by 'consent' of people and clergy in the
Church. Even the teaching he delivered, 'passed on', was
limited by consent. So the life of the Church developed in
the dynamic tension between the bishop's unique, Spirit-be-
stowed role and the living, breathing, consensus of the people of God, also bestowed by the Spirit.

This kind of 'government by leader', he goes on to say,
means that the leader has a right to do whatever the people
will follow and that can imply a much greater power than
'jurisdiction' especially in emergency. He calls this 'declama-
tory' rather than 'coercive' power.

It is clear that Gregory faced the temptation of turning the
pre-Nicene Church into a romantic dream of how perfect
things might be. He tried to avoid this and to be realistic,
acknowledging that nostalgia contributed little to the modern Church. Because it is a dynamic organism the Church
must learn to live its life fully in the twentieth century. As
an historian though, and as someone who had glimpsed a
vision (at least partly historical) of how the Church might be,
Gregory did not want to lose sight of what these early
centuries could teach the Church.

A more specific area of related controversy was the question of Anglican orders. This had always been a personal
concern and one thought about in the context of his possible
submission to Rome. By the time he came to write his *The
Question of Anglican Orders*[1] at the request of Kenneth Kirk, he
was much more calmly convinced of their validity. Perhaps

1   1944, Dacre Press.

the writing of the book itself finally settled the issue for him. Whatever else happened, he believed at that point his own priesthood and those Anglicans with whom he shared it, to be securely in the Apostolic Succession. If for any reason it ever became necessary to leave the Church of England it would still not be possible to deny the validity of the orders he had received.

The book was based on letters on the subject from Gregory's pen, however the material was clearly extensively developed. The original letters no longer exist. The style is accessible and clear and the book was well-received. It seems to have been much used at a time when Anglicans in general and Anglo-Catholics in particular were going through a periodic bout of self-doubt on this question. One of the contexts being the Church of South India issue.

Characteristically Gregory argued that at the time of the Reformation, the Church of England in its Prayer Books intended to carry on doing what the Catholic Church had always done in making deacons, priests and bishops. The fact that a leading contributor to the creation of those Prayer Books, Thomas Cranmer, may have had different beliefs is not relevant. The Church had, and still has, a 'catholic intention'. Dix examined carefully the arguments of Pope Leo XIII's *Apostolicae Curae* of 1896, in which Anglican orders were declared 'absolutely null and utterly void'. He uncovered what he felt were its inconsistencies and assurances that Anglicans could remain confident of the catholicity of their ministry. It has one or two mistakes but generally the book is persuasive and cogent. In many ways, the ground has shifted considerably since then in the light of Vatican II and ARCIC but *Apostolicae Curae* has not in any way been withdrawn.

The preparation led Gregory into areas of specific controversial research where his skills as an historian and scholar were fully employed. He explored the case of James Gordon, a Scottish bishop, who became a Roman Catholic and who asked, in 1704, to have his Anglican orders declared null so that he could receive Roman orders. The details of this case

— were Scottish orders the same as English? Which did Gordon actually receive? Which liturgy was in use? What did the Roman decision actually mean and why was it made? — involved considerable research and were carefully used in the book.

But among the chief themes of the book was Gregory's continued assertion of the catholicity of Anglicanism: 'unless we are "catholics" inasmuch as and because we are "Anglicans" then we are not being "catholic" '. The book affirmed his confidence in his Anglican heritage in the face of all those threats he had been the first to perceive.

A similarly confident tone pervaded Gregory's contribution to the Anglo-Catholic Congress of 1948. Held in London immediately prior to the Lambeth Conference it took 'the Church' as its theme. Ronnie Dix was a chairman of the organising committee and Gregory found himself a major speaker and contributor. Questions about South India continued to focus everyone's attention but Gregory. In addition to presenting his liturgical demonstration of the early Church's worship he also gave a major address on the ministry. Here he argued confidently for the apostolic character of the ministry retained by Anglicans and threatened by the 'levelling out' of the Ecumenical Movement. He returned to his emphasis on the apostolate as the special gift of Christ, his empowering of those who continued to act for him. Their functions in due course were passed on to bishops. His speech was a call for Anglicans to remain faithful to the idea of episcopacy they had inherited because it was apostolic rather than merely expedient.

Overall, the idea of 'apostolic order' takes its place within the web of ideas that surround the nature and purpose of the Church. The web is not to be broken or snapped at any point without disastrous results. 'Order' in the Church is not a convenient administrative device but a sacramental characteristic of the body. More than a limb, a member, it is more like the actual nervous system, essential to the very life-breath. The primitive idea of the Church as sacramentally manifested in its bishop had not been lost by Gregory despite his relationships with contemporary bishops. In fact his passionate vision of what a bishop *might* be made him so scathing about many existing examples. He wanted the Body, the People of God, to feel a deep reciprocity, harmony and continuity with its bishops; to be an organic, living whole. He did know that the days of the Pre-Nicene Church were long gone — not least where he had been too romantic in his vision of those days. Nevertheless he did feel that a restored apostolic ministry was to be struggled for in the setting of genuine ecumenical unity and respect for all the people of God.

The hierarchical ordering of the Church provided for its effective development as a divinely structured society in the world: a community of salvation continuously open to those outside and carefully and gently ordering the lives of its existing members. The web of ministry provided for the proper employment of an authority within the body that was human not rigid, dynamic not legalistic. This applied to the *magisterium*, the teaching structure of the Church, as much as to its disciplinary system. Within this structure the papacy took its proper place and Gregory's image of the papacy as a 'gland' in the body sums up his attitude. He saw it as a natural and naturally developing control within the whole organism: apparently small (even arbitrary in origin) but nevertheless central and persuasive in effect. He argued that its origins in the early Church were in practical action rather than in theory and that, like the general episcopal development it shadowed, it was functional, practical and organic in its influence on the wider Church. Dix the historian worked to see the early papacy in its actual setting rather than through the spectacles of later development but he saw from the very earliest days a real universal dimension to the office of the Roman bishop. What each bishop was for his see, the Pope was for the whole Church.

In a letter to his friend T.F. 'Fish' Taylor in 1937[1] Gregory responded on this issue in the light of B. Kidd's then recent

1   29.4.37.

book on jurisdiction in the early Church. In hasty note form, Gregory succinctly presented the argument he was to maintain:

> Thus when Kidd says 'primacy of leadership' for Pope in Pre-Nicene Christendom he says Pope has over Pre-Nicene Universal Church what pre-Nicene Bishop has over local Church. When bishop acquires 'jurisdiction' so does Pope. Process the same and contemporary.

He went on to add, starkly, 'if episcopalians then papalists'.

It was his articles about this theme that first brought Gregory into contact with Maurice Bévenot.[1] The place of the papacy in the Church was one of the key themes they discussed. We have noted before Gregory's near-romantic, almost mystical reverence for the papacy. It did not mean he could never consider it to be wrong as he demonstrated in *The Question of Anglican Orders* over *Apostolicae Curae* but generally speaking he took the development of the papacy into its contemporary post-Vatican I form as a fact to be accepted within the desire for unity, a factor to be given serious, reverential consideration in any uniting Church of the future.

Gregory expressed these ideas again in his contribution to the *Catholicity* report of 1948. There he was prepared to be slightly more critical of the development of the Roman system since Trent but still, as we saw at the end of chapter three, anything called 'Catholicism' must include a central place for the papacy.

If the papacy is one of the living features of the Church and its ministry, so too is the living reality of the actual people of God, the *laos*, the whole new Israel, the body of Christ. Gregory was never far from this theme of the living community. This is the testing ground of the magisterium, the vital receptive authentication of the ministry's function, the indispensable place for the return of consent to the hierarchy's desire. Gregory spoke more than once (in *The Shape*, for instance, and in *The Apostolic Ministry*) of the laity as a distinct order in the Church in its own right, with its own proper

---

1   'Jurisdiction Episcopal and Papal in the Early Church', *Laudate*, XV + XVI, 1937,38, p. 45 ff.

ministry and functions. He stressed its dignity and authority underlining the mystical significance of its initiatory rites. In a footnote in *The Apostolic Ministry*[1] Gregory wrote: 'It is by the gift of the Spirit in confirmation that the laic is equipped to fulfil the office of his particular 'order' in the Church, just as the cleric is equipped to fulfil the office of his particular 'order' by ordination.'

This important sense of the Church as a mutually supportive community of roles and functions, orders and gifts—each verifying, authenticating and supporting the others—was a consistent background to Gregory's thought. He saw a Church governed by consent and he characterised one of the deepest moments of the Church's life, the Dialogue, the *Sursum Corda*, the beginning of the eucharistic Prayer, as precisely that, a giving of consent. In that opening exchange the bishop, the president, seeks the corporate consent of all the body for his prayer on behalf of them all and, once given, he then proceeds to bless God. At its best the Church is about mutual dependence, about solidarity, about the deep charity of shared-out functions working in harmony together for the good of all.

For Gregory the emphasis on the dignity of the laity implied an equivalent dignity for the rites that initiated them as the people of God — baptism and confirmation. This became for Gregory an area of special scholarly interest but also of some controversial interest both within the Anglican world and on the ecumenical. Here once again he felt he was defending catholic orthodoxy against shallow compromise and expediency.

Two pieces of writing, ten years apart, witness to Gregory's continuing concern over this issue. In 1936 he contributed a paper entitled 'Confirmation or Laying on of Hands?' to a series of Occasional Papers in *Theology*. In 1946, more well-known by now as the author of *The Shape*, he chose to lecture in Oxford, at Professor Cross's request, on 'The theology of Confirmation in relation to Baptism'. He maintained his

1   p. 221.

interest in the intervening and subsequent years by participation in the ongoing debate in the Church in this area. He
joined a committee of Convocation on the subject when he
was elected a Proctor in 1946 and produced at about that
time a Memorandum with Michael Ramsey which stressed
the unity of baptism and confirmation (against those who
were arguing for the sufficiency of baptism alone). They
declined precisely to define the action of the Holy Spirit in
the two rites but emphasised both as necessary prior to Holy
Communion. His notebooks of the early thirties demonstrate that he had taken the trouble thoroughly and carefully
to examine the patristic texts relevant to these themes.

He argued emphatically for the dignity of 'Confirmation'
(in fact an inappropriate name for the equivalent event in
the early centuries) He saw it as emerging from the early
Church's stress on initiation by 'water and the Spirit'. As in
other areas, Gregory was prepared to follow an older and
clearer tradition enshrined in the primitive liturgy but not so
clear from scripture. Again his debt was to Hippolytus whose
description of Christian initiation in the early third century
was seen to have unchanging roots back into the first Christian days. Hippolytus spoke of immersions, plural, submer-
sion in water and, what Gregory considered equally
important, an affusion in oil. Over this whole initiation
process the bishop presided.

Gregory traced this liturgical action back into Jewish practice and argued for a rough parallel pattern: the Jewish
sequence for a convert was circumcision, 'sealing' the candi-
date into the covenant, followed by a purificatory immersion
and the sequence completed by the offering of sacrifice in
the temple. The Christian equivalent became an initial
'sealing' into the New Covenant by the pouring of oil, bap-
tismal immersion and then the Christian sacrifice of the
eucharist. In effect the Spirit (*sealing*), the equivalent of
'confirmation', *preceded* water baptism which seems odd to
modern sensitivities yet Gregory was keen to stress the unity
of the rite. Here was one event, the sealing with oil and the

immersion in water were simply the positive and negative aspects of the same event, initiation into the Body of Christ.

In Dix's theory, the laying on of hands only emerged later as an important element of the rite, and much later as the essential act of confirmation.

Gregory was criticised for various aspects of his theory, not least, again, for lack of genuinely convincing evidence for parts of it. Geoffrey Lampe in particular questioned his equation of 'the seal' of the Spirit with the first anointing of the rite. Gregory developed his ideas but did not essentially change them. Above all he continued to insist on the important of confirmation and its essential unity with baptism as a single initiating event. He traced the history of the separation of the two parts of the rite linking it with the particular development of episcopacy in the west: once the local priest could baptise, 'confirmation' inevitably became isolated as a perfunctory ritual dependent on the increasingly irregular visit of an increasingly distant bishop. It lost most of its significance. Convinced as he was of the awesome honour of the Spirit bestowed on the Christian and their integration into the body, there must always have been a sad contrast in his mind between practice and origin. His experience was of contemporary (indeed his own) confirmation as a perfunctory liturgical affair with little theology other than a general emphasis on a private gift for individual faith. On the other hand, he had a vision of the early liturgy on the night of Easter. There the candidates, surrounded by the whole Church and led by the bishop, made their way through the series of solemn rituals by which they were incorporated into the living community of the Church.

Gregory regretted particularly the individualistic emphasis that had emerged in the mediaeval Church and had been strengthened and developed by the reformers. The Minutes of a 1946 conference he attended at Hawarden on confirmation make clear that he believed it to be about 'bringing into the Church' not about magically 'putting something into' the recipient.

The original association of oil with confirmation had all the appropriate associations of royal anointings. Confirmation was an entering into the dignity of the royal and priestly people of God. The clear link with the poured-out Spirit was then in turn a stress on the life to be lived in the Body. There again the emphasis was on the corporateness of the Church and at the centre, the guarantee of that, the bishop. In the 1936 paper Gregory wrote: 'From a period well before the end of the first century at the latest there is only one fully competent liturgical representative of the People of the New Covenant — the *episcopos*, the bishop....'

Somehow or other, despite all the other changes, the Anglican bishop had held on to the most important part of initiation, 'the Seal', and so there was scope still to emphasise confirmation in the twentieth century as entering, through the bishop, into the life of the Body of which he might still be the focus.

Gregory did not produce detailed proposals for liturgical or theological change in this area in his day, he argued rather that the Church should seize the pastoral opportunity to make the connection of baptism and confirmation clearer, holding onto the connection of confirmation and communion and so rediscovering the sense of initiation into a community, into a life to be lived together in the bestowed Spirit together nourished by the food of Holy Communion.

We have seen here one of Gregory's principles again at work. His first attention was paid to what he could discover of the actual liturgy of the Church, the Body's living worshipping activity, and he took that to be the clearer guide to the life and thought and priorities of the community at any time.

So we come to the central place that liturgy took in Dix's reflection on the Church. It fed that reflection and he fed back into it the fruit of his thought. The liturgy was itself creative — the work of the Church in living action, it was itself creative of the Church, feeding its life and nurturing its growth and development. This was Gregory's deepening conclusion in all his study especially in respect of the early Church. It was also his own personal daily experience participating in the liturgy of the Church through the prayers of his community and in his daily mass. It constituted his personal, spiritual 'home' and its influence and priorities extended through all his work.

In his 1936 essay on Confirmation he could say: 'The history and tradition of liturgy go back into the very Apostolic roots of Christianity in a sense in which it would be hard to say that the tradition of theological theory goes back.'[1] He went on to add, more mischievously: 'It would I believe be possible to put together a considerable monograph under the heading, "The Deleterious Influence of Theologians upon Christian Worship".'

In the same essay he said, 'liturgy is essentially a traditional, conservative popular thing....' and it is because of each of those adjectives that Gregory found himself attracted to working in this area and most suited to it also. Ten years later, in the 1946 paper on confirmation, he made a similar point: 'Liturgy is the vital act of the Church's life, in the end it will mould the ideas of those who live that life.'[2]

This instinct, as well as his research, led him to focus attention on liturgy as used by the ordinary Church: there could be seen religion at work, the real impact of changes, theology alive and active.

In his little book about the development of the reserved sacrament and its use as an object of devotion, *A Detection of Aumbries*[3] he notes:

> The aumbry seemed to put a stop or at least a hindrance to devotional practices which had been growing up in these regions (of the North) for some while, with clerical encouragement, no doubt, but largely out of a spontaneous turn of popular devotion. The use of the reserved sacrament as a focus or object of private prayer was all the dearer to the people and the parish clergy in that it was the outcome of religious instinct and personal devotion, and not of theological reasonings or of the ideas of authority as to what was good

1   *Ibid.*, p. 21.
2   The Theology of Confirmation in relation to Baptism, p. 32.
3   1942 Dacre, p. 36.

for them. The bishops in these regions evidently hesitated to challenge this popular feeling.

Although writing about the thirteenth century here, Dix's words were carefully chosen for the twentieth too. He felt a similar conflict was going on between authority and common feeling on precisely this subject. Gregory wanted to acknowledge some real authority in that popular feeling, allowing a place for the actual living devotion of the people alongside, or even over against, legal and statutory authority. Custom, the prevailing practice of the people, naturally achieved and slowly developed, ought to be a guiding principle. This became more important than canon law or liturgical regulations or even scholarly theory, however precise. All of these should work in conjunction with the former. In observing the Custom of the Church in its liturgy Gregory felt that all the flow and movement and ongoing life of the Body of Christ could be observed. From that observation the appropriate lessons for the modern Church might also then be drawn out.

Gregory never focused his attention exclusively on the detailed study of liturgy. Even when he became acknowledged as a leading exponent of liturgical study with the publication of *The Shape*, he did not abandon all his other interests. Nevertheless he always acknowledged liturgy as a focal point and felt its influence to be crucial, and so in amongst all his reading and study, liturgical texts and studies retained a central place.

He was part, in this sense, of the Liturgical Movement that had begun in the nineteenth century and he very much reaped the benefits of that movement. He was the right man in England with the right interests and instincts and skills to capitalise on the moment when it came.

The Liturgical Movement was very much Benedictine in origin, as monastic communities in France and Germany began to rediscover their musical and liturgical histories, exploring further and further back in the Church's past. By the turn of the century the Movement was wanting to emphasise the active participation of the laity in the liturgy and to underline the way in which the liturgy itself was the primary teacher of the faithful. From this developed the characteristic emphasis of the Movement on the Church as the Body of Christ and as the continuation of his Incarnation — continuing to make with him the Sacrifice of liturgy and life that distinguished the people of God. So the Movement developed a pastoral emphasis rather than a merely academic one, though many were also involved in scholarly research too.

In Anglicanism the Movement was obviously attractive to many Tractarians and some influence is discernible in the revisions of the 1920s. The scholarly work spread its impact too and Gregory entered into the fulness of it, imbibing both the continental and the English-speaking scholars' work. The Movement had its impact on the Parish Communion movement in England and, similarly, the Associated Parishes movement in the USA. In England Gabriel Hebert's books *Liturgy and Society* (1935), and then *The Parish Communion* (1937)[1], to which Gregory contributed, were landmarks in the development of the Movement's influence.

The background of the Liturgical Movement shared many characteristics with Gregory, though probably quite unconsciously for him. It too was scholarly and theological but ultimately focused on the life of the Church, and in particular on the shared life and liturgy of the people of God. The Movement's sensitivity to the formative character of the liturgy and to the need for lay participation were, as we have begun to see, characteristic of Dix's interest too.

In a file of notes which seem to date from about 1930 these ideas were already emerging. The notes may well have been the basis for lectures on liturgy to theological students at Nashdom, if so they provide a fascinating early glimpse into Gregory's own formation. He began by arguing for the corporate nature of the activity: 'the individual is incorporated into a regenerate race by baptism.' He went on to assert that, without sacraments: '... the Passion of our Lord would have

1   SPCK.

no efficacy on our souls since it would have no channels whereby to reach us.'

Here the tone seems to be more scholastic than he would later use but the argument is much the same. His characteristic emphasis on Jewish antecedents is there and in his analysis of the additions the early Church made to its synagogue worship we see already the germ of the later *Shape*. (Here though he seems to distinguish *five* events: (i) bread and wine set before the celebrant; (ii) a thanksgiving; (iii) the blessing of Bread; (iv) the blessing of Wine; (v) the Distribution.)

In writing about the 'Ante-Nicene Eucharist' he frankly admitted: 'We have no complete documents which represent this' but already he insisted that though the substance was extempore, nevertheless by 96 AD, the time of Clement, 'there was already a fixed eucharistic outline.' In a very characteristic way he contrasted the ready-made liturgies of the Reformation and the 'grown' liturgy of the ancient Church. From there he examined what he called the 'four great parent rites' — Antiochene, Alexandrian, Gallican and Roman.

This sketch reveals how long many of his ideas gestated in Gregory's mind, fed by other writers, absorbed from the tradition he was involved in, produced by his own originality of thought.

Between this sketch and *The Shape* lies Dix's continuing research and its first great blossoming in his text of Hippolytus in 1936. At about the same time he contributed his essay to Hebert's *The Parish Communion*. The essay, ' "The Church" in the Primitive Liturgies' outlined the simple shape of the early eucharist and then explored some of the implications of that outline. The themes which would later characterise *The Shape* began to emerge; offertory and sacrifice, action and corporateness, the People of God and clericalisation, the problems of the mediaeval Church distorted further by the Reformation. Above all he was clearly already convinced that the pre-Nicene 'model' was the appropriate paradigm for contemporary reflection. In a contribution to

Philips' appreciation of Walter Frere[1] Gregory reflected on
the older liturgist's influence in the twenties and thirties
especially on the actual development of liturgical revision.
He noted Frere's debt to the oriental tradition as opposed to
the mediaeval western view of the eucharist and then added
in parenthesis: 'In point of fact there seems to have been a
third line of evolution which he never envisaged, but which
may perhaps be that on which *Ecclesia Anglicana* will ultimately set out.'

He meant, we must presume, a return to the most primitive forms of the pre-Nicene model which has indeed become the paradigm for reform in the English Church, and
much further afield too. It was this 'third line' on which
Gregory himself was such a pioneer.

The seeds of *The Shape* were evident again in *The Parish
Communion* essay. Perhaps as he prepared the essay he found
himself reflecting on the need for a fuller treatment of the
many themes he touched on — themes which he indicated
as being closely linked. On the clericalisation of the liturgy
he remarked:

> The history of this revolution has never yet been traced and
> there is no space even to outline it here[2]....
>
> I think that when the history of this momentous change
> comes to be written in full there will be only one conclusion
> possible from the facts, namely, that the change in eucharistic
> theory and practice from a collective to a wrongly sacerdotal-
> ist conception of sacrifice is itself the result of a certain fading
> in the Church's own consciousness of herself as the Body of
> Christ.[3]

As he wrote those words did he perhaps begin to think that
he should be doing something about writing that 'history in
full' and 'tracing that revolution'? Certainly *The Shape*, among
other things, did precisely that.

1   *Ibid.*, 1947.
2   *Ibid.*, p. 132
3   p. 135.

The *Parish Communion* essay ends on a linkage of apparently unrelated themes which focused the essay, and indicated some of Gregory's contemporary concerns, as well as hinting at where his work might lead him:

> There are indications everywhere in the history of a subtle and (to me) unexpected connection between three things which at first sight might be supposed independent questions.
> 1. The conception of the Church as a whole, and not the 'celebrant', as the priest of the eucharistic offering.
> 2. The practice of frequent and general communion by the laity.
> 3. The extent to which the Church, regarding herself as a particular creation of God distinct from the world into which she was created, vindicates her own freedom in choosing her hierarchy in independence of the secular power.
> This last point may seem irrelevant, but I believe that... the abandonment of the choice of the hierarchy by the 'Spirit-bearing' Body of Christ does pre-suppose a very definite change from the idea of the Church held by e.g. Hippolytus. And I think it will be found that wherever and whenever that right has been effectively lost to the secular ruler... there and then with a curious precision it will be found that the practice of frequent and general communion by the laity rapidly declines, and the 'collective' character of the eucharistic sacrifice is soon lost sight of.[1]

Like Hebert and others in the Parish Communion movement and the wider Liturgical Movement, Dix felt that here was a way of rediscovering something of that collective character (even if, as yet, there seemed to be little opportunity for restoring any genuine sense of real choice by the people of their own hierarchy).

So we come to *The Shape of the Liturgy*. In the Introduction, Gregory explained how it began life as a paper read to the Cowley Fathers at their General Chapter in 1941. The original paper is not to be found among Gregory's papers but marked by the characteristic themes we can be certain that it was already noticed in Gregory's treatment of the liturgy

1   p. 135.

and its primitive roots — themes which are so fully developed in *The Shape* itself. He claimed that the book took fourteen months to write and admitted that its scope grew as he wrote it. This was partly because he was deliberately focusing on a 'less specialised public' but also because his work inevitably uncovered and exposed wider and deeper themes inextricably woven into the subject or, simply, areas which Gregory could not bear to leave alone. For instance, we know that the little book *A Detection of Aumbries* began life as a footnote or appendix to *The Shape*. In its published form it would have been an ungainly part of the bigger book both in length and in tone. The same might be said of other parts of the book that were left in. The extensive and not unpolemical treatment of Cranmer and the Books of Common Prayer does not always seem to sit comfortably or tidily with the rest of the book.

It was the book of over seven hundred pages, which came together in those early years of the war. Dense with scholarship and learning it yet holds onto a lightness of touch, especially in footnotes. While pursuing the most obscure minutiae of liturgica the book still constantly brings the reader back to the essential nature and reality of the Church and her worship. Dix scans the entire range of Church history with erudition and a sure hand but the modern situation is never far from the corner of the eye. In the Introduction is acknowledged too the shadow of the War and the uncertain world of the twentieth century.

We know that Gregory began writing while working in his brother's parish in Beaconsfield (this also is alluded to in the Introduction) but in due course it became clear to Gregory (and presumably at his persuasion to the Abbot) that the project required his full attention. He returned to Nashdom, to the Guest House, the monks having departed to West Malling. There he had access to the library and was not far from London and Oxford and their extensive research facilities.

In most ways *The Shape* is not primary research but the distillation of already well-digested scholarship and the dissemination of the work of others. Sometimes Gregory made

the insights of others into an insight of his own, sometimes
a startlingly fresh perception of his own emerged, his attention to the lives and the worship of the members of the Body
of Christ was never far away.

Gregory said that there was much re-writing of the book.
Given war-time conditions ensured it did not actually come
out until very early in 1945 (some copies seem to have been
available late in 1944) published at first by the Dacre Press
and later jointly with A. & C. Black. The *Church Times* noted
in February 1945 in its 'the Passing Week' column, that the
book had sold eight hundred copies in five days (at 45
shillings). Its reputation soon spread, there were eleven
reprints in rapid succession; it has never been out of print
since.

What did Dix himself think he was writing? What did he
feel such a book could contribute? Did he have a sense of its
significance?

The fate of the original manuscript of *The Shape* is unknown but the proofs do contain more than one version of
the Introduction. The original introduction declared the
book to be 'addressed mainly to Anglicans' but this was
clearly too much of a limitation and the phrase was soon
omitted. That highlighted an ambiguity in the book, noted
by Gregory, that the long section on the Cranmerian liturgy
could only be of secondary interest to non-Anglicans while
the rest of the book was truly catholic and accessible to all.

The manuscript of the same Introduction also said that
the book is intended for: 'the intelligent and thoughtful
Churchman — one is tempted to add "or bishop" '. The last
phrase is crossed out, no doubt as too flippant, but again it
suggests some of the tensions of the book. Deliberately
accessible to thoughtful laity as informative history, it is also
a polemical almost a political work. Opportunities to sting
the bishops, if only in a footnote, were not often resisted.

Dix seems to have believed, and no doubt others vigorously encouraged him, that he could write a history of the
eucharistic liturgy which employed all available modern
scholarship and insights, including his own. He felt he had

the appropriate skills to make such a work accessible to an intelligent but lay readership and that this was an important thing to do. In doing so he could also, directly and indirectly, comment on and contribute to contemporary controversies in this sphere.

The book fitted to some extent into his plan, outlined to Bévenot, for making the Church of England more truly or consciously catholic. He claimed in his letters to Freddy Green that this was part of his purpose and he may even have had some success in that aim. But it may be that the book actually worked so well and achieved so much not because of scholarship so much as depth of religious conviction. Whether he wanted to or not, Gregory could not help the quietly passionate force of his own eucharistic devotion pervading the book. Without distorting the scholarship it undergirded it as its unspoken complement until an appropriate moment invited its actual expression. Then the tone of the book adjusted to a new framework and a range of other significances which added a depth, subtlety and attractiveness far broader than any scholarship, however clear and precise. Gregory may have been to some degree conscious of his skill as a teacher of history and as an advocate of particular opinions but somehow his skill in teaching faith and devotion came from deeper within, its very natural-ness and uncontrived importance were his strength and power. These different elements were sometimes in conflict in the book. Some felt puzzled when asked to say just what kind of a book it was in the end. At its best the book fused all these elements into a work that was, and has remained, attractive to an amazingly wide readership, a work deep as well as broad, stylish as well as prayerful and witty as well as profoundly stimulating.

The shape of *The Shape* is not particularly tidy. It is essentially historical. Beginning with the New Testament and the earliest liturgies, it proceeds to discern three 'strata' in the development of the eucharist. The first is the pre-Nicene Stratum, the second the post-Nicene as far as the mediaeval development which becomes a third Stratum. At each level the eucharist acquires accretions which tend to cover up and distort its original shape. Gregory maps these and tries to explore what effect each has on the original shape during this process. At the end of the mediaeval period, with the Reformers, drastic revisions purport to be beginning again but, as is made very clear, what in fact happens is a further distortion of the existing strata. This is not least because liturgical scholarship in the sixteenth century was far from ready to embark on the revolution it knew was needed. At this point in *The Shape* Gregory focuses more or less entirely on the development of the *Book of Common Prayer*. There is somehow a difference of tone to this part of the book from the earlier. He explains his concentration on this, objectively speaking, part of part of a stratum in the introduction to this section[1] but there remains a sense of imbalance and 'mis-shape'. There is little developed treatment of continental reformed liturgies or of the Tridentine reforms. This section of the book does, however, include reflections on the process of liturgical reform — especially in the light of the 1928 attempt. Here Gregory is at his waspish, ironic but accurate best. The book concludes with a sweeping, devout overview that is both deeply theological and inspiringly prayerful. It includes what must be the most famous prose-song in praise of the eucharist in the English language. It is this climax of the book that in so many ways pervades its way back through all that has gone before.

We cannot hope to do justice to this huge work here. That is beyond the scope of the present work and the stated intentions of the author. What I hope to do is to assess the place of *The Shape*, where it fits into Dix's life and, if possible, to discern some of the reasons for its significance.

The themes of the book are many but there are some 'grand' ones and they are the familiar ones here given their fullest and most carefully-argued treatment.

The liturgy is corporate. It is the activity of the whole body of Christ, not of clergy on behalf of the rest, the priestly

1   p. 613.

offering of all the people of God together. This is because Christ's sacrifice enables him to offer eternally to the Father a redeemed race, a restored Body, made up of those who come to join with him in offering themselves. They do so not in addition to his sacrificial offering but inside it, as part of the work he has already done. This bodily-ness, then, this organic community inevitably implies the dignity of all the re-deemed, their special status together, their vital mutual dependence:

> Each communicant from the bishop to the newly confirmed gave himself under the focus of bread and wine to God, as God gives Himself to them under the same forms. In the united oblations of all her members the Body of Christ, the Church, gave herself to become the Body of Christ, the sacrament, in order that receiving again the symbol of herself now transformed and hallowed, she might be truly that which by nature she is, the Body of Christ, and each of her members, members of Christ. In this self-giving the order of laity no less than that of the deacons or the high-priestly celebrant had its own indispensable function in the vital act of the Body. The layman brought the sacrifice of himself, of which he is the priest. The deacon, the 'servant' of the whole body 'presented' all together in the Person of Christ, as Ignatius reminds us. The high-priest, the bishop, 'offered' all to-gether, for he alone can speak for the whole Body. In Christ, as His Body, the Church is 'accepted' by God 'in the Beloved'. Its sacrifice of itself is taken up into his sacrifice of Himself. On this way of regarding the matter the bishop can no more fulfil the layman's function for him.... than the layman can fulfil that of the bishop.[1]

This profound, mystical mutuality of the Church colours the whole book and its steady leaking out of the Church as it becomes increasingly clerical is one of Gregory's recurring laments. It is very much the offertory in the eucharist where this corporateness is made visible in this presentation and, while he is careful[2] to avoid letting the offertory pre-empt

1   p. 117.
2   See Footnote, p.119.

the eucharistic prayer itself, there is for him here a dignified, if almost silent, celebration of the mutuality of the Body of Christ as each member brings their offering to the deacon at the altar.

Gregory's recurring stress on the eucharist belonging to the ordinary worshipper and the importance of popular custom and practice clearly grows out of this same sense of the mutual dignity of all the members. Writing much later in the book, on the possibilities for liturgical reform he underlines the key role of custom:

> From the beginning until the sixteenth century, broadly speaking the sanction in liturgy was not 'law' but 'custom'. In its nature the authority of custom is a self-enforcing thing. If a large number of people cease to observe a custom then it just 'dies out'.... Its authority while it lives is a voluntarily accepted and natural thing, not a compulsive and artificial one. The peculiar appropriateness of such an authority for 'the glorious liberty of the children of God' in their worship of love needs no emphasis.[1]

A little later he adds:

> The depth and breadth and allusiveness of the classical rites comes just from this, that their real author is always the worshipping Church, not any individual however holy and gifted, any committee however representative, or any legislator however wise.... The good liturgies were not written: they grew.[2]

This is common prayer; worship of the people, a key theme in all his thinking, and important to the book at every point. It never, however, means superficial or glib prayer nor is it the 'lowest common denominator'. On the contrary this prayer of the people is where the subtle depths and profound mysteries of life in the body of Christ are to be found. That is, at least partly, why it is so important and so interesting.

This links another of the 'grand themes' of his work and this book in particular, that the Eucharist is an Action to be

1   pp. 716–7.
2   pp. 718–9.

performed, not a set of prayers to be said or a devotion in which to indulge. Dix is stark about this. His famous description of the primitive liturgy transferred from pagan Rome to modern London with the 'grocer from Brondesbury'[1] goes out of its way to stress the brevity of the event, its familiarity and its dependence on a sequence of straightforward actions shared in by all. His analysis of the New Testament material leads him famously to his 'four-action shape' and he continues to stress the action involved here, with the theology and devotion. The liturgy is always work to be done *together*, it is not a passive, remote event to be observed. It is not someone else saying things but an activity requiring positive participation. Again the ancient offertory focused this with each presenting their own 'gift' at the altar and then adding their voiced assent with the others to the dialogue of the eucharist prayer, actively agreeing to the bishop's prayer to God. In this emphasis on liturgy as corporate action lay a wholly different idea of worship and discipleship, a wholly different conception of the Body of Christ.

Gregory was sensitive to the accusation of 'pelegianism' just as the early Church had been. This activity was not to imply that the participants had anything to contribute to the sacrifice they were offering. They were not 'doing' anything directly in their own right to God. Rather the action was all God's and even as they participated in the liturgy it was forming them and creating them as the Body of Christ.

Here is another of the 'grand themes' of the book: the liturgy is formative of the Church. The Church does not make a eucharist for God but the eucharist is the means by which God in Christ fashions a body, a people, the people of God. 'The primitive Church did not create the eucharist. It would be less untrue to say that the eucharist created that primitive Church which preached the paradox of Messiah crucified, the power of God and the wisdom of God.'[2]

1   p. 142.
2   p. 77.

Gregory is convinced of the absolutely fundamental and deliberate connection by Jesus of the Last Supper and the meaning of his death and resurrection. He saw in the actions of Jesus at the Supper the careful provision of a framework for understanding what had happened, a structure within which the meaning could be entered into once again, and a shape of actions which when repeated, would nourish in the participants a life together fed by Jesus himself.

In the eucharist the unity of the Body of Christ is fashioned. Gregory was fond of quoting words of Augustine on this theme, using them in more than one place:

> As Augustine was never tired of repeating to his African parishioners in his sermons, 'So the Lord willed to impart His Body, and His Blood which He shed for the remission of sins. If you have received well, you are that which you have received.' Your mystery is laid on the Table of the Lord, your mystery you receive. To that which you are you answer 'Amen', and in answering you assent. For you hear the word (of administration) 'the Body of Christ' and you answer 'Amen'. Be a member of the Body of Christ that the Amen may be true.[1]

Gregory later adds: 'As the anamnesis of the passion, the eucharist is perpetually creative of the Church, which is the fruit of that passion.'[2]

If these are some of the 'grand themes' which run through the book it is also dense with subsidiary themes and ideas which flow from them. The roughly historical structure of the book does not prevent Gregory from extensive treatment of developing theologies as he progresses, indicating the different stages of development. He deals in detail with the steady assimilation of liturgy to a sense of time rather than its earlier stark focus on the *eschaton*, the kingdom still to come, the primary context of eternity. This accompanies the settlement of the Church into a much closer relationship with the state — in the fourth century and after. With it

1   p. 247.
2   p. 248.

begins the ever greater elaboration of ceremonial, vesture and ornament. In many ways this is already the beginning of the end for Gregory though he continues to detail the developments of the subsequent centuries and to explain them as far as he can. He explores some of the social and moral implications of developments too and, while concentrating on the West, notices the pattern of things in the East as well. Nevertheless the Church of his 'grand themes', the corporate, common, eucharistic Church, simple in its liturgical action, persecuted for its tenacity, constantly renewed by its faithfulness in worship, that Church was the pre-Nicene Church, the primitive community, the glow at the beginning of the book which sheds its light on all the subsequent chapters. Kenneth Stevenson (in *A Portrait of Dom Gregory* a booklet published in 1980) remarked: 'It's a quite extraordinary thing to find a book that reads like a novel but is in fact a serious contribution to scholarship.'

It was certainly this accessibility that made the book so powerful. Many attested in letters and reviews at the time of publication how much they had gained from it and this continued to be the case. In a letter to the Revd. K.C. Millington[1] Gregory claimed to have traced thirty or forty episcopal orders for the book and he said that the Archbishop was recommending all the bishops to read it. One bishop had said to him, 'what you have done — at the very least — is to make it quite certain that the next-time Prayer Book revision is taken up it will have to be a wholly new book, not a revision of the old one, so far as concerns the eucharist.'

Above all, though, the letters show that is was parish clergy and interested lay people who were working their way through the book, absorbing the whole detailed, lively background to the contemporary situation and as a result beginning to enter thoughtfully and critically into the current liturgical debates of the Church. This breaking out of the scholarly coterie of liturgical reflection was the major impact

1   1.9.45.

of the book and entirely consistent with Gregory's feelings about liturgy and about liturgical scholarship.

So the letters came, full of gratitude for the book, with comments and questions and disagreements. They came from far afield. The Bishop of Barbados wrote requesting a consultation on revising the liturgy, continental scholars wrote with queries and doubts. Free-Church and Roman Catholic laity and scholars wrote in gratitude and enquiry. Roman Catholic scholars were not consistently positive, some seeing it as a 'mere tract'. Dom R. H. Connolly's copy at Downside Abbey is notoriously heavily annotated by him. Gabriel Hebert wrote to say that he appreciated the book because it was at once 'critical and believing' and, he added, 'you have lit a candle.'

Not surprisingly the book received good reviews very quickly. The *Church Times* called it 'liturgy made thrilling' and even evangelical reviewers, for example in *The Record*, acknowledged its power while questioning some of its theses. Max Warren, a leading evangelical, wrote in gratitude for the book while defending evangelicals against Gregory's attack over the subject of liturgical reform.[1] W.S. Porter wrote a very positive review for *Laudate* calling it 'the greatest book since Duchesne', and E.C. Ratcliff, himself a leading liturgist, who had seen parts of *The Shape* before publication, was impressed by it, grateful for its reference to continental liturgists and for its new insights into the New Testament material.

The book continued to make its impact, becoming in time a basic text book and one that had to be acknowledged even if to be disagreed with. Dom Benedict Stewart, with whom Gregory had corresponded extensively, published a book in 1953 called *The Development of Christian Worship* and called *The Shape* 'a real summing-up and also a development of the most recent liturgical study'. He saw it as a continuation of the work of the leading liturgist Edmund Bishop and remarked that it had been 'favourably reviewed by the Catholic press'.

1   p. 720.

J.D. Crichton, another leading liturgist said that *The Shape* was 'worthy of taking the place of Mgr Duchesne's *Origines du Culte Chrétien*' and Dom Bernard Botte, editor of a later critical edition of Hippolytus and fellow liturgist acknowledged that 'I recognise that I owe him a great deal.' Maurice Bévenot kept in touch with Gregory through the early days of the reception of *The Shape* and, while arguing with him over certain points, he acknowledges its impact. He reviewed it for *The Month*.' He adds: 'Your intention was only to gild the anti-protestant pill you were administering, the effect has been to consolidate anti-Romanism (to judge from the number of times I have heard of requests for a 'reply' to Gregory Dix).'

It was not only Roman Catholics who noticed the book. Gregory received long letters from non-conformists too including E.H. Robertson, a Baptist Minister in St. Albans. He acknowledged he was using *The Shape* to revise his own Holy Communion service. Gordon Rupp, the Methodist, wrote also in gratitude from Cambridge with suggested reading on Protestantism.

The book, and its ideas, quickly began to affect liturgical revision, though not immediately in England. Ironically, one of the first places to take Dix's analysis seriously was South India. Steadily, through the 1950s, the structure he had outlined began to be seen as the appropriate shape for revision. In a different way, too, John Robinson at Clare College in Cambridge acknowledged his debt to Gregory's work in his book *Liturgy Coming to Life*[1] where he describes how the college chapel developed the Prayer Book service into a much more communal event, using Gregory's four-action shape.

Inevitably the book led Gregory into controversy, perhaps most famously with G.B. Timms in *The Church Quarterly Review* on the subject of Cranmer. He was challenged then, and more recently, for his overconfident assertions about the earliest period when the evidence was really too scant. He

1   Mowbray 1960.

was criticised for over-simplifying a very complex textual and
theological situation and for a lack of objectivity, particularly
when it came to Cranmer and the Book of Common Prayer.

In his recent book *The Search for the Origins of Christian
Worship*,[1] Paul Bradshaw shows that Gregory was generally too
confident with his theories. There is, for instance, just too
little evidence for the character of first-century synagogue
worship for confident assertions to be made about its universal similarity with the first part of the early Christian liturgy.
The assertions can often, at best, be only hypotheses and
possibilities. Nevertheless Bradshaw acknowledges the pervasive influence of Gregory's ideas especially about *The Shape*
and the Jewish connections.

So now we can go back to the book and look at some of
these important ideas in a little more detail.

Was it full of new and revolutionary ideas? As so often with
books that make this kind of impact it was a combination of
some new ideas presented with those of other scholars,
worked together into a succinct and fascinating picture that
was persuasively and attractively presented. Again, some of
the ideas were very simple and actually obvious but, unnoticed before, they now seemed revolutionary.

How radical was Dix prepared to be? He wrote as an
'orthodox catholic' and part of his purpose was precisely to
further that cause, but he was not afraid of Biblical criticism
nor using the theological and philosophical insights of recent
years. He acknowledged his debt to scholars like C.H. Dodd.
He was prepared to depart from catholic pious theology and
accept that the Last Supper could not itself be a eucharist
(this led to some vigorous correspondence) and he seems to
have been quite radical on the question of 'the Second
Coming' as we shall see later.

But his simplest, most fundamental themes are radical
enough. He brought to an end the search for the original
prayer-forms of the Christian eucharist. He argued that it was
not words that were original but a shape which he maintained

1   1992 SPCK.

was discernible everywhere. He drew out the four actions of the eucharist also stressing the 'activity' of the Taking of the bread and wine, the Blessing of the bread and wine, the Breaking of the bread, the Sharing of the bread and wine. Scholars have argued in different ways about each of the four actions and about whether they should have equal weight, but the simple pattern has become extraordinarily influential both in the study of liturgy and in its revision and creation. Less of a discovery than a careful piece of analysis, it did transform the liturgical scene.

The Shape emerged from Gregory's analysis of New Testament and other early texts in the light of his interest in the Jewishness of the early Christian community and of the importance of what could be learnt from Jewish prayers and structures and institutions of the same period. In his enthusiasm Gregory sometimes read too much out of scant material but nevertheless it allowed him to be critical of theories of Greek mystery and other obscure pagan influences so early on. The first community was made up of Jews following a Jew and this inevitably remained a powerful factor. Thomas Talley, the liturgical scholar, recalling the first time he had heard Gregory lecture in the States remembered his emphasis in an article in *Worship*,[1] 'From Berakah to Eucharistia: a Reopening Question.' 'I can still remember [verbatim it seems] his opening sentence: "Our understanding of our forms of worship underwent a radical transformation some forty years ago when it finally occurred to someone that Jesus was a Jew." '

Gregory argued that the *Synaxis* (the first part of the Christian liturgy made up of readings and psalms, sermon and prayers) was simply the Christian community continuing to do what it had always done in the synagogue. This part of the liturgy was at first distinct from the eucharist though often in fact held immediately prior to it. The eucharist itself he argued was descended from the *Chaburah* meals Jesus held with his friends. The *Chaburah* was a particular form of

1   1976, p. 50.

association for a group of friends or colleagues; it involved special meals together and those meal times included special fellowship prayers and graces. Such meals were shared together by the apostolic band with Jesus during his ministry. On the night before his death he made particular provision to share such a supper with them and during that supper transformed all such future suppers for ever. Gregory was insistent that it was Jesus who instituted the Eucharist and that he did so deliberately. It was not a later invention of the early Church. Thus the occasion was not in fact the Passover meal, for all its powerful connotations, but just a special supper which would have included both the ordinary graces of any Jewish meal and a special grace over the cup at the end for this special group of people, the *Chaburah*.

Dix was soon attacked for lack of evidence for the *Chaburah* in this period. He continued to argue that it was likely but maintained that, even without the details of that 'institution', his analysis of the origins of the eucharist need change very little. What Jesus instituted was, in fact, nothing new: they were to continue to do what they had always done in blessing bread and sharing the cup. What was stark and new was a sharp and deep meaning for the events provided by the two phrases 'This is my body', 'This is my blood.' The command to 'Do this' was not new. Jesus could expect they would always continue to share meals in this way but now transformed by the phrase 'in remembrance of me'.

In Gregory's theory the early Church in fact very quickly left out the actual meal part of the eucharist (perhaps this was Gentile influence) and reduced what had been seven actions with the bread and cup separately to the classic four actions in which the bread and wine are taken, blessed and shared together, and the bread broken, as Jesus commanded 'in remembrance of me'.

Looking behind the earliest eucharistic traditions, Gregory discerned further Jewish influence in the prayers themselves, even though he continued to argue there was not one standard original prayer. The prayers echo the *berakah* of the Jewish tradition: the prayers blessing God and in particular the *Birkat ha-mazon* or grace after a meal. He followed other scholars in making this suggestion but it fitted well with his thesis, drawing out again the Jewish character of the early liturgy. In particular it stressed that the early eucharistic prayer was characterised by thanksgiving, the universal theme of these prayers, blessing God for his goodness. Only after this opening series of Thanksgivings to God and in consequence of them is any petition made.

Gregory believed that this continuity with Jewish institutions and the continuing influence of the Jewish world on the early Christian world had made a huge difference and needed to be much more widely acknowledged. In a lecture in Edinburgh in 1949 on *Changes in Christian Worship in the First Century AD* he acknowledged how accusations of 'Hellenisation' of 30 years ago had given way to a recognition of Paul's rabbinic, Pharisaic and Jewish antecedents. He could now foresee a coming over-emphasis on 'Judaising' with 'the rabbinising of a Galilean gospel'.

He argued that the meeting of this powerful Jewish development in the Christian sect with the world of the Gentile Graeco-Roman institutions and thought, was explosively creative at a moment of maximum potential for the two coming together.

Certainly the Jewish dimension of Christian origins has become a major area of study even if, inevitably, scholars have become more and more cautious about what can be positively said of the period.

Three further related themes are worth commenting on briefly within this context; *anamnesis*, sacrifice and eschatology.

Jesus said, 'Do this in remembrance of me.' Behind 'in remembrance of me' lies the Greek word *anamnesis* over which Gregory reflected much. His thoughts on this concept have contributed much to general considerations about what the eucharist is actually for and how it 'remembers' Christ and his action. In his contribution to Hebert's book on *The Parish Communion*[1] Gregory wrote:

1   1937, SPCK.

> The eucharistic sacrifice in the early writings and liturgies
> hinges upon the word *anamnesis*, which is not easy to translate
> adequately. Words like 'memorial', 'remembrance 'have in
> English a connotation of something which is itself 'absent'.
> *Anamnesis* has, on the contrary, the sense of 're-calling', of
> making a past thing 'present' again, so that it is here and now
> operative by its effects.... It is as the *anamnesis*, in this active
> sense, of the Paschal Sacrifice of Christ, as the 're-calling' of
> it before God and man so that it is here and now operative
> by its effects, that the Eucharist is the effectual offering by
> the Church of the Sacrifice of Calvary, the 'solemn proclama-
> tion of the Lord's death till He come.'[1]

Dix identified this sense of 'active re-calling' as originating
in Jewish thought-patterns and it continued to be a basic
assumption behind his thinking in *The Shape* and elsewhere.
The idea implies activity and stresses the present moment
rather than the past and also something done collectively.
The command of Jesus to his followers to 'Do this for the
anamnesis of me' is a command for a collective action on the
part of those who will be his continuing life, his Body. In
obeying the command and 're-calling' into the living present
the action of Christ they will be creating themselves, or
allowing themselves to be created, as the living reality of
Christ.

Here the concept of *anamnesis* leads into the theme of
sacrifice. The word sacrifice in connection with the eucharist
was, and still is, fraught with partisan sensitivities. Mediaeval
ideas of the priest's sacrifice had allowed people to see some
kind of re-slaughtering of Christ. The reformers had studi-
ously and consciously emphasised the once-for-all nature of
the sacrifice of Calvary (as Cranmer does in the Book of
Common Prayer). In the catholic tradition, however, the
sacrifice of the mass remained an important idea and one
dear to Gregory. He wanted to explore how it should be
re-thought within a restored and refined catholic liturgical
theology. The way ahead here seemed to be through the
concept of *anamnesis* especially in connection with the offertory.

1   Hebert, pp. 120, 121.

Without going into detail on the sacrificial system of the
Old Testament (Hebert thought he should have done) Dix
maintained that it expressed the relationship of the people
of Israel, as a people, with God. The system was fulfilled in
Christ, and his death and resurrection were given a sacrificial
interpretation very deliberately by Jesus at the Last Supper.
So the process of *anamnesis* involves specifically the 'recalling', the 're-presenting', of a sacrifice. It is this sacrifice
which creates, and keeps on creating, the Church. Within it
each Christian member of the body has the dignity of presenting him or herself to become part of that recreated
Church, in becoming part of the sacrifice. As each present
their offertory of bread and wine they present themselves to
be sacrificed and renewed. When the bishop-president, on
behalf of all, recites the prayer which recalls the sacrifice of
Christ that sacrifice is again presented to God and in it are
taken up the self-offerings of all the people. All together are
transformed and 'returned' in the sacrament of the Body and
Blood which feeds the Body with new life and so makes it
the one Body of Christ. The sacrifice of the mass is an
offering of the whole community within the one offering of
Christ: it is not a repetition but an 'entering-again-into', it is
not a priestly privilege but the natural and normal activity of
the Body of Christ in its eucharistic liturgy.

At the very end of *The Shape* Gregory wrote:[1]

> This (the Eucharist) is the whole life of the Church and of
> the Christian expressed, fulfilled, done, in an action; for as
> Goethe (I think) says somewhere 'the highest cannot be
> spoken, it can only be acted.' The more we can learn to think
> of our own worship at the eucharist not in terms only of
> assistance at a pleading or recollection of a redemption two
> thousand years ago, nor yet in terms only of 'my communion'
> (however true these partial understandings may be) but in
> terms of the 'pan-human' fulfilment of the Messianic sacri-
> fice, the nearer we shall be to entering into the mind of the
> apostolic Church about the eucharist and the further from
> most of our present controversies.

1   pp. 751–52.

The third concept which was always part of the shape and
context of Dix's thinking and writing was eschatology. He
felt the importance of reflecting on the eucharist in the
framework of a Jewish concept of time with its clear sense of
the End, the *Eschaton* to come with the Messianic Age. For
Christians the Messianic Age had already been inaugurated
by Christ and the eucharist is the Messianic banquet, it is
already the place where destiny is fulfilled and the End-Time
is entered into and experienced. This is the special work of
the Spirit, given in the eucharist, and keeping alive in the
Body the reality of the kingdom. It was with the Peace of
Constantine in the fourth century and the Church's accommodation with the world and the State that the long, steady
atrophying of that dimension began. Rediscovering by reflection on the eucharist this sense of the 'End of Things'
experienced now, of a world renewed and tested here, of a
kingdom to be lived in royally and immediately, was part of
Gregory's longing for the Church and one of his underlying
motivations.

Further and perhaps more radical reflections on eschatology were focused in two footnotes of *The Shape*. Turning to
the idea of the 'Second' Coming of Christ, usually associated
with Christian eschatology, he pointed out that the New
Testament and early Christian writers never speak of a 'Second' coming but only of 'the Coming':

> Speaking tentatively and with a due sense of the difficulties
> of the matter, it looks as though for the original Christian
> eschatology we have to get behind the teaching of S. Paul,
> for whom the *parousia* or 'Coming' of our Lord is always in
> the future, at a 'last judgement' at the end of time. This is
> an adaptation for the benefit of gentiles.[1]

Then in a fascinating footnote:

> Yet that S. Paul himself shared and understood the more
> Jewish eschatology seems clear from 1. Cor. X. 11. where he
> speaks of Christians 'upon whom the ends of the ages are

1   p. 262

come.' As Fr L.S. Thornton C.R. points out: '... a better translation would be: "For whom the ends of the ages overlap." ' 'The present age' and 'the coming age' meet in the Church. And I would add, especially at the eucharist.

In the immediately preceding footnote he explored this territory a little further by reference to an essay of W.K. Lowther Clarke called *The Clouds of Heaven*. Interestingly many of these themes were to be explored later by J.A.T. Robinson in his book, *Jesus and his Coming*.[1] In the footnote Gregory quoted Lowther Clarke as saying:

> When our Lord said: 'Ye shall see the Son of Man sitting at the right hand of power and coming in the clouds of heaven', He referred to his Ascension, not to a Descent; to this vindication by the Father and only indirectly to a judgement of this world. The true meaning of His words was gradually lost until in the second century they were taken to mean 'a coming from heaven.

Dix then commented:

> So far as I have any means of judging, the materials assembled by Dr Clarke entirely bear out his contention, which seems to me in line with much in the Jewish pre-history of Christian eschatology. But such a view calls for a drastic revision of current theories about primitive Christian messianism and eschatology generally, and in particular of the relation of the 'second coming' (*parousia*) to the paschal sacrifice of Christ in his death, resurrection and ascension together.

He had little opportunity to explore this much further but the notes reveal his permanent spirit of careful enquiry and his strong sense of rootedness in the eucharist.

All this taken together suggests how important he thought the Jewish background to the early Church. He observed and documented how this came into tension, sometimes fruitful and sometimes not, with the Graeco-Roman world, its ideas and institutions. He traced the impact of the 'Peace of the Church' and the advantages and compromises that devel-

1   SCM, 1957.

oped from the 'Christianisation' of the empire. This was seen as a crucial event, deeply and permanently altering the Church's life throughout the whole mediaeval period, the Reformation and Counter-Reformation and on, still powerfully, even into the twentieth century. In all this he consistently noted the conservatism of the Roman liturgy itself. Focused on the papacy, always the last to incorporate accretions and innovations, it is often a unique resource for echoes of the most ancient liturgical practices. In certain liturgies, such as the liturgy of Good Friday, it preserves intact something pure and primitive. There is a reverence here for the Papal, an affection for the Roman as the natural and proper guardian of the primitive and the pure together with an element of nostalgia and romanticism.

The liturgy in its developing strata was inextricably entwined with the growing clericalisation of the Church's worship performed by the priest for the people. The laity found other things to do since they were no longer part of the action (not even the communion). Gregory explored the developing devotional provision for lay people within, but distinct from, the liturgy; the private prayers to say, the individual and personal devotions to make. He examined the late mediaeval text, Langforde's *Meditations in the Time of Mass*, widely used in the fifteenth century. This he compared directly with Richard Baxter's seventeenth-century Reformed liturgy pointing out the considerable similarities. Here he noted an emotional intensity and individualistic piety which has been substituted for the collective, active participation of the primitive liturgy. (In other places in his writings he identified this emotionalism and individualism as a specifically Germanic, Teutonic or Northern European trait.) The underlying idea of the Church, and the place of the laity in it, had completely changed: liturgy has become a very different activity.

This led in the next chapter of *The Shape* to Gregory's treatment of the Cranmerian Prayer Books and the state of official liturgy in England. One of the more polemical portions of the book deserves some further consideration. There were other matters of controversy too, however, to be noted briefly first.

We have referred already to the offertory and noticed that Gregory wanted to avoid any idea of pre-empting the Eucharistic Prayer. Nonetheless his promotion of the importance of the offertory remains a point of contention and controversy. He saw the bringing up of the people's gifts, their presentation by the deacons and their offering to God by the bishop as constituting together the single first action of his shape, the Taking of the Bread and Wine. He included the 'imposition of hands' by the bishop and presbyters on the gifts[1] but did not distinguish that as a separate event (the real Taking) as some scholars have wanted to do. For Gregory the first great dramatic and symbolic Action of the Eucharistic liturgy is what he calls the offertory, this collective presenting of the Bread and Wine. The controversy over this, especially among Evangelicals, concerns the apparent implication that here the Church does have something independently and in its own right to bring to God, rather than coming empty and wholly in need. Dix maintained that the dignity of the Church by baptism and confirmation and the continuous sense of participation in Christ meant that the offertory was not only justified but singularly appropriate both theologically and scripturally. Nevertheless this controversy continues and some believe that Gregory's emphasis has unduly influenced modern liturgies.

A second area of controversy concerns the epiklesis: words in the eucharistic prayer invoking the specific action of the Holy Spirit to make the Bread and Wine the Body and Blood of Christ. This invocation was a feature of Eastern liturgies and theologies and had occurred in the 1928 Prayer Book eucharistic rite. Walter Frere considered it important but Gregory believed that it was a late development, and not authentic in the text of Hippolytus. He argued both in his essay in *The Parish Communion* and in *The Shape* that in origin it was a prayer not for the changing of the bread and wine but

1   p. 111.

for the *communicants*, on whom the Spirit came down in the communion of the blessed bread and wine. So the Holy Spirit is seen as *in* the elements by reason of the consecration, it is not the Spirit who consecrates as a result of a specific invocation.

The controversy was significant because it related to the idea of a specific moment of consecration during the eucharistic prayer rather than to the idea of the entire prayer being consecratory. Gregory wanted to defend the unity of the prayer though he stressed too the central 'consecratory' importance of the Words of Institution; very much a Roman and mediaeval emphasis. It was significant to him that, as he saw it, the primitive Roman prayers contained no such special invocation of the Holy Spirit.

Once again the controversy continues with *epiklesis*-like prayers in or out of modern liturgies, in various positions, indicating a variety of theologies of consecration and a variety of attempts at compromise.

Gregory argued that the reformers were too close to the distorted liturgical developments of the late middle ages to be able adequately to escape from them and prepare truly primitive liturgies. It might equally be argued that for all his sensitivity to primitive liturgies Gregory was himself still too close to the heritage of the Prayer Book to offer a detached critique. All the ecclesiastical and parliamentary difficulties of the 1928 Prayer Book were still fresh in people's minds and Gregory had decided opinions about that book and the Church-State situation. But it was not just recent history that undermined Gregory's objectivity: he seems to have found it difficult to be historically objective about Thomas Cranmer.

Back in the mid 1920s in his notebooks as a history lecturer, at Keble he presents Cranmer as time-serving and hypocritical: 'Cranmer recanted to save his life and only returned to Protestantism when he found he was going to suffer in any case.' Other occasional comments in the following years reveal a lack of sympathy and a readiness to blame

Cranmer in large measure for the difficulties of the Church of England.

By the time he came to write *The Shape* however, Gregory would seem to have decided that he could more effectively damn Cranmer with faint praise than by an open expression of his real dislike. The treatment of Cranmer is an important part of *The Shape* because he is properly acknowledged to stand behind the modern English liturgical situation as still its major influence. Gregory was more than ready to acknowledge Cranmer's beauty of language, clarity, and the careful correspondence between his theology and its expression. In a lecture to the Chelmsford Diocesan Worship and Art Association in 1945[1] he spoke of Cranmer's liturgies having: 'exquisite beauty and craftsmanship... not only in their noble language which makes them a superb piece of literature but in their delicate liturgical construction'.

He argued that Cranmer was deliberately clear about what he intended the eucharistic rite to be — a reminder of Christ's sacrifice, an *aide-mémoire* and very definitely not a sacrifice, an *anamnesis* or a mass. In the same lecture he went on to make this point — and to add a twist from his theories about North European influences:

> They [Cranmer's liturgies] are not disordered attempts at a catholic rite. On the contrary they are the crown of medievalism in religion, the climax of that mediaeval development of eucharistic devotion which for three centuries had been steadily drifting away from primitive practice and understanding of the liturgy towards that purely subjective interpretation of the eucharist which came into its full growth in the sixteenth century. They are neither Syriac nor Greek in their understanding of form, but mediaeval — for emotionalism is the great discovery of the Middle Ages in religion, the infusion of the Teutons, into the Christian Church.

Everything Cranmer did in re-shaping the rite from 1549 to 1552 was deliberately to exclude any perception of the new rite as a mass, as a continuity with any of the theology of the

1   18th Sept.

old rite. Gregory supported his argument with extensive reading in, and quotation from, Cranmer's own writings and demonstrated, certainly to his own satisfaction, that Cranmer had come to follow the more radical teachings of the Swiss reformer Zwingli. He argued that he had in fact reached this position by the mid 1540s so that all his subsequent work was coloured by it. He went on to argue that, nevertheless, the Church of England itself never formally accepted that theology and continued, in fact, to maintain a much 'higher', if less explicit, doctrine.

The modest revision of 1559, after Cranmer's death, added the following words to the administration of communion: 'The body of our Lord Jesus Christ which was given for thee preserve thy body and soul unto everlasting life.'[1] This effectively undercut Cranmer's theology and restored a quite other layer of theological meaning to the rite but a layer entirely consistent with the Church's intention as opposed to Cranmer's. What matters, of course, is what the Church intends, not any of its individual members, and so Dix could argue that, despite Cranmer's Zwinglianism, this did not ultimately alter the catholic continuity of the Anglican rite. In this way he was able to distance himself completely from the theology Cranmer espoused while at the same time maintaining the catholicity of Cranmer's Church. Gregory has been criticised from more than one direction for this. Many have argued that Cranmer was far less clearly Zwinglian than Gregory maintained and, in particular, that Cranmer's rite is much more ambiguous. Equally others have argued that there is a much less clear division between Cranmer's intention and that of his Church. It was controversy over his attitude to Cranmer that led Gregory into a famous debate with G.B. Timms after the publication of *The Shape*. Controversy was, of course, inevitable. Many Anglicans had been persuading themselves for a long time that Cranmer had intended to create a 'half-way house' between the Catholic and Protestant positions, a middle way, liturgi-

1 *BCP*, Holy Communion.

cally and theologically. Now to be told, cogently and authoritatively, that Anglican liturgy set out to be radically protestant was something of a shock.

Gregory had problems with Cranmer for more than one reason. He recognised that Cranmer's Nominalist philosophy meant that he had difficulty with the idea of transubstantiation and he saw how this underlying philosophy continued to affect his work in the Church generally and the liturgy in particular. More than anything else, however, Gregory could not understand or excuse Cranmer's erastianism, his readiness to cede to the king complete control over the Church and the spiritual realm. This linked directly with the strength of Gregory's feelings about Church and State and he was ready to assign to Cranmer much of the blame for the Anglican settlement and its continuing effects.

In an extraordinary passage of *The Shape* he draws together his feelings about Cranmer and the Church situation of the sixteenth century and presents them as if through the mind of Cranmer as he went to the stake in 1556. The writing has a 'stream-of-consciousness' quality to it which might be expected to mean sympathy for the subject, Cranmer. In fact the effect is the opposite and we begin to feel him a pathetic, self-absorbed and unattractive character. On his way to the stake Dix pictured him thinking of those who had also died in the same way including many in whose executions he had been instrumental:[1]

> They had all died, almost every one he had ever known—and thousands more unknown—and many others still to die —in these quarrels about the bread and the Body—that could never have blazed so fiercely in England or spread so far but for his work.—If he had used his position as archbishop altogether otherwise, to reform the old religion, not to make a new prevail?—Impossible! If a man saw the truth so clear, it was a duty to impose it—if the king were willing. —Would English Christians always be rent henceforward? — (Here was the stake at last) — This was what it all came

1   pp. 673–74.

to in the end — the bread had nothing to do with the Body
— That was what he was dying for.'

One might feel there is more of Gregory's mind in this
passage than Cranmer's and that in fact we are being ma-
nipulated. There is little sensitivity to the very different
world of the sixteenth century — the value of life, the role
of the monarch and state, the place of religion. Rather the
writing invites us simply to see Cranmer as responsible for
many deaths, for a 'new' religion and for the divisions of
English Christians. His summary of Cranmer's thought, 'the
bread had nothing to do with the Body', is at best crude, at
worst perverse. His skill is used in imaginative writing in a
way that begins to go against his own best principles. He
found it difficult to be objective about Cranmer because
Cranmer came to represent for him all that was wrong with
the Church of England. His feelings here were not merely
academic and intellectual but ultimately deeply personal and
spiritual and from the very core.

The Shape was written in the wake of the failed attempt at
reform in the 1928 Prayer Book. Liturgical development and
reflection had not gone away, if anything it had intensified
right across the Churches. The book provided extensive
background material for that development, some of it quite
new, and a controversial reflection on the Book of Common
Prayer. Gregory went further and, with his tongue somewhat
in his cheek, made suggestions about what the process of
reform ought to be. These ideas are contained in an 'Additional Note: The Present Liturgical Position in the Church
of England' added to chapter XVI.[1] He suggested that a group
of bishops could authorise a new rite for experimental use in
their dioceses for seven years, during which time clergy and
laity could make suggestions and alterations in the light of
practice which would then be considered as part of the
development of a renewed liturgy. The emphasis therefore
was on a developing *custom* in liturgy, a liturgy that grew with
people's use of it rather than being imposed from above.

1   p. 699.

Here again was Gregory's intense dislike of 'worship according to statute' and his promotion of the key principle of popular custom and liturgy as a natural growing and developing in the community of God's people. Whether his suggestions have been explicitly tried anywhere is difficult to say but certainly in the decades since *The Shape* some Churches have seen the importance of experiment and 'trial use'. Gregory's 'seven years' would not seem to be nearly long enough. The thirty or forty years from the first new liturgies of the 1960s to the end of the century may prove to have been something like the necessary period of experiment. For the most part, final decisions on liturgies have continued to remain, sometimes uncomfortably, with synods and lawmakers.

Dix never seems to have ventured to say what a renewed liturgy would actually in detail look like. He was frequently asked, especially after *The Shape*, to make suggestions and actually to compose rites. Requests came from Canada and Bermuda, from the Bishop of Ripon with regard to English liturgies, and from many individuals in England, South India and elsewhere. He was perhaps wise to resist. His reluctance was certainly consistent with his principles. In *Theology* in 1938[1] in an essay on 'Primitive Consecration Prayers' he wrote: 'all liturgies are the continuous product of the organic life, not only of individual Churches, but in some sense of the whole Church. The liturgy is too great a thing to be controlled by individual men.'[2]

This was his argument in *The Shape* too. In the meantime he went on saying his Roman Tridentine mass day by day.

In a letter to Marcus Stevens in 1936 he revealed something of his own liturgical taste:

Personally, I detest Pontifical Mass. It is such a commotion. I know it's mostly all very primitive and all that (though that is to my mind irrelevant. 'Primitiveness' is merely the rod Jezebel has laid up in pickle for her own back and which I

1   Vol. 37, p. 261.
2   p. 282.

shall always most joyously brandish.) But I think the Middle. Ages effected two vast improvements in devotion — frequency of Confession and a solitary Low Mass. However, I suppose since the Church requires it Pont. Mass must be right and my faults of taste and devotion will no doubt be corrected as I come to understand her mind better. But — there is a lot of palaver!

The Shape was not about the detailed ingredients of a renewed liturgy nor even about a comprehensive presentation of the background to the modern liturgical situation. It was that, but it was much more too. It became for him a celebration and affirmation of the crucial central place of the eucharist in the life of the Church and so in turn of the world. When he had ground all his axes, and the book does have axes to grind though the main one is probably Cranmer, he moved instead into writing that is quietly passionate in its devotion. There is little in the book that is merely archaeological while on the other hand the opportunities are often taken to move from detached scholarship into the devotional. Here again is the effect of Gregory's imagination. He could see always, because he was a monk, because he was a priest, because he was a man of faith, the implications for the Church of what he was presenting from his scholarship. And his imagination saw always that organic unity in all its variety which is the Church, the Body of Christ. He could not bring himself to write only for one fragment of the Body, for its scholars or its controversialists, he found himself being led always on to the widest screen, the biggest canvas and he painted appropriately.

Most readers of *The Shape* have favourite passages which demonstrate Gregory's imagination at work. Certainly the most famous is the passage towards the end of the book where he celebrates the Church's faithful obedience through the centuries to Christ's command: 'Do this.'[1] He picks his way down the centuries in careful, measured but intense prose, selecting the widest range of eucharistic celebrations

1   p. 744.

in order to demonstrate how the eucharist has become the
heart of all the Church's life — from the most splendid to
the most ordinary, the grandest to the most personal. The
contemporary references to the war and the Church of his
day only make the passage more poignant. (He must have
thought of his own brother serving as a war chaplain as he
wrote about 'the beach at Dunkirk'. Ronnie Dix later recorded his own distribution of the eucharist on the 'D' Day
beaches at the end of the war.)

For Gregory the purpose and climax of the passage is that
what is being made is the *plebs sancta Dei*: 'the holy common
people of God'. The next paragraph ends:

> The sheer stupendous quantity of the love of God which this
> ever-repeated action has drawn from the obscure Christian
> multitudes through the centuries is in itself an overwhelming
> thought. (All that going with one to the altar every morning!)[1]

This, though, is only the most famous example of Gregory's
imaginative writing. We have seen others, when he writes
about Cranmer, for instance. The last pages of the book are
intense with this developed application of his thought and
concentrate particularly on the singularity of redeemed humanity, this new collective human being before God in which
each of us has a place. It is when he writes on themes of this
kind that Gregory is at his most intense and his imagination
seems to be most fully engaged. What matters to him ultimately is the solidarity of the Church before God and her
solidarity for the world.

There are other 'favourite' passages. The Grocer from
Brondesbury[2] is one or this passage selected as a favourite by
John Robinson in *Liturgy Coming to Life* and by others. Gregory
marks what was for him a very great turning point in the life
of the Church; the fourth century and its end.

> There is a sort of pause in events round about the turn of the
> century while that whole ancient world — still so magnificent

1   p. 745.
2   p. 142.

— waits for the stroke of God, and trusts him though it knows
He will slay. It is like some windless afternoon of misty
sunshine on the crimson and bronze of late October, when
time for an hour seems to stand still and the earth dreams,
fulfilled and weary, content that winter is at hand. The whole
hard structure of the *civitas terrena*, the earthly city that had
once thought itself eternal, was now ready to dissolve into a
different future. Gibbon was right. The foundation of the
empire was loosened by the waters of baptism, for the empire's real foundation was the terrible pagan dream of human
power. Its brief Christian dream of the City of God which
alone is eternal was broken by the roaring crash of the sack
of Rome by the Goths in AD 410. The world went hurrying
into the darkness of seven long barbarian centuries, but
pregnant now with all the medieval and modern future. It
was the achievement of the Church in the single century that
had passed since Diocletian that, though all else changed in
human life, it was certain to be a Christian world, that centred
all its life upon the eucharist.[1]

Dix's very great concern that his scholarship should be at the
service of the wider Church is demonstrated not only by the
tone of his writings but in other activities too. One of the
most interesting was his development of the 'liturgical demonstration'. When it became clear in his visit to the American
Priory in 1947 that he would need to spend time there raising
money for the new foundation, Gregory began to put together lectures and other projects that would give him entrance to the public lecture circuit and enable him to raise
money. One of his most popular devices, captured in a series of
photographs in the magazine *The Living Church* and used many
times during the lecture tours, was the liturgical demonstration. With a small amount of training beforehand, he showed
people how he conceived the pre-Nicene Church to have
celebrated the eucharist. Concentrating on the second part
of the celebration (as in the 'Grocer from Brondesbury'
passage in *The Shape*[2]) he had the men and women separately

1   pp. 395, 396.
2   p. 142.

bring their offertory of bread and wine to the deacons (and children bring water). The gifts were then offered by the bishop with the presbyters joining in and the bishop using the prayer of Hippolytus before the deacons again distributed the consecrated bread and wine. Gregory, standing in the pulpit as commentator on this, emphasised the brevity, the simplicity, the action, the participation. It became a classic teaching device, an example of the imaginative presentation of a theme in a way that was accessible to the largest number of people. Again it demonstrated Gregory's widest possible concern in the application of his scholarship. The demonstration became a major feature of Gregory's tours and he was invited to present it at the Anglo-Catholic Congress in London in 1948. Using it again in America in 1950 he was quoted as saying:

> You could give your life to God, they believed, only by giving it into the Church. You could receive it back only by receiving it through all the other people's offering to the Church. It was something you could not do without. It was something that could not be done without you.

He used the demonstration again in his lecture tour of Sweden in 1950.

The use of this popular teaching aid focused a great deal of Gregory's concerns — the eucharist, its simple and direct origins, its corporateness, the action, and the importance of bringing alive now the same importance it once had. The very practicality and accessibility of the demonstration became symbolic of Gregory's concerns.

Many of these themes and concerns recur in the talks and lectures Gregory gave at this stage in his life in the United States, Sweden and Britain. Here, in the popular lectures especially, his concern was to enhance the place of the eucharist in the life of the Church, to bring closer a solidarity in the Church like his vision of the Church's primitive solidarity. And the same thread runs also through more academic lectures (for instance on confirmation) and through retreats and devotional addresses given to religious. It is clearly in the *Retreat on the Rule* given to his own community referred to in chapter two.

Retreat on the Rule is another example of Gregory's writing at its most characteristic. Informed by careful scholarship, witty, personal but devout and prayerful, it is full of the themes of the Church and her life which characterise all his best work. It is deep, thoughtful, imaginative.

But still the most characteristic of all his writings is *The Shape*. The balance of scholarship, wit, devotion, politics reflects most accurately the balance in the man. It seemed to allow things to come from deeper within Gregory than perhaps he consciously intended, infusing the book and contributing to the great impact it made.

He intended to write other things. We have noticed that he referred to other ancient liturgical texts which he hoped to edit — more on Hippolytus, the *Didache*. From early on he seems to have planned a shorter version of *The Shape* which might have tidied up the long section on the Prayer Book but this version was never produced. The trips to America and illness got in the way of further writing and any revision of *The Shape*. There were things Gregory wanted to change in the light of criticism and developing scholarship in the seven years or so between the publication of the book and his death. Some small addresses and other devotional material were published, some posthumously,[1] but Gregory clearly thought his way ahead was in working more closely on the early Church. His lecture series on *The Sub-Apostolic Church*, delivered in Sweden, was to be the next major book, later published as *Jew and Greek*[2] edited by Canon H.J. Carpenter.

In *Jew and Greek* we can see where Gregory's thoughts were turning, only to be cut short by illness and death. He focused attention on what he called the 'problem of the sub-apostolic Church'. By 'problem' he seems to have meant the extraordinary growth of the movement, its shift to a Gentile world

1 *The Image and Likeness of God*, 1953 Dacre Press; *God's Way with Man*, 1954 Dacre Press.
2 *Jew and Greek*. 1953 Dacre Press. ed. J.H. Carpenter.

but its clear retention of a distinctively Jewish character. He dealt in general first with the prevailing cultural situations in the Greek and Syriac worlds of the first century and used his resources as a classicist and an historian to distinguish the two cultures. He compared, for instance, the 'two temples' of Athens and Jerusalem — one for beauty, he says, and the other for worship. Similarly he distinguished two starting points for the two approaches — the Greek works from the cosmos to an organised world, the Syriac beginning from 'the Living God.'

Dix acknowledged the role of other thinkers like Karl Barth and Feuerbach in making this wider analysis but here risked more general theories than he did in *The Shape* and, to some extent at least, his argument proved the less effective for being less particular. His emphasis on the continuing Jewish character of so much of the 'new religious movement' remained characteristic and convincing. The argument ultimately led to the assertion that the force of the personality, teaching and action of Jesus himself continues to dominate Christianity. It is not subsumed in some Greek philosophical mingling of other ideas and ceremonies.

Certainly some of the distinctive themes of Jesus have been, at least partly, lost sight of. He singled out the Davidic claims for his Messiahship and noted how the character of the Messianic theme was adapted to the Gentile world in the course of time. But even Paul, Gregory claimed, never very successfully absorbed the Greek approach and the Greek mind and so for him it always continued to be a gospel 'for the Jews first and also to the Greek'.

The first Jewish decade of the Church's life when Jesus was proclaimed as 'Messiah' within Syriac Judaism (30–40 AD) ensured the abiding Jewish features of the faith and the Church. It was 'the Way' as opposed to a cult or a philosophy, a corporate body with a new covenant life as the 'New Israel of God'. It was a common life, faith, a morality, a common worship 'in Jesus — Messiah'.

Within this setting, in the face of persecution as a superstitious accretion to Judaism, began to emerge the gospels

and in particular, first of all, Mark's. It was to this section of
the book that Gregory returned even while he was dying,
adding notes on the authorship of the second gospel and
examining the earliest evidence for Mark as the writer. But
the ideas remain Jewish even into the later gospel of John
where, Gregory argued, 'St John's God — "the Father" — is
no relation to the Unmoved First Mover.' To have life in
himself is the energy of Deity, echoing the ever-repeated
'The Lord liveth' of the Old Testament.'

Even so, by the time of his gospel, 'The tragedy in St John
is not Israel's rejection of the Messiah but the far wider one
of "the world's failure to know the Word".'

Gregory continued to examine the persistence of the
Syriac ideas and to trace them ultimately back to Jesus.
Although the Hellenic world soon became the only world
open to the gospel yet the Jewish character of the gospel
remained. He highlights three main reasons for this. First,
the Jewish scriptures remained a powerful and controlling
influence. Early worship continued to be based on syna-
gogue-style worship and retained its strong scriptural emphasis. The sermon (rather like the letter to the Hebrews)
would have been the place for Christian explanation.

Secondly, the importance of Mark's direct reception of the
gospel from Peter was asserted and in consequence the
power of the sheer attractiveness of the story of Jesus.
Thirdly there was the influence of worship — both the
regular meeting of the community and its special rites such
as Initiation when the use of the Creed, for instance, pro-
tected distinctive Jewish-Christian ideas such as 'the flesh'
as opposed to the anti-materialism of Hellenism.

The eucharist, itself, emerged as a major distinctive feature here with its very name a translation of the Hebrew
berakah, and *agape* as a translation of *chaburah*, the brotherhood
meal which *The Shape* had focused on as the root of the
eucharist.

Again he made his distinctive point about the prayer of the
Church being the clearest hallmark of its life. The 'springs
of her history' are in her prayer and worship.

This book then saw Gregory pursuing his interest in the origins of the Church and in what controlled and determined its emerging life. There is, almost inevitably, an anti-liberal edge to the book, with its insistence that the distinctive features could and must be traced to Jesus himself in the end. All his emphasis on Jewish characteristics was part of this assertion and it ultimately enabled him to see the Catholic faith as·a continuing and a single whole, emerging finally from Jesus himself.

Dix is at his most compelling and engaging when he turns to the subject of worship, its origins, their implications, the developments. Here his writing comes most alive — most personal, most clear, most attractive.

Jew and Greek is the much less significant book than Gregory's reputation as a writer rests on *The Shape*. Now, fifty years since it was published, how does it look? Did Gregory make a permanent contribution with his *tour de force*?

It is less in the innovative discoveries of Gregory's writing that his impact was made and more in the accessibility of presentation and the imaginative·style of his writing. The book is the assimilation of current thinking, attractively presented and opened up for the Church. There is no doubt that the book's influence was subsequently enormous. A standard text for decades in theological colleges and still in print it contributed profoundly to the liturgical develop-ments that began at the end of fifties and came to a climax in the sixties and seventies. No other single book made such an impact.

In a letter to Green,[1] Dix said: 'Ratcliff who read it for me wisely said that it would take nearly ten years to make its full impact on the study of liturgy and that it would be the basis of a new start in the subject.'

From this distance we see how the work helped to re-establish the centrality of the eucharist. This was a com-mon theme of the liturgical movement and crucial to the work of Gabriel Hebert and the Parish and People (Associ-

1   Letter 1945.

ated Parishes in the United States) movement as well. Fifty
years later it is virtually taken for granted again in most of
the denominations that the heart of Christian worship is in
the eucharist, though it takes different forms in those different settings. The model for this universal pattern has largely
been the pre-Nicene one derived from Hippolytus which was
so basic to *The Shape*. Following Gregory and others, liturgists
have gone back behind the Reformation, behind the Oriental
and the Latin rites, to something that looked like an origin,
a common core, free of the perils of later controversies. That
subsequent scholarship has become more unsure of the
evidence for a clear original does not detract from the success
of the model across the Churches in recent decades. Gregory's writings were a major contribution to this steady and
profound change.

Closely linked to this renewed emphasis on the eucharist
itself was his analysis of the simple shape of the earliest
eucharistic worship — the four actions of taking, blessing,
breaking and sharing. With this outline Gregory avoided the
pitfalls of looking for an original prayer and released subsequent liturgical development from a fruitless search. *The
Shape* has been remarkably faithfully adhered to in all major
revisions, a clear testimony to its simplicity, accuracy, and
usefulness.

There has been an underlining of the integrity of the
whole eucharistic prayer. Dix was keen to emphasise this
unity and to avoid ideas of consecratory phrases or special
moments. The whole prayer effected the change of the gifts.
This emphasis has not been as thoroughly absorbed into
subsequent liturgical development as some others but it
remains a logical consequence of Gregory's argument and is
part of the simple power of the Prayer at its most primitive,
to which he was so sensitive.

One of the main results of these different themes, taken
together, has been to renew a sense of the Church as a
corporate entity, an organic whole, the Body of Christ. The
emphasis on the eucharist shared in by everyone, at communion but also in the offertory and other parts of the rite,

has stimulated a deeper sense of corporate identity. This was a theme crucial to Gregory's writing and thinking. *The Shape* made a major contribution to the process of exploring this basic idea.

The expression of this 'bodily-ness' in the offertory has had a more mixed reception. Evangelicals in particular have been wary of the idea of being able to 'offer' God anything. Even so an offertory procession remains in many Churches the ideal opportunity to picture the people of God playing their part in the drama of salvation, liturgically expressed.

Dix might well have been surprised to see these features of the present liturgical scene linked to his book since he made very few direct connections with contemporary practice. However the book was so full of a lively, refreshing faith — stimulating and inspiring — that readers were bound to ask how these ideas might be implemented now. So the book made its partly indirect yet somehow all the more powerful impact on the life of the Church.

The Shape of the Liturgy is in many ways a very English piece of writing. It is accessible, but not by trivialising or by being superficial. It is applied theology, almost popular theology, because Gregory could not stop his imagination leading him to consider the widest contexts, the largest group of people, the setting of the whole Church.

He could not suppress his personal commitment and what we might call his 'sense of mission' in the service of detached and 'pure' scholarship. Despite his own claims he was always more than merely an historian and his 'programme' to make the Church of England more catholic was never far from his mind.

It is in this way that Dix's writings and scholarship generally fit into the context of the rest of his life. The fit is somewhat untidy and irregular. Some have regretted that Gregory did not have the opportunity for more writing rather than the fund-raising lecture tours of the United States or the extensive involvement in Church politics in the 1940s. He, however, was not designed to be the reclusive scholar-monk. His imaginative intelligence was better suited to making connections between history and the contemporary Church, between theology and practice, between study and action. The Religious life fitted into this too. He saw the Religious Orders as the sensitive moderators of the Church, setting the pace, checking authenticity, adhering faithfully to catholicity, as well as quietly contributing the continuous offering of prayer.

He hankered sometimes for the quiet monastic life but he knew that, in fact, he was also made for the fray — with the wit of a practised politician but also with the precise pen of a scholar.

Kenneth Kirk, the Bishop of Oxford and Gregory's friend, writing at the time of his death, called him 'the most brilliant man in the Church of England'. He used that brilliance unevenly — the consequence of his personality but also of circumstances, especially in the context of his religious community. Nevertheless, his brilliance shines through in his writing and especially in *The Shape*. It is a brilliance of careful study, clear application to the wider Church and an imaginative sensitivity to the ordinary people of God in their liturgical life.

5

Travels: America and Sweden

*... Those who are sent on a journey should not omit
the canonical hours, but, to the best of their ability,
should perform them where they are, and not neglect
the obligation of their service.*

Rule of St Benedict, Ch. 50

In a letter to his friend Marcus Stephens at Kelham, Gregory
describes listening to the Coronation of King George VI on
May 12th 1937. Throughout the day he has been observing
the awed effects on what he calls 'our Americans'.

The letter gives a little glimpse of the Nashdom community in the mid-thirties. Within it, as part of it, were three or
four Americans living the life in order to learn the life for
themselves. The Americans arrived in 1936 and some remained until the beginning of the war. They returned to the
United States to inaugurate the daughter house of St Gregory's, Three Rivers in Michigan. Presumably the idea was
that, the small community, suitably formed in the religious
life by living at Nashdom, could be transplanted and would
grow in its own soil, attracting new members, becoming
gradually more and more independent until, in due course,
it would be an independent autonomous abbey.

The development was not quite as smooth as that, and
Gregory's visits to North America, including Canada as well
as the United States, were part of the attempt to sort out the
problems. Today St Gregory's Abbey is a stable independent

221

Anglican Benedictine abbey within the Episcopal Church of the USA. The history of Catholic recovery and revival within the Episcopal Church of the USA is slightly different from that in Britain but the desire within it to recover a monastic life is exactly parallel. As in Britain, during the last years of the nineteenth century and the first decades of the twentieth, Religious communities for women and men were emerging all over the United States and Canada. Some were directly connected to communities in Britain, such as the Society of St John the Evangelist, others were entirely autonomous. St Gregory's was intended to be autonomous, in the Benedictine way, but rooted in the great tradition of Benedictinism and nourished and encouraged by the English mother house.

The site on which the monks eventually settled after their return is magnificent. Three Rivers is not far from Kalamazoo in Michigan. The monastery is now a complex of slightly austere but comfortable wooden buildings. At the centre is the impressive wooden chapel with its high roof and quietly numinous atmosphere for which Gregory worked so hard in fund-raising. But the monastery buildings are only part of the place. It is built near a lake surrounded by trees, some parts of the terrain have been cultivated and gardened for the monks but other parts are left undeveloped. Huge trees form long avenues to the lake, or lead quietly and gently to the monastic cemetery, a secluded opening in the forest.

Gregory knew the site, though without the developed buildings, and called it 'magnificent'. He went fishing on the lake and caught enough fish for a meal. It is possible to feel there, as he perhaps felt in amongst all his busy-ness, a proper continuity of nature and human living, of the earth and the Religious life, some kind of harmony and balance.

The first visit to St Gregory's in 1947 was not long-planned and in many ways did not fit in easily with his own activities and plans. The little plant transferred to America seemed not to be thriving and Abbot Martin, as Superior of both communities, decided that they needed further direct support from the mother house. In consequence, he sent Gregory.

Gregory had stayed in touch with the American brethren after their return to the States, and one long letter of 1946 to one of them, Dom Paul Severance, indicates both that their friendship remained intimate and Gregory's interest in the American daughter house remained lively. In the letter, however, there is no hint as yet of a future visit.

Why was the visit necessary? The American monks on their return to the States had become involved in running a parish in Valparaiso in the diocese of Michigan. It proved, however, too soon to be involved in this kind of work. The community had not developed any stability or a life of its own and needed first to concentrate on that. In time the bishop saw this and effectively pushed the monks out to force them to get on with developing the Religious life itself. In the meantime, however, Dom Paul Severance, the Prior, had a stroke and things seemed to be faltering badly. They needed help to establish the life, but it was also becoming clear that they would need help to finance the venture. Sending Gregory provided help on both counts — he could help to form the life but he was also famous enough to be able to earn money as a lecturer and speaker.

Dix left for America by plane at the end of February 1947. He arrived at New York, where he was due to preach on the following Sunday but as the plane was delayed he found himself pausing only briefly in New York before going on by train to Three Rivers. It was obviously something of a shock when he got there. The beauty of the place in the snow was a pleasant shock but the smallness of the house and the disarray of the community caused him some dismay which he candidly passed on to the Abbot. His organising skills, used tactfully, even subtly, immediately came into play and he began to outline to the Abbot what he felt was necessary. The building was so cramped that there could be no possibility of the community's growth without more space both in living accommodation and in the chapel. Gregory saw immediately that he was ideally suited to help raise the necessary money by responding to requests already made for lectures and sermons, retreats and consultations.

Had he seriously expected to be able to 'sit quietly at Three Rivers', as he later suggested to Kenneth Kirk, his hopes quickly evaporated into a whirl of busyness and extensive travelling. This would help the fund-raising, but the community's stability was a more complex problem. In some ways they would have benefited more if Gregory could have 'sat quietly at Three Rivers'. As it was, he found himself providing much-needed support for Dom Francis, something of a foil to Dom Paul, and carefully advising the Abbot that more senior support was needed from Nashdom to help to establish the community.

By the middle of March 1947 the gravity of the situation dawned on Gregory. Writing to the Abbot he outlined the difficult financial situation. Dom Paul needed to be in a nursing home but that would need money; there was a mortgage of $8,000 and they needed urgently to erect a new chapel and cells, costing, at the cheapest, $10,000–$12,000. In the weeks up to Easter, Gregory set about organising an increasingly extensive lecture tour through, almost non-stop, to August.

The timing, more or less by accident, was perfect. *The Shape of the Liturgy* and *The Apostolic Ministry* had been published and issued in the States just long enough for Gregory to be famous and in demand. There was even a sense of the American Church welcoming Gregory in a way the English Church would not: 'I am embarrassed here', he said in a letter home, 'by being treated as a prophet outside my own country. It is painfully marked.'[1] He discovered that a considerable party of the press had been waiting for him at New York, only avoided by his delayed plane. He realised he could capitalise on this.

The Abbot was, on the whole, not going to argue with him. His ideas were clearly, even forcefully, expressed, though in the politest tones of obedience, and the Abbot, acknow-

1   17.8.50.

ledging Gregory's better information 'on the ground', could only agree. Dix found it necessary to advise about the community too and similarly the Abbot had to heed what he said.

Ironically, Gregory was sacrificing once again the stability of his own Religious commitment, this time for the sake of the stability of the new community. After the frantically busy year of 1946 Gregory might have hoped to settle back down into the rhythm of his vocation. He wrote saying as much to Dom Paul Severance in 1946. It was not to be. It needs to be said that Gregory lapped it up. Whether it was simply that the opportunity to organise and to communicate, the chance of large audiences and eager listeners, the excitement of a quite new world, its challenges and risks all simply gave wonderful scope to his talents, he certainly responded. Or whether he longed for the quiet life but decided, since the opposite was unavoidable, to enter fully into it, it is difficult to tell. No doubt the truth was the combination, however contradictory, of the two.

Dix rose to the occasion. He had the skill to capitalise fully on his reputation, the charm and wit to use his status and 'curiosity value' to the full and the sense and good humour not to get too carried away or lose his sense of proportion. In a letter to Abbot Martin during his second visit he wrote: 'I have already decided that I will tolerate being made a circus of where I am paid to be a circus, but will not allow myself to be "lionised" — of which there are signs — except to raise money for St Gregory's.'[1] This clearly was an attitude he developed from quite early on in his first visit.

In all of this, he had no formal status in the American community. He was not prior and not even strictly a member. Clearly this had disadvantages in that at every point he could only advise, suggest, persuade and cajole — both at St Gregory's and to the Abbot at Nashdom. Equally, though, it had advantages. It left him free in persuading Americans to support the community to emphasise that it was not for

1   9.7.50.

himself, that he could not commit the community, that he was merely fulfilling his vows of obedience.

In all, combining his 1950–51 trip with the 1947 trip, Gregory seems to have raised between $20,000 and $30,000 to add to the other appeals and money-raising efforts made by the community. In this he depended on American generosity. Even though the war was not long over, the American situation was better than the British. Dix could appeal to a combination of generosity towards a Religious community under a vow of poverty, a sense of religious revival and new commitment amongst Anglican catholics, the appeal of a new and yet deeply traditional venture, and even a measure of pity for the war-torn English. He is reported to have said: 'You have before you the unique spectacle of a Britisher asking for dollars to be spent right here in the USA!'

He knew, of course, how to use to the full his unique combination of the eccentric, the charming and witty, the clever but intelligible and articulate, the quietly passionate and devoted, the imaginative and the unerringly practical. That dazzling combination was calculated to mesmerise any audience but especially an American one.

The first tour took Gregory from lecturing at the University of Chicago to the General Theological Seminary in New York, to the leading of retreats for Religious communities in Canada, to Long Island, New York again, Cleveland Ohio, Chicago again and then down to New Orleans, Texas and back to Connecticut and New York, finally returning to Three Rivers in July. More tours followed as the opportunities arose and as his reputation grew. He found he could command fees of $600 for a set of lectures in the academic establishments. Parishes and other groups varied much more.

What did he speak about? Some of the texts of lectures and addresses remain and there are many other references. His main subject was the liturgy, though he also spoke about the ministry. These were natural subjects in the light of his published work. He made his academic impact. Thomas Talley, later to be a leading American liturgist himself, records an early experience of liturgological study in Texas, referred to in the last chapter:

> I gathered with an enthusiastic crowd of clergy and laity at a summer camp in the diocese of Dallas to hear a series of lectures by Dom Gregory Dix.... I can still remember his opening sentence: 'Our understanding of our forms of worship underwent a radical transformation some forty years ago when it finally occurred to someone that Jesus was a Jew.'

He spoke also, however, about the Religious life and about its Benedictine expression in particular which clearly gave him the opportunity to promote the cause of Three Rivers. Some of his addresses included more general theology and we have quoted already, at the end of chapter one, a reference made in an American lecture to the theology of the nature of God. Some of the remaining lecture notes are incomplete or extremely brief, suggesting that he soon developed a pattern of things he wanted to say and needed fewer and fewer developed notes.

One address on the eucharist exists in two forms, taken down by different people in different places. The two reveal a similar structure and a pattern of themes he wanted to stress. He distinguished first the two halves of the Service — the first part with its roots in the synagogue, the second a private Christian function. He used Paul's account in 1.Cor.11 as the most primitive and went on to show how, within the next few years, the actual meal disappeared from the celebration and the seven actions were telescoped into four. His major emphasis was on the Jewishness of the action. Jesus did nothing new but gave it a whole new meaning by linking it to his death, the 'new covenant'. Jews for centuries had broken bread and often shared the cup of Blessing but now the actions had a new significance and by continuing to 'do this' the Church entered into the offering of Jesus. So we find ourselves, not unexpectedly back with one of Gregory's favourite themes — the body, its offering, its worship.

He later told Kenneth Kirk that he only gradually developed the ability to speak extempore — but develop it he did, no doubt of necessity. He found himself speaking at dinners

and social events, at diocesan functions, at summer schools.
He found himself asked to conduct parish missions. His
disclaimer that he was really only an academic belied his skill
in personal and imaginative communication. He said in a
letter that: 'I can't do the hot gospel stuff the way that brings
the crowds in'[1] but in actual fact 1,300 people turned up, in
the rain, for a day on the liturgy, and in the evening 1,050
people witnessed his demonstration of the primitive liturgy.

This liturgical demonstration was the dramatic acting out
of the primitive liturgy described in chapter four. It is difficult to say when he first introduced it, but he may well have
tried it in America before using it at the Anglo-Catholic
Congress in 1948 in London. Certainly he used it on his
second visit to the United States as the series of photographs
in the Episcopal Church magazine *Living Church* record.

The imaginative use of such a directly accessible device
with Gregory's careful, pastoral and devout commentary
indicates one of the major themes of Gregory's teaching and
speaking — the action of the liturgy as the Church's corporate, bodily offering of itself to God. All his concern for the
Body of Christ as a Body, all his sensitivity to the dignity and
integrity of lay people in the Church emerges here. These
transparent concerns not surprisingly meant that he became
a popular speaker with non-academic church groups as well
as with clergy or university and seminary audiences.

These practical and pastoral concerns brought Gregory
naturally into contact with groups working for liturgical development in the American Church. Like the Parish and
People group in England, the movement called Associated
Parishes had begun working to apply new liturgical insights
to the regular life of the Church. The movement was a
natural ally for Gregory and he spent a 'week of conversations' with them in August of 1947 during which he told them
that they were the first group he knew to be putting the
liturgical revival into practice in parishes. In amongst all this,
not unnoticed by these American allies, Gregory continued

1   6.11.50.

with the apparent contradiction of his own daily Tridentine mass.

Once again the combination of the intellectually and academically stimulating with the pastorally and devotionally relevant in a powerfully imaginative manner made Gregory a very attractive speaker. Some of the retreats Gregory gave to communities in Canada and the United States reveal this very well. In an address on Patience, a virtue he mused on more than once in the US, he invited his hearers to think of the Wise Men after the night of ecstasy and adoration:

Then comes the anticlimax and the secret flight for home. And after they got back, the explanations to the other magicians in the common-room of the Zoroastrian Temple — the others who had also seen the Star and had not followed. 'Well, did you find what you sought?' 'Oh yes, we found it, in the end.' 'And was it very far?' 'Oh — we found — a young child and his mother.' 'Oh! it seems not so very much, after all that way — but then — ?' 'Well — then we came away. There was some trouble with the police.' 'It seems to have been a disappointing business — but still, if you're satisfied' and the little smile that says so much! And the overheard remark afterwards: 'I never did think much of old Balthasar's system of interpretation. It seems to have led him a nice wild-goose-chase this time. I only hope he won't bring the police here looking for him.' — And after that, the long grey years at home, with occasional news that some Herod slightly more disreputable than the last had just succeeded to a throne or been kicked out of a tetrarchy in Palestine — and, if they lived to hear it, in the end news of an execution at Jerusalem.... Don't you think the question must sometimes have risen in their minds — 'That journey — it was extraordinary. It seemed very wonderful at the time. But I wonder — were we really wise?' In the Religious life there comes to all of us the desperate days when one wonders — 'True, there was a Star, and it led us — once. But it seems to have set — long ago now. True — there was that time when I knew — but it was years ago now. And I have given all my gold, and my incense is all burned away and my myrrh was used for a burying....'

During the lecture tour Gregory returned to Three Rivers from time to time and found himself involved in organising the community for which he was raising money. When he returned in late April he felt even more strongly the need for support from Nashdom and perhaps especially a novice master with someone alongside to support him. He found they needed instruction in Latin (or else an English office). By the middle of May 1947 the Abbot had agreed to send Dom Patrick Dalton and Dom Maurus Benson. Two or three postulants were also on their way. Gregory's lectures had raised enough money for the chapel and Gregory was even acting as cantor at the services. By July 1947 Gregory petitioned for Dom Francis to replace Dom Paul as the Prior since he felt the latter's influence was so unhelpful. His contribution to the founding of the new monastery was not, then, only in terms of fund-raising but also establishing its identity and helping to form its life.

From the beginning the community had devoted help from interested Americans. A leading supporter was Gregory Mabry, rector of a leading Episcopalian Church in New York. With a similar mischievousness of spirit to Gregory he quickly became a friend and worked alongside Gregory arranging tours, raising money, maintaining contacts. Gregory made other lasting contacts too among the bishops, clergy and leading lay people. He was grateful for extensive positive support and coverage by *The Living Church*, which enthusiastically helped with the Priory's appeal. He became adept at approaching the rich, and brazenly begging. In a letter home he wrote: 'I have been making love to the lavatory-pan Queen of the Middle-west... and extracted from her an offering in kind....'[1]

In another letter,[2] to the Abbot, Gregory expressed the feeling that St Gregory's had 'turned the corner' — his lecture tours were continuing and he believed that the money raised would make all the difference. Combined with

1   15.5.47.
2   Late May 1947.

the expected arrival of monks from Nashdom, the picture looked much more hopeful. Dix returned to England on September 10th 1947 — it had been hard work. He told Kenneth Kirk he had never worked so hard in his life but it had been worth it.

In all of this Gregory himself never seems to have questioned the rightness of establishing the new monastery. No doubt this was partly out of a sense of obedience but behind all his efforts lay also his own determined commitment to the Religious life — and to the religious life in the Anglican communion. At times Gregory found the American Episcopal Church almost as exasperating as the Church of England, but he remained committed to the catholic vision. Not surprisingly St Gregory's had to cope with the accusations of 'Romanising' that Nashdom also faced and Gregory found himself having to persuade bishops and others that the community was not about to 'go over' at any moment.

He clearly enjoyed himself. He was attractive to his American audiences and glowed in the attention. The zest with which he entered into all the different aspects of the American visit must also have put him under considerable strain. In more than one letter he claimed to be in excellent health but he admitted to an inevitable tiredness. At the end of May 1947, returning from Canada, he managed to rest for a day and a half at Niagara. 'The worst of a waterfall is that it has only one trick....' he commented in more than one letter '... in this case a very majestic trick I admit....'[1]

He had hoped for a holiday in the West Indies on his way home but this was not to be. He returned to the fray in England. Perhaps the sheer energy and intensity of all he was doing kept ill health at bay.

Frequently in the letters he spoke of homesickness. He became very attached to St Gregory's but still: 'I think of Nashdom and my father and brethren at least 30 or 40 times a day — so that is obviously where my roots are.'[2]

1   29.5.47.
2   15.5.47.

Most of what we know about Dix's experiences in America comes from these letters. He was a wonderful correspondent. From the very beginning they are witty, full of detail, frequent, precise (legible) and long. He tells stories, recounts annoying thoughts, often repeated to more than one correspondent — indulges his imaginative gifts. The letters to the Abbot read often as if they are intended to be read by the community — or to them all. The actor was at work but they must have felt themselves in close contact with all that was happening through those letters. The very first letter sets the tone. Written from Ireland where the plane was delayed, Gregory found himself in the company of the Roman Catholic Archbishop of Port of Spain who was busily commandeering limousines and dispensing everyone from the keeping of Lent. Gregory comments: 'That's the way to run a Church, fairly stomping on the faces of the laity.... And I shall never travel without an Archbishop in future. They are so useful!'[1]

Correspondence meant of course that Gregory could also stay abreast of affairs in England where he was still involved in so many matters. Keeping up with the English Church while lecturing in the American Church only added to the complexity of life. In many ways he was glad to be away from it. Writing to Freddy Green after his return he said: 'It has been an immense rest to get away from the ecclesiastical hubbub and deal with purely monastic problems for a bit.'

Yet he could not resist the invitation to join the American ecclesiastical hubbub. He gave the Commencement Day address at Seabury Western Theological Seminary, one of the leading colleges, and spoke of the uselessness of the Lambeth Quadrilateral as a basis for ecumenical development. He encouraged the American bishops to promote instead the earlier Chicago form of the Quadrilateral.

At the time there was pressure to be back in England to work for the cause in person. Preparing for his return he outlined what awaited him — Convocation, Church Assembly and the Lambeth Preparation Commission; the Baptism

1   2.47.

and Confirmation Commission; a commission to meet with non-conformists in the light of Fisher Cambridge sermon; other committees of Convocation; the subjects' committee for the Anglo-Catholic Congress coming up in 1948, things promised to publishers. Gregory seemed to be able to keep it all going with hardly a falter.

To Dom Hilary Powell he wrote:

> I am snatching half an hour I can't really spare from a paper promised for Ealing Church Week which must go off by Air Mail. (I had an agitated cable from Ronnie [who was to deliver the lecture] last week about it asking if I was watching the Calendar. I have just expended the Community's money on a cable reading: 'Working Julian Calendar stop Happy Easter stop Retain hair stop Paper coming.' I will not be badgered by my younger brother.)

Somehow he sustained the same zest and energy throughout his visit. The challenge stirred him and America appealed to him. It was far from obvious that Gregory would like the United States. He might be expected to feel comfortable in the more English and old European parts of the States and Canada, but he thoroughly enjoyed himself in 'the deep South' too, apart from 'the attitude to the negro' which he called 'abominable'. Everywhere he remarked on and appreciated the warm hospitality and the eagerness to learn. He admired, and was only too ready to respond to, American generosity. To Freddy Green Gregory said: 'Only in this preposterous but extraordinarily likeable country could even Divine Grace bring off such a ridiculous story within 6 months.' Somehow he managed to find just the right wavelength to evoke the maximum response. This dark, small, rather ill-looking, very English monk in his Benedictine habit, and with a twinkle in his eyes, found himself with a new home, not only at St Gregory's Priory but all over America.

After the whirlwind tour and his careful advice to the Abbot, it was hoped that the community in America would settle down with two English monks to help and money raised for the next phase of building. In the course of the

next two years Abbot Martin at Nashdom resigned and died,
and Dom Augustine Morris was elected Abbot, appointing
Gregory as his prior. This should not have affected life at St
Gregory's but as time went by it became clear that all was
not well. Gregory, as Prior of Nashdom, maintained a correspondence with the Prior of St Gregory's — Dom Patrick
Dalton. From this correspondence, which we looked at in
chapter two, it becomes clear that the American initiative
was not yet over all its hurdles.

In the meantime he was involved in many things including
preparations for more travelling, this time on a lecture tour
of Sweden in early 1950. Dix went out at the invitation of
the Swedish Church to lecture for a month in the universities
of Uppsala and Lund and in various other places around the
Kingdom. Gregory saw the lectures as a counterblast to
Bishop George Bell's recent lecture tour in Sweden. He
intended to show the Swedish Church the real Anglican
Position. Again we owe our knowledge of this visit to Gregory's letter-writing both to the Abbot and to Kenneth Kirk.

The Swedish Church, like the English, is a national institution that maintained a continuity at the time of the Reformation. Its ethos is distinctly Lutheran even though it has
retained much that makes it look more catholic. It is interesting, therefore, to watch Gregory himself observing a
Church on the surface similar to his own Church but in which
he finds many differences.

He told the Abbot that the Church seemed even more out
of touch than the Church of England, there was 'an appalling
stiffness and deadness'. He insisted on continuing to say his
daily mass, something unheard of in the Swedish Church,
and he was given an altar in the Cathedral in Stockholm to
do so. He said a daily mass in Uppsala also and in Stranghus.
He found himself with an 'audience' of curious onlookers and
also some communicants. He had to contend, as so often,
with accusations of 'romanism'. A professor of Dogmatics
said that: 'his ideas are Papistic though very subtle.'

He presented the liturgical demonstration of the primitive liturgy, and so stirred up discussion and reflection as well as controversy.

Here too he found himself in discussion with leading theologians and Church officials as well as speaking to Church congregations, students, and attending more social gatherings. He travelled extensively and the lectures he gave became the posthumously published book *Jew and Greek*. Gregory was welcomed and listened to and he was critically observant in response. He told Kenneth Kirk: 'What they need is daily mass and weekly communion and morning and evening prayer daily in Church to make it all come alive.'[1]

The letters are full of his entertaining humour. Remarking on the language he says to Kenneth Kirk: 'A notice "Damfrising" which I took to be a reasonable comment on the weather (-9° at present) turned out to be "Ladies Hairdressing".'[2]

His first letter to the Abbot from on board ship describes the hilarious pantomime of his drunken cabin-mates and their attempts to get into the bunks: 'rather like a parody of Conrad' he says. The next day: 'Hanssen and Johannson (it sounds like a music-hall) have each come and apologised very charmingly (which meant a lager with each).'[3] As in America, the schedule was hectic and Gregory's health was far from perfect. He succumbed to 'flu and, although he struggled on, it took time to overcome it.

Dix returned to England towards the end of February. It was obvious to him that many people wanting to see the revival of the Swedish Church felt that contact with Anglicans was a valuable way of helping their Church to grow. In many ways the whole background was too protestant for Gregory. 'If I ever hated Luther,' he wrote to Freddy Green, 'I hate that psychological monster three times more now that I have seen his results!' But he did show them and spoke to them of what it might be like to be a catholic in a reformed Church.

1   2.2.50.
2   *Ibid.*
3   4.2.50.

Later in 1950 Gregory had to return to the United States. As before it was in response to a crisis of leadership. The Abbot had lost confidence in Dom Patrick Dalton as the Prior at St Gregory's and some kind of 'trouble-shooting' became necessary once again; it seems to have been longer planned than the first visit but still the response to a problem.

He arrived back in the United States in July 1950 and was to be there for nearly a year. This time the territory was familiar, the community was somewhat more established. But this time also the crisis was greater and Gregory's health was already poorer.

The immediate problems were to do with finance and buildings. At once Gregory had misgivings, confirmed by Gregory Mabry, about the plans for the chapel, the site, the design, the debts being incurred. At the same time he felt the life of prayer was being established in the community though there was some 'stagnation'.

The tension apparent in the correspondence between the two priors — Gregory and Dom Patrick Dalton — described in chapter two, made Gregory's situation a difficult one. He felt that, with Patrick recalled to Nashdom, he still had to be deputy both to the Abbot and to Dom Patrick. At the same time it was becoming apparent that Dom Patrick had not been the most efficient business manager. To help with the financial situation Gregory asked for permission, 'to write a short book of some kind in the next few weeks'.

This, combined with an imminent speaking tour, meant that Gregory was returning to the frantic schedule of his previous visit. As the days went by it became apparent that the financial situation was more confused than at first thought. There was confusion about the size of the Church to be built — three bays or seven. Gregory felt seven was too ambitious. $24,000 would be needed to create a six-bay Church, their appeal could stretch to $20,000 and Gregory would need to raise the other $4,000 by lecturing.

At the same time he continued to feel confident about the internal life of the monastery.

In the next weeks Gregory re-wrote *The Power and Wisdom of God* for publication in America with the royalties going to St Gregory's. He began work on a translation of the Spiritual Exercises of John of Fécamp OSB[1] and planned a Dacre Press series on Benedictine Spirituality. Even so he poured joking scorn on an idea of a volume of his sermons: 'You can print one if you like, he told his abbot, I shall be ribald if you do.'[2]

Gregory kept up good spirits in the letters of this period but on the whole there was less wit, fewer stories. Sensitive to the tension between himself, Dom Patrick Dalton and the Abbot he struggled to keep the balance. He found himself obliged to be openly critical of Dom Patrick's attitude to Gregory Mabry but he also quickly took the opportunity to let Mabry see the growing stability of the community, attributable to Dom Patrick, and in that way to soothe Mabry's and Patrick's bruised sensitivities.

Dix embarked on a lecture tour which once again included his liturgical demonstration. The photographs in *The Living Church* date from this period, and in them Gregory looks more haggard. There was good cause. After his return from America he wrote to Green: 'By the end of October (1950) I felt like death and early in November saw a doctor who sent me to a big New York surgeon who told me I had got cancer.'

He was sure he couldn't tell the Abbot, because he would be called home and the money would never be raised in time but he said, determined to stay: 'I was very frightened... the really horrid thing was not being able to consult anyone.' In addition to all the other pressures of the situation Gregory was living with this most alarming and secret pressure of all: the pain of illness, and the thought of dying. He desperately needed a rest. Finally he was able to take up the invitation to go to the West Indies from a friend from Oxford days, then Bishop of Antigua, Newnham Davies. Early in 1951 he flew to the Caribbean.

1   1078.
2   20.7.50.

American friends gave him for Christmas a substantial diary, and for the first few weeks of 1951 this was carefully kept. The holiday is described in detail including rough sketches. He travelled to Montserrat via Antigua and called it a 'near earthly paradise'. It reminded him of Africa though the people seemed less happy. Apart from one preaching engagement, it was 'a gloriously restful holiday'. He described the view from the bedroom window in Montserrat as: 'exactly like the backdrop of a theatre badly painted in impossibly crude colours.'[1] He commented to Green later that he felt Newnham Davies was alone in suspecting how ill Gregory was.

On January 26th he flew back to Miami and returned to St Gregory's ready to begin the lecture tour which he hoped would provide the money for the chapel. His travels once again took him all over the North East and then later to Kansas City, Illinois, Louisiana and New Orleans with return visits to New York for Good Friday and Three Rivers for Easter.

In the meantime Dom Patrick Dalton returned as prior to Three Rivers. At the beginning of February this led to something of a crisis for Gregory. No doubt the pressure of illness and everything else he was already involved in made its contribution, but Dom Patrick's return was something of a catalyst. Gregory openly admitted to the Abbot that Patrick was 'extremely tiresome', though he excused him. Gregory began to wonder if he had been away too long, should he return? Worse, he went on to say: '... it has been suggested to me that I tend sometimes to come between the Abbot and the community', worst of all, he offered to resign as prior.

This was a low point for Gregory. The offer to resign must have been connected with Dom Patrick's return but also his painful, serious and still untreated illness. It suggests a not surprising loss of Gregory's usual self-assured confidence and sense of purpose. There was even a hint of pique in it. The point was not referred to again. Gregory regained his footing

1   1.51.

but the relationship with Dom Patrick seems only to have deteriorated. By mid-March Gregory wrote: 'I did value his affection and confidence greatly, now they are gone.'

This was not unconnected to the fact that the financial situation continued to be unclear. No one seemed to know how much was in the accounts. In Holy Week 1951 the crisis came to a head. Gregory finally received from Dom Patrick details of the accounts — sent on scraps of paper — which indicated that the 'estimate for completion' was $37,802. Gregory's agitation is evident in his normally very even script. He thought they risked having to stop the building and that the dedication in May looked impossible. He found no sense of regret in Dom Patrick. A week later, writing from Three Rivers, he disclosed more of the details of the situation and began to think of solutions — loans, lectures, an increased appeal... and in the same letter: 'I am well flustered and I had a beastly experience in Holy Week of the "Potiphar's wife" variety... it left me very tired and nauseated.'

Tired, tense, torn by the situation at Three Rivers and desperately ill, Gregory delivered in New York at the Church of the Resurrection, the devotional addresses referred to earlier for the Three Hours on Good Friday which became the book *God's Way with Man*. He was struggling to prepare them when he had to write to the Abbot about the latest shock from St Gregory's. His words become all the more poignant when we know all that was crowding round his mind at the time — and that they were to be his last addresses on Good Friday:

> There is only one way: to let go of self, to give oneself to God out of love, the love that responds to His, manifested and demonstrated to the end on Calvary.

By now Gregory was living with pain. To Green he said that after Easter 1950 'my insides went rather to bits'. Providentially he was sent three very large donations at just this point — $50,000 then $10,000 and then $7,000. This would provide for the whole developing monastery, not just the chapel. In eleven months Gregory calculated that he raised

$130,000. 'I hit the film-stars level of income!' he said. It is possible he exaggerated his own direct rôle in this money-raising but with the help of American friends and benefactors, the priory's own efforts and Gregory's continued lecturing until his return to England in May, St Gregory's survived its crisis and slowly and steadily established itself. He, of all people, knew the reality of the situation but he remained convinced of its absolute rightness. To the Editor of *The Living Church* in 1950 he wrote that the prayers and sympathy and interest of good Christian people were what would spread the influence of Benedictinism in the Episcopal Church.

> And (thanks be to God!) I think it is taking root. There is something strong and fresh growing up in the life of the community which as it gets a little older and more settled in the life will be worth contributing to the Church. When I compare it with the desperately struggling little spark I left three years ago I am filled with thankfulness. God has been good to us!

Others also felt it was taking root. Kenneth Kirk visited Three Rivers in 1949 and said it was 'the steadiest thing he had met in the Episcopal Church'. And the Bishop of Bath and Wells also remarked: 'Your priory in America has an extraordinarily high reputation... a complete absence of pose.'

Gregory played his part in laying the foundations for that reputation. There is something fitting about its dedication to St Gregory — a reminder, in the very name, of what the monastery owed to Dom Gregory's commitment and energy, his skill and devotion, his health. He stayed for the grand dedication of the chapel on May 3rd 1951 and then flew home the next day — to see a doctor.

'A monk out of his cell', said St Antony of Egypt, 'is a fish out of water.' The monk who stood, robed but so ill, at the triumphant dedication of St Gregory's chapel in May 1951 was thousands of miles out of his cell. It had been exciting and stimulating, it had been important, even fun, it had also been costly in vocation, in distraction, in health. It became in the end a kind of sacrifice, an offering. On a card inside the diary they gave him for 1951, Gregory's American friends (probably Mabry) inscribed a verse:

> Our hopes maybe are most sanguinary
> That you will have a full itinerary:
> And at the end, if not quite dead you'll
> Here recall your U.S. SCHEDULE.

The last two lines now have a far sadder irony than ever they had when written.

6

Death and Life

... *let them prefer nothing whatever to Christ; and
may He bring us all alike to life everlasting.*
Rule of St Benedict, Ch. 72.

The history of Gregory's illness is not especially well-documented. There are occasional references in many of his letters to continuing gastric trouble, and those who knew him well were aware that he was sometimes in considerable discomfort and pain. Some have made the connection with the illness that developed while he was in Ghana towards the end of the twenties and with which he was eventually invalided home to spend time in hospital then. Problems rumbled on. In 1935, in a letter to a friend, at Wells, he says: 'I have spent part of this morning in vomiting but am now recovering.'

This, recounted in a matter-of-fact way, implied that it was not a unique or unexpected occurrence. Gregory's habits of hard work and sometimes very late hours can't have helped. All came to a head in the United States when his increasing pain took him finally to a specialist consultant who diagnosed cancer of the bowel.

Gregory returned home from the consecration of the Three Rivers chapel the next day to see a doctor who arranged for him to have urgent hospital treatment including surgery. Gregory was in hospital for some time. On the whole he does not seem to have been a particularly good patient though he certainly retained his sense of humour. Stories are told in the community of Gregory continuing to smoke his pipe as a man went berserk in the public ward where Gregory was recuperating. The doctor subsequently criticised Gregory's pipe-smoking to which he replied: 'What do you expect in the front stalls of the circus?' On another occasion an inventory of stock on the ward was being made and one operation stocking was found to be missing. Gregory claimed that a nurse had pulled off a leg and thrown it away but had kept the other stocking for fear of the inventory. He wrote to Freddy Green in September of 1951: 'I did twice try to get into Purgatory on the day of the op.', he went on to describe visiting Oxford in a bath chair and going to Cornwall 'to learn to walk again'. At that point he anticipated tests every three months for the next two years and he added, characteristically: 'The bon Dieu is really very neat in his ways and so reliable.' Gregory spoke further about his hospital experience in a letter later that year[1] to Maurus Benson at Three Rivers.

> Fortunately, my guts are doing fine. The Drs spoke of my alimentary canal after my last X-ray in terms normally reserved for show bits of Venice. I have to go for another, with a 'sigmoidoscope' exam thrown in, in Nov. sometime. (A kind of searchlight cum periscope (with radar attachments for all I know) which they push up one's behind. Mercifully under a 'Gen. Anaesthetic.') This isn't because anything is now likely to go wrong with the works but in case there is a recurrence of the Cancer. If so they want to treat it at once with ray-therapy if they can, instead of going on slicing off sections of my bowels like a Bologna sausage. At present there is no sign whatever of recurrence. My weight is steady, I have even some colour in my cheeks, I get quite happily through a day of 6.30 a.m. – 10 p.m. each day. I am full of wicked but most enjoyable thoughts and feel much better than for some years.

1   8.10.51.

Gregory appears to have healed up very quickly after his operation and to have been able to spend time in July recuperating in Cornwall where he claims in a letter to have walked a mile. He returned to Nashdom while the Abbot was absent for part of the summer and resumed some of his duties as Prior. When he wrote to Maurus Benson in October, he was waiting to be able to go and spend three or four weeks in the Scottish Highlands. He told Green that he was hoping to make a 'snob's progress' — a deer forest in Inverness, a castle on the Isle of Colonsay, and ten days with the Bishop of Argyll and the Isles at 'the most beautiful spot I know in the world — looking down the Firth of Larne'. For all his buoyant spirits he was, nevertheless, avoiding public engagements of any kind and even contemplated not seeking re-election to Convocation, though the Abbot thought he ought to remain for the sessions of January 1952.

During November 1951 Gregory stayed with Kenneth Kirk, then Bishop of Oxford, who, in a letter to friends[1] remarked on how bright and happy he had been. Everyone clearly felt he was on the road to full recovery and the eventual return to all his work and activity. Gregory might not, however, himself have been totally convinced of this. For all the jolliness of his letter to Maurus Benson there is also something very final about the ending of the letter: 'And to yourself my greetings and abiding affection and gratitude for a great many things in these 15 years and my apologies for many others. Yrs ever in Dno Gr. D. O.S.B.'

It is as if enforced rest and time alone in convalescence by the sea in Cornwall and in the mountains of the Highlands were forcing on Gregory some sense of the need to face his mortality and not forget the seriousness of his illness. He had, in fact said to Green: 'It is a great waste my being alive at all really, because I shall never again be so well prepared (and even quite content) to die as I was in May after expecting it for 7 months. But I find that I quite enjoy being alive, all the same, in this peace.'

1   26.2.52.

By February of 1952 things do indeed seem to have turned for the worse. In the letter referred to above[1] Kirk revealed his concern for Gregory. He asked for their prayers:

> The second is my closest and oldest friend and the most brilliant man in the Church of England — Gregory Dix. He had a major internal operation last year and for a while everything seemed most hopeful... now something — they don't quite know what — has gone wrong and there is a prospect of a series of more operations, all of them difficult and dangerous. He is being wonderfully brave, but is very weak and tired.[2]

By this time, the end of February 1952 Gregory was back in hospital and the situation steadily became more critical. A series of telegrams towards the end of March graphically illustrate the crisis. Here are the contradictions and tensions of an emergency, the hopes and the realism — and still Gregory's wit and detachment and desire not to make life difficult for the Abbot. On March 20th the Abbot had to fly to the States again but he left Gregory apparently comfortable, installed in Grovefield House near Nashdom with the Russell-Smiths, friends of the community. Bridget Russell-Smith was a nurse.

Gregory's condition worsened however and the community cabled the Abbot: 'Summers says one week.' (Summers was the community's doctor.)

On Wednesday March 26th at 11.40 p.m. Ronnie Dix sent a telegram to Abbot Augustine in the United States:

> Gregory indignant about previous cable... requests you ignore one-week theory ... says he is improving and doctor has misinterpreted symptoms on renewing acquaintance with case ... original abscess still draining good thing ... later quotes Brown's [Gregory's own doctor's] support for saying week's notice fantastic ... truth is Brown noncommittal... might be tomorrow or fortnight... nurse thinks about 3 days believe

1   To Dorothy and John Henry, 26.2.52, quoted by Eric Kemp in his life of Kenneth Kirk.
2   p. 204.

Gregory's persistence probably due to shock... still quite clear-headed so expect much more than one week... salute brethren. Ronny.

A telegram the next morning from Mrs Russell-Smith is more terse and less optimistic: 'Burnham. 10.20 a.m. Thursday 27th. Condition critical... Brown reports nothing more can be done. Bridget.'

The Abbot replied with a telegram to Gregory: 'Please get better but should God will otherwise farewell Alleluia. Brethren here as at Nashdom surround you love prayers. Long to be with you but believe duty remain. Tell Nashdom. Deepest love Blessing. Abbot.'

Two days later a telegram arrived from Gregory himself: 'From Nashdom, Burnham, Bucks. — 8.12 p.m. March 30th. To Fr Abbot — I try to obey. Temperature, pulse etc. plumb normal. Treatment resumes tomorrow: so it may be *au revoir*, *Laus tibi, Domine*. Many prayers and much love to brethren. Of course, remain, Gregory.'

The immediate crisis appears thus to have been over, but Gregory was dying and his care and treatment from this point on were set within the framework of that realisation.

He must have been increasingly preoccupied with the prospect of dying, quite apart from dealing with pain and discomfort, for which drugs were some help. At the beginning of May he received a letter from one of the bishops he had come to know in the United States, the Bishop of Western Michigan, who clearly felt he was writing to Gregory for the last time: 'The hill grows steeper near the top', he said, 'and the breath comes shorter.'

Perhaps Gregory remembered what he had written himself for the Three Hours devotional service only a year before in New York when he was already conscious of carrying a death-dealing disease in his body. The talks were posthumously published in 1954 as *God's Way with Man*:

It is not time now to speak of the Resurrection of the Body, but St Paul said, 'We shall all be changed.' The Christian doctrine of resurrection is not merely the immortality of the soul. The rending of the soul from the body is a terrible thing because it is unnatural, and so it is always regarded in Holy Scripture. Death is a solemn and serious thing, even for those who are full of faith and are prepared to die. It should be a ritual act, an act of worship — a personal return of life to the God who gave it — to the Lord of all life who is its fount, its master, and its end. It should be an act of solemn oblation and worship, an act of acknowledgement, an act of adoration, the pouring out of the whole being to Him whose rightfully it is. Supremely it is an act of sacrifice to God.[1]

Gregory was now preparing this final rite, this worship, this act of adoration.

Abbot Augustine Morris returned from America in April and in the next weeks spent a great deal of time with him. After Gregory's death in early May the Abbot wrote down a detailed account of the last few days of Gregory's life and sent a copy to the brethren at Three Rivers, as well as to others.

The weeks following my return from America were full of ups and downs but the general tendency was down. Increasing doses of opium were necessary to keep the colostomy in order: he was becoming so thin as to be almost emaciated. Nevertheless, although his speech slowed up probably owing to the opium, his mind remained bright and he was keen to know everything about Nashdom and St. Gregory's and the details of my American visit. I had to take him step by step on a mental tour of the monastery. He was able to enjoy dipping into Vincent Taylor's new book on St Mark, and Dr Summers was extremely surprised to find him sitting in bed with this heavy tome in his hands.

On Saturday May 10th he took a turn for the worse: that evening I prefaced an address to the community with a warning that it was now probably a matter of days for him. It was that evening, as Dom Gregory knew, that I was appointing Dom Benedict to succeed Dom Godfrey as novice master.

That night as on the previous two nights I kept the car ready at the front door. At 2.45 a.m. the telephone rang. Hearing someone else on the way to answer it, I began immediately to dress. His brother and Dr Summers were also

1   p. 73.

summoned. The doctor arrived soon after me and warned the patient that the end was at hand. There was an internal haemorrhage and a good deal of pain. Summers said that he would leave me with Dom Gregory and then administer an injection of morphia. I then arranged for the Blessed Sacrament to be brought. He was able to make his confession lucidly and coherently. Dom Godfrey administered Holy Communion.

Dom Godfrey Stokes, in fact, recalls taking communion to Gregory at this point and in administering it saying '*Corpus Christi*' instead of '*Viaticum*', the words at the Last Rites. It was obvious to him that Gregory noticed this variation.

We then waited for his brother's arrival and left the two brothers alone for a space after which the doctor gave the injection. The two brothers and I prayed together for a space and then, as the morphia was beginning to take effect, I said the first part of the prayers for the dying. Ronnie came up to Nashdom to say mass at 6.30 and I sang the conventual mass at 9.20 and had breakfast. Dom Benedict asked leave to accompany me back and said the Sorrowful Mysteries of the Rosary silently at the bedside. He then gave the patient a blessing with a cross given him by the Abbé Couturier. Dom Gregory opened his eyes and after looking at Dom Benedict for a moment said 'Novice master', remembering the appointment that had just been made. After Dom Benedict's departure, we prayed together for a little with the crucifix and lighted candles at the foot of the bed.

While he was still in hospital, in a corner bed opposite his own was a bad hat, with a good deal of goodness and charm, 'the Major'. They had had not a few conversations on religion and the Major, who lives not far away, had visited him at Grovefield House. Dom Gregory was working towards getting him to his first confession and in fact had a few days before received his promise of a first confession. While I was having coffee downstairs towards the end of the morning, I was told that Dom Gregory was repeatedly asking for the Major. I therefore rang him up and he promised to come round. Meanwhile, the nurse, Mrs Russell-Smith and Sister Watters, a New Zealand girl, were very anxious to administer another injection, fearing that an internal collapse would cause acute pain.

After a little I persuaded the patient to agree to this,
knowing that he would have 20 minutes before it took effect.
The Major then arrived and I left him alone with Dom
Gregory, myself waiting outside in the passage. After some
time I looked in and received a decided 'No' from the bed.
After some minutes I opened the door again and Dom Gregory said, 'Could you please get the purple stole from the
suitcase.' I gave it him, cast it round his neck and went out.
After some minutes, however, the Major came out in deep
distress and said, 'I don't think it is any good: he can't do it.'
I went in and found Dom Gregory still eager to finish. I told
him therefore to rally his remaining strength and I would get
the Major to come back. He did, but I remained outside the
door to see if I could hear the sound of voices. It was obvious
that there was difficulty, so with the Major's permission, I
entered and assisted the patient to complete the transaction.
I should make it clear that this was very definitely a voluntary
act, although assisted by my prompting. I will add at this
point that the Major attended the funeral. His wreath was
marked: 'In a short space of time I have learned to respect
and love a great man.' To perform this last priestly act, Dom
Gregory had to fight not only pain and death but a heavy
injection of morphia.

Somewhat later, about 12.30 p.m. when Ronnie and I were
with him, he thought that Monday had come. On Monday
afternoon he was hoping to see his publisher Mr Newth. I
rang Newth up and he agreed to come over at 2.30. While we
were waiting for him, Dom Gregory referred to the Wild Cat
lectures which I had taken him some days before. 'I don't
think they are worth publishing: they are not in a fit state.' I
assured him that it would be possible to carry out a sufficient
revision and suggested that he might try to expand one
passage of which he had talked to me about St. Mark. He
then succeeded in dictating to me fairly coherently a sample
of what he wanted, containing references to Eusebius, Jerome,
Theodoret, Victor of Antioch and the *Corpus Inscriptionum
Latinarum*.

A further note in the Abbot's handwriting survives and shows
Gregory making the case for a distinction between Mark the
author of the gospel and John Mark of Jerusalem who appears
elsewhere in the New Testament. He wanted to argue for a

gospel author close to Peter in Rome. At this stage, twenty-four hours before his death, his mind was clearly still lucid enough to remember authors and documents of the early Church though some of the dictated material becomes confused and is incomplete.

Newth arrived directly after this and Dom Gregory began to discuss with him the future of *The Shape*. They then discussed mutual friends and the idiosyncrasies of dons. Dom Gregory complained that it was not he who was making all this fuss. 'I did not send for Father Abbot or Ronnie or had anything to do about it. It is all their fault!' After a little, I gave Newth a significant look and he said, 'Well, I had better be leaving you in peace.' A characteristic reply came from the bed, 'Sorry I have bored you.' After this there was nothing to do but stay a few minutes longer and then Newth took his leave. 'Well if the foot in purgatory slips over, farewell', said Dom Gregory, 'but if not, *au revoir*.' He then had another injection and I came up to Nashdom for a couple of hours. When I returned, he seemed to be ready to settle down to the business of dying. He was most grateful to God for allowing him to do what he could to tie up the loose ends. He remembered particularly a young man on the British Embassy staff whom he had met on the ship returning from Sweden and who had poured out his troubles. Last February this man wrote a letter of gratitude on the second anniversary. Dom Gregory could feel a certain sense of fulfilment and completion for which he was deeply thankful. He closed with a very Gregorian remark, 'God is so tactful.'

In the intervals of consciousness, we generally said a few prayers. Ronnie remained with his brother from 10 p.m. to 2 a.m. while I slept on a sofa and at that hour Mrs Russell-Smith and I replaced Sister and Ronnie. Towards 3 he rose and pointed a finger at each of us in turn and said 'You, and you.' He clearly recognised us. We prayed together a little: I said the Holy Name and he said to me, 'Keep on saying Jesus.' At my prompting he said in a firm and fervent voice, 'Jesus, into Thy hands I commend my spirit.' He then paused and I think his thoughts turned to his brother, a Cambridge man: 'in spite of being a Tab.'[1] I felt I could wish that that might be the end

1   'Tab', short for *Cantab.*, the opprobrious name given by Oxford men to those from the younger university.

but there were a few other snatches of prayer and conversation. When conscious he mostly looked upwards. Just before
10 a.m. he roused and saw me at the foot of the bed. 'Father
Abbot', he said. I bent over him and he tried to tell me
something but had to give up. This was I think his last
conscious moment. At about 10.30 I think that something
disastrous happened inside. Each breath was a heavy groan.
Slowly the groans changed to sighs and the sighs grew quieter
and slower until the end came shortly after 12.30.

Abbot Augustine's account is invaluable for its comprehensive and detailed recording of Gregory's last hours, but other
evidence shows there were other visitors too, prior to these
last hours and there was even controversy. Having happily
lived in the thick of controversy in his active life it may not
have escaped Dix that he was dying with a touch of it.

It is clear that a number of friends visited Gregory during
the final weeks of his illness. Kenneth Kirk missed seeing
him by an hour. Writing later to Dorothy and John Henry[1]
(quoted again in Eric Kemp's biography[2]) he said:

Gregory's death is a sad blow to many of us, but he had a
happy and wonderful end. In the last few hours there was no
pain; he knew he was about to die; but he saw quite a number
of friends (alas I did not get there till an hour after he died)
he helped at least two people with much needed spiritual
advice, and he even interviewed his publisher. I met quite a
number of those who had been with him during those hours;
it was clear that he had made them even happier at the end
than during his lifetime — and he had always spread happiness. He was one of the saintliest people I have ever known
and, though he died young, the mark he left on the Church
of England will live for a long time.

Among the others who visited Dix earlier in those last weeks
was Christopher Butler. Gregory seems to have known Butler
from Keble days and Butler was, for a time, a chaplain of
Keble before he left the Church of England and became a
Roman Catholic. In due course he became a Benedictine

1   27.5.52.
2   p. 206.

monk and by the time of the visit, had become Abbot of Downside. Towards the end of July, Abbot Butler wrote to Abbot Augustine to say that he believed the *Catholic Herald* was reporting Butler's visit to Gregory as if it had been an opportunity to invite Gregory to join the Roman Catholic Church. Butler apologised to Abbot Augustine for any pain this may cause and offered to write to the papers explaining it was the visit of an old friend at Butler's own request. The incident was subsequently reported also in the *Church Times*, where Abbot Augustine, in writing to solicit information for a Memoir, took the opportunity to deny these suggestions which had appeared in *The Universe* as well as *The Catholic Herald*. The *Church Times* editorial noted what it called Butler's 'half-hearted apology' for this and quoted Butler's phrase: 'he died in the conviction that he ought not to submit to the claim of the Catholic Church'.

This, said the newspaper, was 'graceless'. Subsequently Butler wrote both to the *Church Times* and Abbot Augustine explaining that he had no need to apologise since he had not 'originated the report or the rumour'.

For Gregory himself the question of submitting to Rome had been real for many years but latterly it seems to have been much less significant. He had resolved the question and the prospect of death does not seem to have stirred up old questions. In fact, the opposite seems to have been the case and he was able to die secure in his faith, an encouragement to others, supported by the prayers and devotion of his religion. A little flurry of controversy does not seem inappropriate at the end of such a life not least as it was resolved without any animosity or difficulty among the remaining friends.

As soon as his death was known the tributes began to flow in to the Abbey. Obituaries appeared in *The Times*, the *Church Times* and many other newspapers and journals. Many of them noticed the way he combined the work of scholar and Church politics with the life of a priest and monk: some saw that this had been a difficult combination to sustain. Harold Riley in *The Church Union* commented 'I think sometimes people

leaned on him too much and imposed on him too heavy a
burden.'

Gregory Mabry, his friend and helper in New York, seems
to have had a hand in a number of the obituaries that
appeared in the United States. He may have been responsible for some of the inaccuracies such as the suggestion that
he spent part of his boyhood in France.

The obituary in *The Times* called him 'extreme' but noted
also his 'impish sense of humour and a streak of sheer
naughtiness'. The obituary writers (Michael Ramsey may
have been one) commented on his 'highly original cast of
mind' as well as on the fact that he could be 'intransigent'.
'The bishops have lost a salutary gadfly', an obituary commented, but added: 'the single-hearted sincerity of his personal religion was unmistakable.'

Many letters indicated that requiem masses were to be
said for Dix both in the United Kingdom and in the States.
The Abbey arranged for requiems in London at All Saints',
Margaret Street and in Oxford at St Mary Magdalene's with
the Bishop of Dorchester preaching. The Bishop of Oxford
and other Church men and women, including the Major,
were present for the funeral at home in the Abbey where, on
Friday May 16th, in perfect weather, Gregory was buried in
the cemetery of the monks.

On the day of his death, his friend Dom Maurus Benson,
wrote from the United States: 'I think he is one of those souls
who will be surprised at how high up he finds himself now. I
think that when he really thought of death he always was
humble to the point of underestimating himself. That is
what I always thought when he spoke of his interior life.'

For weeks tributes from all over the world flowed in. There
were letters from Roman Catholic communities as well as
Anglican, from soldiers and bishops, from lay men and
women, from grand institutions and unknown individuals.
Many spoke of the privilege of knowing Gregory and working
with him or studying his scholarly work. Many witnessed to
a sense of shock and dismay about his early death.

Some writers chose to concentrate on Gregory's scholarship and learning. John Robinson from Clare College, Cambridge gave thanks 'for his making the meaning of the eucharist clearer to us' and a 'converted Unitarian' wrote wanting to record her debt to *The Shape* — 'the deepest help, historically and spiritually'.

Other letters focused on his personality and charm. The Primus of Scotland said: 'he charmed everyone — not least those who most disliked his position', and another writer addressed the Abbot concerning: 'your *enfant terrible* who was the joy of the whole Church'. Many tributes came from those who had experienced Gregory as a confessor or spiritual director — many nuns, lay men and women, who knew Gregory in a kind of secret way but spoke of his spirituality and devotion: 'As a spiritual director he could hardly have been excelled; always firm but always gentle, always candid, but always loving, always patient and always kind.'

Tributes written at the time of death, especially a death so untimely and sad, are inevitably not an objective appraisal of the significance of a life and work but they do pick up some of the threads that together form the shape of Gregory Dix. They focus our attention on the facets of the man which attracted (or repelled) people and begin to outline the overall impact and impression that he made.

In beginning to see the whole man and in trying to fit the facets of him together it is vital to acknowledge again the gaps that exist in the information, gaps both accidental and deliberate. This is particularly true of Gregory's family. He remained in close touch with his brother who frequently visited Nashdom and was there at the end. A nice little 'vignette' survives at the Abbey, perhaps because it was amongst the papers of another monk, Dom Patrick Dalton. It is a small hand-made book of drawings and photographs, rhymes, jokes and songs full of private humour with pictures of Gregory and Ronnie as children. From Ronnie and Eileen Dix, it poked fun at Gregory and the monks and was a gift to a *friend*. It is a little flash of insight into family loyalties and affections and humour. 'The Poopsies own Annual' it is called 'of 1937'. Beyond this we know that both their parents had been dead for some time (1932 and 1936). What is not at all clear is how much contact there had been earlier on especially between Gregory and his mother. It seems clear from the two letters that survive from Gregory to his mother that there must have been others, a regular correspondence. Where are those letters? Did Gregory destroy them? Did Ronnie? Did they disappear after Ronnie's, or his wife Eileen's, death? Here is a gap and we can not assume that because they did not survive they never existed. The same applies to other correspondences. Many stop abruptly and sometimes begin again, they survive almost arbitrarily and can trap us into over- or under-estimating their significance.

In a slightly different way Dix's friends appear unevenly in this account. Some are represented by correspondence or other documents, the importance of others is indicated much more indirectly. Gregory had the reputation of a gift for friendship. His charm, candour and the general attractiveness of his character made him a fascinating companion. Apart from old college friends and members of the community like Patrick Dalton, Augustine Morris or Maurus Benson, it was these qualities that endeared him to men as different as Maurice Bévenot and Gabriel Hebert.

There was also another group of men (there seem to have been no close women friends) with whom Gregory had a distinctive relationship. These were older men to whom Gregory reacted like a pupil, a younger brother or son. Perhaps Gregory felt he needed the influence of an older generation especially after his father died in 1932. This group of older friends included Kenneth Kirk and Walter Frere. It certainly included Freddy Green who had been his college chaplain at Oxford and to whom he wrote in 1940 (aged 39) that he found himself working only with younger men but was:

> looking for a lead: which drives me to a lot of self-questioning. That is why I am writing to you because, though I am over the question of poping for the present, I do want somebody

more mature and trustworthy to judge and criticise my mind
for me and say where I am wrong.

The same mixture of affection and admiration and 'looking
for a lead' clearly touched his relationship with William
Temple, too, with Abbot Martin and perhaps even with the
Abbé Couturier. He himself seems to have fulfilled the older
role occasionally especially with younger monks like Marcus
Stevens.

Did Gregory have time, while he was ill, to sort out his
papers, to remove controversial or sensitive material, to
organise material that had potential? On the whole this does
not seem very likely but it reminds us again forcibly to take
account of 'the gaps' and remember that there is no such
thing as omniscience in the world of biography. All history
has an awkward arbitrariness to it, however recent, however
seemingly comprehensive.

This book, as a whole, should witness to the energy of the
man, his range of abilities and skills, his zest for life and
passion for the causes he espoused; it should provide some
taste of his wit and humour and charm and some testimony
to his widely-acknowledged gift for friendship. It should bear
witness, however inadequately, to his brilliance in writing
succinctly, intelligibly and persuasively in *The Shape* in a
scholarly contribution which really did change the Church.

There are sharp edges left, gaps and spaces and inadequacies but through it all shines something of the sparkling
shape of the liturgist, the controversialist, the monk.

We have noted how Kenneth Kirk — a brilliant man
himself — referred to Gregory as 'the most brilliant man in
the Church of England'. Geoffrey Curtis CR in his book
about the Abbé Couturier said of him:

> Gregory Dix was one of God's best gifts to the Church of
> England in this century. It would be difficult to do justice to
> his charm, brilliance and versatility... serving the whole
> Church by his theological writings at once erudite and sparkling,
> the Church of England in particular by his piquant and often
> wise counsel, a host of friends by his inimitable wit and

refreshing sympathy and many souls by his prayerful understanding.'[1]

Dix made his contribution to the Church in many ways and
alongside many other people, but his singular outstanding
offering was *The Shape of the Liturgy*. Here, probably more than
he realised himself, he strengthened the catholicity of the
Church of England and made a lasting mark on liturgical
development everywhere in the course of the next decades.

Curtis went on to say: 'I sometimes felt that one had there
Sir Thomas More, Erasmus and Dean Colet all rolled into
one, not without an occasional touch of Rabelais.'[2]

One might add a touch of Thomas Cranmer too, even
though Gregory disliked him so much. He shared Cranmer's
intense interest in liturgy but he also shared his passionate
devotion to a cause and the readiness — for which Gregory
disliked Cranmer so much but which he did not wholly avoid
— the readiness sometimes to allow his principles to serve
his cause.

Here was a complex man. Romantic, imaginative, shrewd,
mature, charming, mischievous, tenacious, he was ultimately
struggling to work out his own salvation as a monk in a
community and seeking to fulfil the longings and aspirations
of his personality. In many ways those longings and aspirations were cut short by illness and early death, but in another
sense his impact was already made. When death came he
could, in the words of the Rule he knew so well: 'persevere
in Christ's teaching in the monastery until death... by patience share in the sufferings of Christ... and merit to be a
partaker of His Kingdom.'[3]

Imagine him at his most typical, going in the early morning
to say his daily mass. Day by day, at one of the side altars in
the chapel at Nashdom, or wherever he happened to be, he
would repeat that solemn celebration. Standing alone at the
altar in the converted ballroom of that princely house, with

1   pp. 169, 170.
2   *Paul Couturier and Unity in Christ*, Geoffrey Curtis CR, SCM, 1964.
3   Prologue, *Rule of Benedict*.

only a server to accompany him — in traditional vestments and, leaning over the vessels on the altar, muttering quietly the so-familiar Latin words. He had said them, or heard them, at least once each day of his life in the community, words of prayer and devotion. He knew them also because he had studied them over and over again — studied the actual words, their order, the shape of the prayers, their meaning and origin. These were words lodged deep in every part of his life — intellectual, critical, devotional, prayerful. In fact, he also knew what was 'wrong with them' — how they had developed away from their original shape and purpose, how, adjusted, they could better serve the Church and be the vehicle for the prayer of the people. He knew what they had meant to ordinary people through the centuries, how they had entered deeply into people, into himself... all this he took with him to the altar day by day. He perceived how those words, those actions, could even more effectively serve the Church and inspire people, could if suitably changed to reflect current knowledge, but his practice was faithful to authority and the tradition. It was another part of this complex personality standing at the altar that, whatever his personal conclusions about the eucharist, what was celebrated was what the Church commanded. The further twist of irony was, of course, that 'what the Church commanded' referred in this context to the authority of the Roman Catholic Church. The Church of Gregory's ordination actually provided quite other words for priests to say which Gregory had to use from time to time, and to which no doubt he brought then the weight of the same critical mind as he said them. Home, though, was that quiet, muttered daily Latin mass in such contrast to his liturgical demonstrations. Here everything came together, scholar, catholic protagonist, priest; here, day by day it could all be handed over, was offered: the untidiness and uncertainty of things absorbed, the basic inspiration for his work and prayer returned to, the day begun again.

And so coming to *Qui Pridie*, to the moment which he acknowledged to Dom Patrick Dalton he always reached with the greatest intensity and concentration, 'on the day before he suffered'. Here, each day, he entered into the sacrifice of Christ with the whole Church, with all of himself. He joined 'the eternal gesture of the Son of Man towards his Father as He passes into the Kingdom of God'[1] — the gesture which is the eucharist.

Perhaps as he reverently elevated the Host, he smiled and remembered a small boy with a fish slice. Perhaps, in contrast, his mind turned also in awe to those words which, as he said, squeezed his heart out:

> O Christ, who now beneath a veil we see,
> May what we thirst for soon our portion be,
> To gaze on thee unveiled, and see thy face,
> The vision of thy glory and thy grace.

'*Domine, non sum dignus...*' he said, bowing over the altar before his communion, and there was perhaps a twinge of pain in his stomach? — a reminder, a warning: 'but speak the word only and I shall be healed....'

Steadily and quietly his mass would come to an end and his mind fill again with all those for whom he prayed, St Gregory's Priory in America coming first and affectionately into his mind, his brother, his own community, his friends... and all those lives he had been able to touch. As he stepped back from the altar entering for a moment the silence of heaven, he may have felt, perhaps for a moment, all the levels of his life, all the arbitrary and uncoordinated elements of it, all its layers, held together in that place.

'God is so tactful', he might have thought with a smile, as he bent to reverence the altar and leave.

God is so tactful.

The End

1   *Shape*, p. 266.

Select Bibliography

Life

The Rule of St Benedict, Various editions.
The Jubilee Book 1914–1964, Benedictines of Nashdom, Faith Press.
The Call of the Cloister, P.F. Anson, SPCK 1955.
The Rivers of the Flood, Dom Anselm Hughes OSB, Faith Press 1961.
Kenneth Kirk, Eric Kemp, Hodder and Stoughton 1959.
Dom Bernard Clements, E.M. Almedingen, John Lane at the Bodley Head 1945.
Walter H. Frere, ed. Philips, Faber 1947.
Cosmo G. Lang, Lockhart, Hodder and Stoughton 1949.
Michael Ramsey, O. Chadwick, Oxford 1991.
T.B. Strong, H. Anson, SPCK, 1947.
Paul Couturier and Unity in Christ, Geoffrey Curtis CR, SCM 1964.
William Temple, Iremonger, Oxford 1947.
Archbishop Fisher, E. Carpenter, Canterbury Press 1991.
Saraband, Memoirs of Eric Mascall, Gracewing 1993.
Fisher of Lambeth, W. Purcell, Hodder and Stoughton 1969.
Raymond Raynes CR, N. Moseley.
Anglo-Catholicism, W.S.F. Pickering, Routledge 1989.
Christian Monasticism, Dom David Knowles, Cambridge 1969.
A History of English Christianity, 1920–90, Adrian Hastings, SCM 1991.
Unfinished Agenda, Leslie Newbiggin, Eerdmans.

Rome and Canterbury through Four Centuries, B. & M. Pawley, Mowbray 1974.

Leaders of the Church of England 1828–1978, David Edwards, Hodder and Stoughton 1978.

Liturgy and Theology

Liturgy Reshaped, ed. Kenneth Stevenson, SPCK 1982.

Gregory Dix, 25 Years On, K. Stevenson, Grove 1977.

Liturgy and Society, Gabriel Hebert SSM, SPCK 1936.

Parish Communion, ed. Gabriel Hebert SSM, SPCK 1937.

Catholicity: a report, Dacre Press, 1947.

Christian Worship: its origin and evolution, L. Duchesne, SPCK 1903.

Liturgy Coming to Life, J.A.T. Robinson, Mowbray 1960.

The Roman Primacy to AD 461, Kidd, SPCK 1936.

The Search for the Origins of Christian Worship, Paul Bradshaw, SPCK 1992.

A History of Anglican Liturgy, C.J. Cuming, Macmillan 1982.

Liturgy and Worship, Lowther Clarke, SPCK 1932.

The Study of Liturgy, Jones, Yarnold, and Wainwright, SPCK 1978.

Worship, Church and Society (on Hebert), C. Irvine, Canterbury Press 1993.

Appendix I
Bibliographical Data

1927

1. Review: *Religio Laici* by Sir Henry Slesser, in *Laudate* V.20 (Dec. 1927), pp. 282–3.
2. Review: The Gospel Apologetic by the Rev. M.C. Elphinstone, in *Laudate* V.20 (Dec. 1927), pp. 283–4.
3. Review: *The Christian Attitude* by James Wareham, in *Laudate* V.20 (Dec. 1927), pp. 285–6.

1928

4. Review: *Effects of the Reformation on Ideas of Life and Conduct* by the Rev. F.C. Chaplin, in *Laudate* VI.21 (Mar. 1928), pp. 52–53.
5. Review: *Normal Development of Ordinary Mental Prayer* by the Rev. W.H. Longridge, and *Some Difficulties in the Practice of Frequent Confession and Communion* (*id. auct.*) in *Laudate* VI.22 (June 1928), pp. 115–6.
6. Review: *Lives of the Popes in the Middle Ages* by Mgr H.K. Mann, in *Laudate* VI.24 (Dec. 1928), pp.239–241.

1929

7. Review: *La Chretiente Medievale 395–1254* by Augustin Fliche, in *Laudate* VII.26 (June 1929), pp. 121–2.
8. Review: *Dictionary of English History* publ. Cassells in *Laudate* VII.26 (June 1929), pp. 122–3.
9. Review: *The Primitive Church* by B.H. Streeter, in *Laudate* VII.27 (Sep. 1929), pp. 154–74.

10. Review: *Mysteries of the Soul* by R.M. Freienfels, in *Laudate* VII.28 (Dec. 1929), pp. 245–47.
11. Review: The *History of Kirby Underdale* by the Rev. W.R. Shepherd, in *Laudate* VII.28 (Dec. 1929), p. 252.

1930

12. 'The Revealing Church', in *Laudate* VIII.29 (Mar. 1930), pp. 24–46.
13. Review: *The Bishop's Register* by the Rev. J.C. Offer, in *Laudate* VIII.29 (Mar 1930), pp. 57–8.
14. Review: *Caliban in Grub Street* by Ronald Knox, in *Laudate* VIII.30 (June 1930), pp. 115–6.

1931

15. Review: *The Fullness of Sacrifice* by the Rt. Rev. F.C.N. Hicks in *Laudate* IX.33 (Mar. 1931), pp. 57–8.
16. Review: *The Mystery of Faith and Human Opinion* by the Rev. M. de la Taille SJ in *Laudate* IX.33 (Mar. 1931), pp. 65–6.
17. Review: *Church, State and Study* by Ernest Barker, in *Laudate* IX.36 (Dec. 1931), p. 266.
18. 'The Twelve Apostles and the Gentiles' a series of four articles in *Laudate* IX.36 (Dec. 1931), pp. 228–39. and X.37, 38, 39 (Mar. June and Sept. 1932), pp. 41–55, 89–96 and 168–80.

1932

19. Review: *The Lives of the Popes in the Middle Ages* (vols. 16–18) by Mgr. H.K. Mann, and *The Decline of the Medieval Church* by A.C. Flick, in *Laudate* X.40 (Dec. 1932), pp. 258–263.
20. 'The Use and Abuse of Papias on the Fourth Gospel' article in *Theology* XXIV.319 (Jan. 1932), pp. 8–20.

1933

21. Responses to Bp. Palmer on Lay Celebration: *C. U. Gazette* 1932, vol. LXIII no. 746, 749 (1933).

22. Review: *Liturgy and Worship* by W.K. Lowther Clarke and Charles Harris, in *Laudate* XI.42 (June 1933), pp. 116–121.

23. 'Didache and Diatessaron' article in *JTS* XXXIV.135 (July 1933), pp. 242–250.

24. *The Counter-Reformation 1550–1660* by B.J. Kidd, in *Laudate* XI.44 (Dec. 1933), p. 246.

25. 'Nordic Spirituality' review article in *Laudate* XI.43 (Sept. 1933), pp. 152–162.

26. 'Northern Catholicism' review article in *Laudate* XI.44 (Dec. 1933), pp. 208–27.

1934

27. 'Origins of the Epiclesis' articles in *Theology* XXVIII 165, 166 (Mar. Apr. 1934), pp. 125–37, 187–202

28. 'The Grandfather of Nonconformity' article in *Laudate* XII.47 (Sept. 1934), pp. 166–184.

29. 'The Epiclesis: Some Considerations' article in *Theology* XXIX.173 (Nov. 1934), pp. 287–94.

1935

30. Review: *The Council of Trent and Anglican Formularies* by H.E. Symonds, in *Laudate* XIII.49 (Mar. 1935), pp. 57–8.

31. Review: *The Order of the Holy Qurbana of the Orthodox Syrian Church of Malabar*, trans. by the Most Rev. Mar Ivanios, in *Laudate* XIII.49 (Mar. 1935), p. 61.

32. 'The Christian Passover' article in *Laudate* XIII.49 (Mar. 1935), pp. 2–18; published as *Mass of the Pre-Sanctified* (see 33 below).

33. *Mass of the Pre-Sanctified* (pamphlet published by CLA, London 1935) (see 32 above).

34. 'The Gospels in the Second Century' article in *Laudate* XIII.50, (June 1935), pp. 97–120.

1936

35. Review: *Reconstruction of Early Christian Doctrine* by H.J. Bradley, in *Theology* XXXII.187 (Jan. 1936), pp. 48–51.

36. 'The Blessing of Holy Oils' article in *Laudate* XIV.56 (Dec. 1936), pp. 231–40.
37. Review: *Almsgiving*, a handbook by W.K. Lowther Clarke, in *Laudate* XIV.56 (Dec 1936), pp. 251–2.
38. 'Confirmation or Laying on of Hands?', *Theology* Occasional Paper No. 5 (SPCK, London 1936).

1937
39. *The Apostolic Tradition of St Hippolytus* (Vol. 1 only) (SPCK for Church Historical Society, London 1937), 2nd edn. (ed. Henry Chadwick) (SPCK, London 1968).
40. Review: *Liturgy of St Peter* by H.W. Codrington, in *Laudate* XV.57 (Mar 1937), pp. 60–61
41. 'The Idea of "The Church" in the Primitive Liturgies' an essay in *The Parish Communion* ed. A.G. Hebert (SPCK, London 1937), pp. 95–143. (Also published as a pamphlet (see 42 below).)
42. *The Idea of the Church in Primitive Liturgies* (pamphlet by SPCK, London n.d.) (reprint of 41 above).
43. 'Jurisdiction Episcopal and Papal in the Early Church', articles serialized in *Laudate* XV.57, 58, 59, 60 (Mar., June, Sep., Dec. 1937), pp. 45–55, 101–24, 157–73, 232–50: and *Laudate* XVI.62, 63, 64 (June, Sep., Dec. 1938), pp. 107–18, 166–81, 231–43: published as a pamphlet *Jurisdiction in the Early Church*, CLA, London 1975 (see 69 below).

1938
44. 'Primitive Consecration Prayers' article in *Theology* XXXVI1.221 (Nov. 1938), pp. 261–83.

1941
45. Correspondence on 'Anglicanism and the Papacy' with Sykes, in *Theology* XLII.255 (Sep. 1941), pp. 165–76.

1942
46. *A Detection of Aumbries* (pamphlet, Dacre Press, London 1942).

1944

47. Question of Anglican Orders: *Letters to a Layman* (pamphlet, Dacre Press, London 1944).
48. Review: *The Influence of the Synagogue upon the Divine Office* by C.W. Dugmore, in *Theology*, XLVII.209 (July 1944), pp. 158–60. 1945
49. Contribution to 'The Liturgy' Essays from a clergy conference at Tewkesbury 1938. SPCK ed. K. Mackenzie. G.D.'s essay on consecration.
50. *The Shape Of The Liturgy* (Dacre Press, London, 1945).

1946

51. C.T. article: 'Is the English Church uncommitted?' 13.4.45 (re C51)
52. *Theology of Confirmation in Relation to Baptism* (pamphlet, Dacre Press, London 1946) delivered as a lecture at Oxford Unviersity, 22 Jan. 1946).
53. Correspondence on 'The Church of England in India' with Bentley, Jalland and Willis, in *Theology* XLIX.313 (July 1946), pp. 207–16.
54. 'Ministry in the Early Church' an essay in *Apostolic Ministry*, ed. K.E. Kirk (Hodder and Stoughton, London, 1946), pp. 183–303.

1947.

55. 'The Liturgist' an essay in *Walter Howard Frere, Bishop of Truro: A Memoir* by C.S. Phillips and others (Faber and Faber, London 1947), pp. 121–146.
56. *The Power and Wisdom of God* (Broadcast Addresses) (pamphlet, Dacre Press, London 1948).
57. 'Dixit Cranmer et non Timuit' article in *Church Quarterly Review* CXLV. 290 (Mar 1948), pp. 145–76: CXLVI. 291 (June 1948), pp. 44–60. (Also published as a pamphlet, see 58 below.)
58. *Dixit Cranmer et non Timuit* (pamphlet, Dacre Press, London 1948) (see 57 above).

59. '"The Seal" in the Second Century' article in *Theology* LI.331 (Jan 1948), pp. 7–12.
60. 'The Christian Shaliach and the Jewish Apostle: a Reply' article in *Theology* LI.337 (July 1948), pp. 249–257.
61. Unsigned contribution to 'Catholicity' Report for Abp. of Canterbury, Dacre Press 1947. (G.D's essay on Post-Tridentine Roman Catholicism).
62. 'Correspondence on "Shaliach" with St John Hart in Theology LI.340 (Oct 1948), pp. 385–6, 1949.
63. Contribution to essays from the Anglo-Catholic Congress, 1948 on Ministry, Dacre Press 1948.
64. 'Correspondence on "The Ministry"' with Mascall in *Theology* LII.347 (June 1949), pp. 219–24, 1951.
65. 'The Church of the Early Martyrs up to AD303 (broadcast talk) (published in *The Story of the Christian Church*, Mowbray, London 1951).

Published Posthumously

1953

66. *Jew and Greek*, A study in the Primitive Church (Dacre Press, London 1953), (prepared for publication by Canon H.J. Carpenter: being lectures delivered at Uppsala in Feb 1950, and subsequently in America).
67. *The Image and Likeness of God* (Dacre Press, London 1953) (retreat addressed prepared for publication by Dom Augustine Morris OSB).

1953

68. *God's Way with Man* (Dacre Press, London 1954): Good Friday addresses New York 1951; Foreword by Michael Ramsey. (Published in USA as *Power of God*).

1975

69. *Jurisdiction in the Early Church* (CLA, London 1954): being *Laudate* articles 1937–8 (see 43 above). Foreword by Dr T.M. Parker.